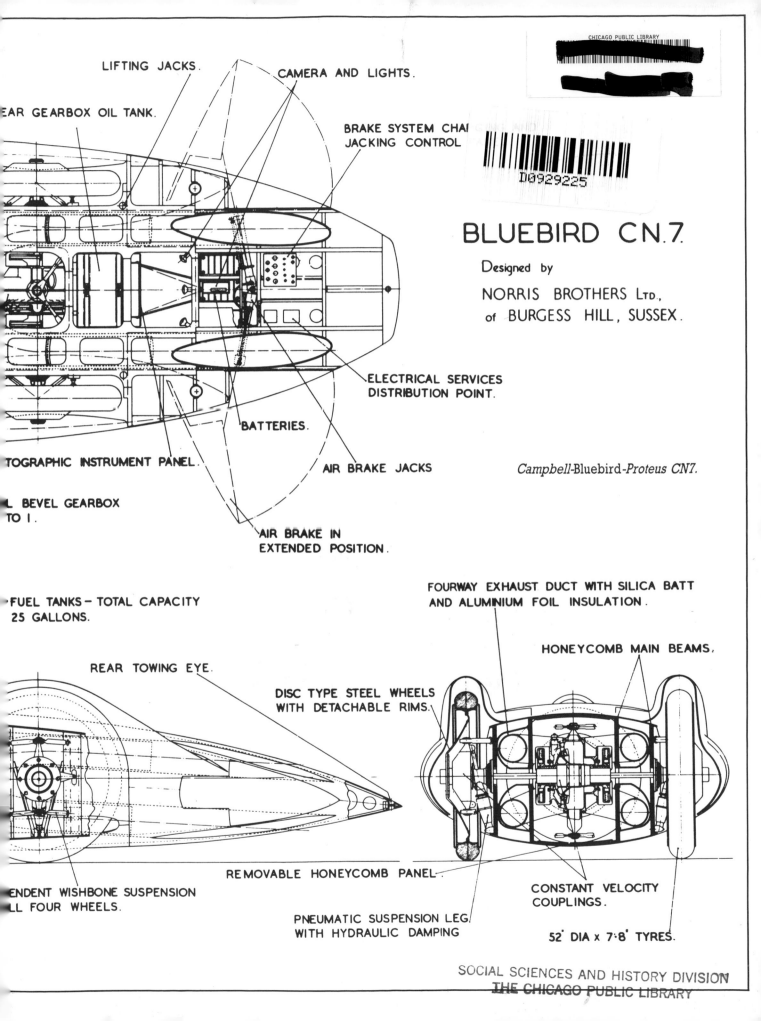

BLUEBIRD CN.7.

Designed by

NORRIS BROTHERS Ltd.,
of BURGESS HILL, SUSSEX.

Campbell-Bluebird-Proteus CN7.

The Land Speed Record

The Land Speed Record

Peter J.R. Holthusen

Foulis

Haynes

Dedication

With love to my devoted wife Jean, and our beloved daughter Sarah; my great partners in this project

ISBN 0 85429 499 6

A **FOULIS** Motoring Book

First published 1986
© Peter J.R. Holthusen 1986

Published by:
Haynes Publishing Group
Sparkford, Nr. Yeovil, Somerset
BA22 7JJ, England

Haynes Publications Inc.
861 Lawrence Drive, Newbury Park,
California 91320 USA

British Library Cataloguing in Publication Data
Holthusen, Peter J.R.
    The land speed record : to the sound barrier and beyond.
    1. Automobiles, Racing—Speed records—History
    I. Title
    796.7'2 GV1030
    ISBN 0–85429–499–6

Library of Congress catalog card number 86-81747

Editor: Mansur Darlington
Page layout: Tim Rose
Printed in England by: J.H.Haynes & Co.Ltd.

Contents

Foreword

In man's conquest for challenges there have been certain particular feats which have captured the imagination of both man and boy. One might recall the attempt and success of the first man to climb Mount Everest, to swim the English Channel, to run a four minute mile, to break the speed of sound in an aircraft or to go into space. Oh! to be one of those fortunate enough to attempt such a feat, let alone the first to accomplish such a task. "Sir – twenty miles an hour upon a coach? No man could rush so fast through the air and continue to draw breath!" Dr. Johnson's belief in the suffocating effects of speed upon man were unfounded as history has recorded in the physical sense, but in another sense he was correct. Many a man has lost the breath of life in the pursuit of speed. The aura of speed has captured both the hearts and minds of men, along with all the resources that they might be able to muster. The advent of this search is not new to man; I suppose that it could have started when man found himself pitted against both beast and his fellow man in an effort to survive or, perhaps, it could have begun with the pleasure that man felt as he ran with the wind against his face. None the less it progressed with the equation 'time versus distance' which equals the pace. From the days of the horse-drawn chariots to today, with our horseless carriages, to extend the boundaries has been, to a small breed of men, an insatiable race. As I read of the accounts of these adventurous men a list of whose names are too numerous to mention, I cannot help substituting myself in their place as I try to visualize the challenge and the fears that were peculiar to each of their fates. I think of the vast amount of energy that has been expended, the time logged in dreaming, planning, figuring and all the hours of fabricating and assembling. The blood, the sweat, the tears, the unfulfilled dreams and lost years. All to extend their realm of speed. If one could calculate the cost, I'm sure it would prove that indeed, it has been a formidable assault.

On 17 December 1979, I found myself in a most unique place. When I was a youngster I used to sit and daydream, contemplating life and perhaps the contribution that I might make. Even then, I felt that it would be unusual, something out of the ordinary, perhaps in some strange and distant place. Little did I realize then, how close were my thoughts to what actually God had destined as my fate. Here I sat, strapped in a multi-thousand horse-powered rocket vehicle with a Sidewinder missile as a booster ready to blast across a dry lake at Edwards AFB. This same lake bed is used by the space shuttles as they, and crew, return from outer space. This strange stage where brave men acted out their roles and met their fate, flying higher and faster in a quest to extend their boundaries, where countless scores of experimental aircraft for decades were put through their paces. Here, where men accepted the challenge victoriously while others paid the ultimate price, leaving behind an audience of dedicated crew, friends and families, void of victory, scarred for life, leaving them with unanswered questions of what might have been.

What a sobering moment as I looked before me at that dry lake bed where so many of these committed men had lost their lives with fixity of purpose in their faces. That dry lake bed lay before me like a dormant volcano ready to erupt with a firey explosion of twisted metal and broken dreams, claiming, perhaps, My Life! As I contemplate what lies before me, I wonder from what source did they draw their hope, their strength?

I feel as David must have felt as he committed himself to face his giant, confident not in his strength, but in God and the strength of His might. I can remember very vividly as I looked out of the windshield down the fuselage of the rocket and the vastness in front of me as the crew busied themselves with the task of readying the rocket for its sternest test. I felt the quiet assurance of strength in my relationship to God. Neither I, nor anyone else knew what might happen. God alone knew what course this battle was to take from the beginning and what the outcome would be. I only knew that there was a giant out there waiting and it was time to do battle. Peter Holthusen's book covers the quest of this subject as no other book has. It has been a labour of love for him and I'm confident that no other man living today has a broader knowledge or a better understanding of this subject.

My thanks to my friend, Peter, for his contribution to the preservation of the efforts and sacrifices of all the men and their families who share in the success of surpassing the speed of sound. The only thing that separates them from me is Time and Distance. Mark Twain once wrote, that ''Someday, when man can go 700 miles an hour, he'll again long to go seven miles an hour.'' For some this may not be the case, but then again I have been there and beyond.

Stan Barrett

Introduction

Almost always the most difficult section to write of any book is the Introduction. When the aim has been, from the outset, to create an all-embracing volume to cover the entire history of the Land Speed Record, the task is even more complicated.

The history of the Land Speed Record is as long as that of the motorcar itself, ranking high in importance amongst man's greatest endeavours.

The very early years saw contests of speed between electrically-powered vehicles, then briefly steam, before the internal-combustion engine became ascendant, reigning supreme, as it did, until the first decade after the Second World War.

It was in the early sixties that the 'modern' age of land speed record-breaking dawned, when appeared rocket-powered, and jet-powered vehicles, no longer driven through the wheels, but by the direct thrust of their engines. And it is this era of the Land Speed Record with which this book is primarily concerned.

Thus, though much detail can be found in the following pages on the wheel-driven record attempts—indeed, it is to be hoped that such achievements have been treated with their proper importance—, these have been chronicled chiefly to place in context the 'jet-age' cars which followed and—of no less importance—those that are even now being readied for the great challenge ahead: exceeding the speed of sound, then achieving the magic 1000mph.

This book has been written as a testament to those intrepid pioneers of speed, who progressed from unmetalled roads to beaches, and from those treacherous sands to the crystalline salt and dry lake beds of the High Sierras, always in pursuit of greater power and greater speeds.

It is also a testament to the courage and support of their families and friends, some of whom shared the fruits of victory, and some the burden of unfulfilled dreams and tragedy.   **Peter J.R. Holthusen**

In 1903 Camille Jenatzy entered the 4th Gordon Bennett Cup race on the Ballyshannon course in Ireland, with the Mercedes '60'. Jenatzy's land speed records of 1899 launched him onto a career path in road racing.

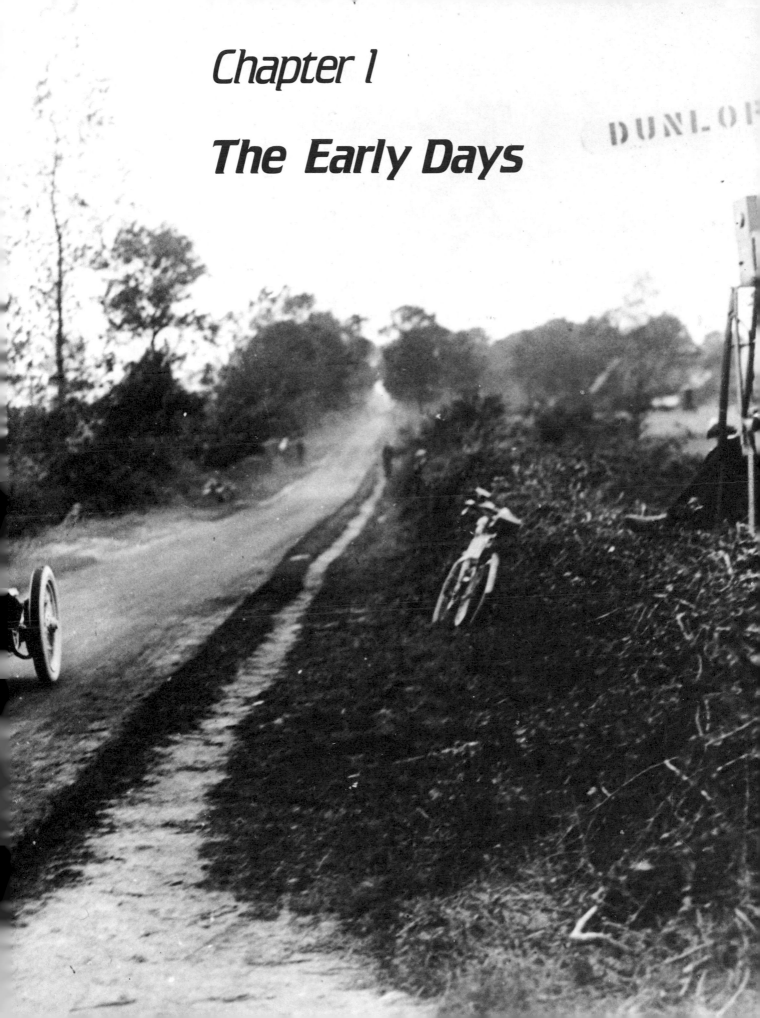

Chapter 1

The Early Days

There is a tradition of the exhilaration and of the lure of speed which dates as far back as the great Roman and Greek messengers, and the concept of speed is one that continues to fascinate humankind. It is of no surprise, therefore, that evidence of this condition can be found at the very dawn of motoring. Reporting on the Paris-Rouen reliability run of 22 July 1894, Gerald Rose, in his classic *A Record of Motor Racing 1894-1908*, notes that, "many now well-known people were present at the start, amongst them Mr James Gordon Bennett, the proprietor of the *New York Herald*, who sent a special reporter on a bicycle to follow the race through to Rouen".

Le Petit Journal, the newspaper that sponsored the Paris-Rouen trials, considered them a success. A large crowd saw the start on the Boulevard Maillot. Reports in the archives of the Automobile Club de France indicate that the lunch stop at Nantes was enjoyed by both the townspeople and participants and a remarkable seventeen of the twenty-one starters completed the 78.75 mile run and hill climb.

The inception of the automobile speed record on 18 December 1898 was owed entirely to the introduction of motor-car reliability trials and hill climbing to the Paris-Rouen area by the debonair Count Gaston de Chasseloup-Laubat.

Count Gaston de Chasseloup-Laubat was the younger brother of the

The bullet shaped La Jamais Contente *shortly after Camille Jenatzy established a new World Land Speed Record of 65.79 mph (105.904 kph). The car was powered by two electric motors driven by Fulmen batteries by way of direct drive to the rear wheels.*

Léon Serpollet was one of the world's most talented steam car exponents, observed here in his streamlined 4-cylinder, single-acting steam-powered car at the start line on the Promenade des Anglais at Nice, where he broke Camille Jenatzy's land speed record at 75.06 mph (120.79 kph) on 13 April 1902.

Marquis de Chasseloup-Laubat, who had founded the now legendary Automobile Club de France (ACF).

It was cold and wet on the morning 18 December 1898, when the dashing Count took his chain-driven 40 horsepower Jeantaud electric motorcar to the lonely Achères road outside Paris. He made a single run through a measured kilometre in 57 seconds for an average speed of 39.24 mph (63.13 kph) and claimed an official world record. The seeds of rivalry had been sown; doubtless someone would soon come along and have a go at beating it ....

The news that a Frenchman had done such a thing struck like a thunderbolt at the heart of a patriotic Belgian electric car inventor, the red-bearded Camille Jenatzy. He sat down and penned a challenge to the Frenchman; they would duel with their electric motorcars in what was to be the world's first road race.

They met on the Achères road on 17 January 1899. Jenatzy, the challenger, was the first to be timed. He passed through the measured kilometer at 41.42 mph (66.65 kph), the electric batteries of his motor car giving out just after he crossed the terminal timing line. The French Count, however, recorded an elapsed time of 43.69 mph (70.31 kph) to beat him, subsequently burning out the motor of his Jeantaud with the overburdening surge of power he had applied in his quest to regain his record.

De Chasseloup-Laubat and Jenatzy agreed to meet again at Achères, and both intrepid drivers went home to build bigger engines for the race. Jenatzy won the next challenge round at 49.92 mph (80.33 kph) ten days later. By this time the titanic struggle between the two electric car drivers had attracted so much interest that the Automobile Club de France organized rules and appointed official time-keepers and marshals for the now famous runs.

The Frenchman next returned to Achères alone in March to establish yet another new record, 57.60 mph (92.69 kph). Jenatzy confidently continued working on a new idea that he felt certain would win him back the record. He developed an electric motor with secondary coils that would turn at 900 rpm, something not possible it was thought at that time. He christened his new car *La Jamais Contente* (Never Satisfied), perhaps to remind himself that he would not submit to his French rival. Once again, he challenged the Count, and the run was set for 1 April 1899. Jenatzy, once again the challenger, was to go first as was the custom, but he started his run too soon. When he reached the end of the timed kilometre, officials there were still measuring the distance and had not marked the exact spot for the vital timing recognition. Jenatzy was sure he had broken through the 100 kph barrier, but due to the lack of urgency shown by the ACF officials and timing marshals, the feat could not be recognized, and he could not repeat the run having totally exhausted his batteries on the first run.

Jenatzy returned to the same lonely road on 29 April, but this time the Count Gaston de Chasseloup-Laubat was present as one of the large crowd of spectators lining the track. The Belgian admonished the time-keepers and

Henry Ford driving his 1902 racer at Empire City Raceway, New York, while mechanic 'Spider' Huff walks the running-board after beating Alexander Winton.

Henry Ford (left) driving the famous Ford 999 in a wheel-to-wheel with Harry Harkness in the Mercedes-Simplex at Grosse Point, Michigan.

received their assurances that there would be no slip-ups on the course this time. They were so intent on accuracy, in fact, that after the run they were still checking their timepieces after Jenatzy had dismounted and stormed up to them demanding to know his speed. It was a new record, 65.79 mph or better than 105 kilometres per hour. He had broken the 100 kilometre barrier. Jenatzy held the World Land Speed Record for nearly three years, and the speed record for electric cars for more than half a century.

When the record was broken, Léon Serpollet, a Frenchman, did it in a steam-powered car, using for his track the famous Promenade des Anglais at Nice, because the Achères road was too rough for such high speeds. Serpollet drove his streamlined steam car, *La Baleine* (The Whale), to a speed of 75.06 mph (120.79 kph), holding his breath nearly all the way through the kilometre. He allegedly remarked after the run that he literally had to turn his head to inhale.

The World Land Speed Record inched slowly upwards, while sportsmen like American millionaire William K. Vanderbilt Jr, the great Henri Fournier, the Hon. Charles S. Rolls, whose name, coupled with that of Royce, epitomized British motoring at its best, Baron de Forest, and Arthur Duray held official and unofficial records for short periods of time. The World Land Speed Record was a European possession, even though the famed Ormond Beach, Florida, near Daytona, had become recognized as the best of the great beach courses. In fact, the Ormond Beach garage became the first American 'Gasoline Alley', housing the great racing machines of the day, and today, is the home of the legendary Birthplace of Speed Association.

It remained for a Mid-western auto mechanic, however, to be the first American to drive an American-built car on American soil and set the new record. Henry Ford had just resigned his position as a general superintendent of the Detroit based Edison Company to build his own gasoline-powered automobiles. Noting the success of Alexander Winton, Frank Duryea and Ransom Olds, who promoted their cars through racing, Ford built two racing cars, the Ford *999* and the famous *Arrow*. Henry Ford stated his feelings about competition, writing in his autobiography, "Almost everyone proceeded from the premise that a first class car would automatically develop the highest speed''.

In Ford's first challenge of the fabled Winton, he won a match race. Next, Ford hired as a driver a bicycle racer, Barney Oldfield, who went out to race Winton and won again; the first time he had ever sat in the driver's seat of an automobile. (Oldfield later recalled that he did not know how to handle the car and so had driven flat-out through the corners due to pure ignorance of the way of the automobile.)

Ford had one more speed stunt to pull off: breaking the World Land Speed Record, which at that time was 84.73 mph (136.35 kph). Although not a racing driver himself, Ford took his *Arrow* out to Lake St. Clair, Michigan, on 12 January 1904. Not far from Detroit, Lake St. Clair is a smaller stretch of water amidst the Great Lakes region, connecting Lake Huron with Lake Erie, and upon its frozen surface a mile was measured out. Ford made a test run, and then proudly announced to the spectators and time-keepers that man and machine were ready to make an attempt at the record.

With aide Spider Huff at his side, Ford inched onto the frozen, hard-packed ice covering the lake, his spindly pneumatic tyres spinning on the hot cinders that were spread for adhesion on the melting surface. He hit the first crack, bounced, and almost lost his grip on the frozen steering wheel. Fighting to regain control as the four-cylinder, 70 horsepower engine continued to force more power to the wheels, Ford held on grimly while *Arrow* hit another crack and bounced higher into the air. Slipping and sliding across the frozen lake, the car flashed through the measured mile at an average speed of 91.37 mph (147.04 kph), Ford said in retirement many years later that he had scared himself so badly on that run, that having broken the record, he never again wanted to climb into a racing car.

The impetus of Ford's world record, albeit on ice, which was flashed from coast-to-coast by the telegraphic news service, enabled him to get his

The popular Belgian sportsman, Baron Pierre de Caters in the 90 hp Gordon Bennett-type road racing Mercedes with which he set the record at 97.26 mph (156.52 kph) on 25 May, 1904, on the Ostend to Nieuport road.

Henry Ford calculates his timing while mechanic 'Spider' Hutt attends to the 4-cylinder, 16.7-litre engine shortly after the record attempt.

A rare and historical photograph of American Automobile Association Contest Board secretary Samuel Butler, centre, inspecting new timing equipment at Ormond-Daytona in 1906.

While the European manufacturers were building bigger engines and heavier cars to carry them, the Stanley brothers of Newton, Massachusetts, entered the land speed record sphere in 1906 with their remarkably advanced racer with the rear-mounted steam power unit. Christened the Stanley Rocket, it raised the World Land Speed Record to 121.57 mph (195.64 kph) at Ormond-Daytona Beach. Driven by Fred Marriott, head of their factory maintenance department, the flying mile was timed at 127.66 mph (203.83 kph).

fledgling automobile manufacturing business off the ground. He never forgot the lesson that people equate quality with speed in a motor car.

The World Land Speed Record continued creeping upward toward the 100 mph barrier. The world's first true drag racing exponent, France's Louis Emile Rigolly, liked to duel wheel-to-wheel from a standing start. He competed in a long series of contests with Arthur Duray, Baron Pierre de Caters, and P. Baras, culminating in a dramatic showdown meeting alongside the canal running from Ostend to Nieuport in Belgium on 21 July 1904.

Having been defeated by Baras in a standing mile race, Rigolly was determined to do something spectacular. He roared through the flying kilometre in the 13,500 cc Gobron-Brillié at a speed of 103.55 mph (166.64 kph).

Rigolly's car was one of the behemothic fuel-devouring devils of the day, typical of the early speed mechanics' approach to achieving more

Fred Marriott streaks through the measured-mile at Ormond Beach in the Stanley Rocket. *With no gearbox, the car was driven by a twin-cylinder horizontal, rear-mounted steam power unit, driving the rear wheels direct through connecting rods. The streamlined body was of cedar construction covered in taut canvas, with a full-length underpan.*

speed – make the engine bigger and more powerful. Vanderbilt's sleek Mercedes, however, had an 8,700cc engine; Duray's Gobron-Brillié had a 13,500cc displacement and Ford's *Arrow* was a powerful 16,708cc.

While the European manufacturers were building bigger and bigger engines and even heavier cars to carry them, the Stanley brothers of Newton, Massachusetts, took a very different approach. They wanted to set a record to promote the performance of their ill-fated steam car project, the *Rocket*. Rather than recruit a professional driver like Barney Oldfield or Clifford Earp, the Stanley brothers selected Fred Marriott, head of their factory maintenance department, to drive their new creation. He would make the record attempt on the vast sands at Ormond Beach.

Since the first speed trials had been made on the 23-mile stretch of Florida coastline in 1902, Ormond Beach had become the traditional home of

Fred Marriott (top photo in duster and goggles) poses with one of the Stanley brothers before setting his record speed in the Stanley Rocket *in 1906. Trying to better the record the following year, Marriott crashed at around 150 mph (240 kph), and was lucky to escape alive. The engine (on the left of the lower photograph) was notably intact.*

18

Louis Chevrolet, driver of the 22.5-litre, 200 bhp, V8 Darracq was the Stanley Brother's most formidable rival at Daytona in 1906.

American millionaire William K. Vanderbilt, Jr, not only held the land speed record twice, but his books on touring were among the very first and finest of the day. He was also the founder of the celebrated Vanderbilt Cup series.

land speed record attempts. It was there that the great Alexander Winton and Ransom E. Olds raced side by side at 60 mph, and the line judges declared them dead-heat finishers. It was to nearby Daytona that the artful Vanderbilt had slipped his Mercedes by charter boat, because there was no dependable route by road. When the skipper eyed the sinister-looking driving machine suspiciously, Vanderbilt offered to drain the highly inflammable petrol from the tank before putting her aboard. Vanderbilt actually emptied the radiator instead of the fuel tanks, because he knew there was no gasoline in Ormond. The boatman didn't know the difference.

Ormond Beach was not a smooth course, but a friable, rippled one that frequently changed its contours as the ebbing tides and continuous sea breeze sculptured the shoreline. The crowd was a partisan one, favouring cars powered by the internal combustion engine, as Fred Marriott set off in his steam car across the sands of 26 January 1906. The car hissed quietly to itself; as if to gain the favour of the spectators it gave off very little sound. Marriott was timed at 127.66 mph (205.44 kph) in the mile, and just for good measure he made a return run through the flying kilometre at 121.57 mph (195.64 kph). Both are records that still stand today in the category for steam-powered cars.

Contemporary newspaper reports reveal the undercurrent of prejudice against the Stanley *Rocket,* a large proportion of the local and indeed National press condemning it as a freak. Even though Fred Marriott became the first man to travel at the rate of two miles per minute, he was robbed of his moment of personal glory, for another driver was crowned speed king of the meet that year.

The Stanley brothers knew the value of publicity to be gained from setting a World Land Speed Record, and they knew too well the sceptics and detractors were still far from impressed by the fact that their car had, in one swoop across the sands at Ormond, raised the all-time record by more

The spectacular barnstorming American, 'Wild Bob' Burman who, in April 1911, claimed to have broken Barney Oldfield's flying-mile record at Daytona Beach, with a one-way run through the mile in 25.40 seconds, or equal to 141.37 mph (227.51 kph). The European ACF naturally rejected the 'one-way' record; the Americans accepted it ... the inauguration of an era of controversy between the rules and ultimate speed timing.

than 18 miles an hour, running well below full potential power. They returned to Daytona for Speed Week, 1907, determined to prove the car's true land speed potential.

The Stanley *Rocket* was rated at only 50 horsepower, but the car, which looked like a torpedo on wheels, weighed a mere 1,600 pounds. For the 1906 run, Marriott had used only 900 psi of steam pressure, but this time he had the boiler up to 1,300 psi, and the car had a better gear ratio. The rippled sands, however, were in a terrible condition as Marriott steamed away from the starting line. Taking almost nine miles for his run-up, he entered the measured mile at speeds estimated at between 132 mph and 190 mph on the first run and between 196 and 198 mph on the second run, when disaster struck.

Approaching the 197 mph mark, Marriott hit one of the troublesome gullies running across the beach. The nose of the *Rocket* lifted like a kite, the car rose some 10 feet in the air, twisting sideways as it careered down the course, smashing to the beach 100 feet down range. The boiler exploded on impact, the car disintegrated, hurtling debris across the Ormond course. Fearing the worst, rescuers were astonished to find the driver unconscious but alive, with four cracked ribs, a fractured breastbone, facial injuries, and his right eye hanging out of its socket. A Mexican doctor who happened to be holidaying close to the crash scene took him to the nearby Coquina Hotel for attention, there slipping the eyeball back into place with a sugar spoon; Marriott quipped, "Now it's the best eye I have ... Thanks Doc!"

Tommy Milton, who, although blind in one eye, was among the great names at Indianapolis in the 1920s. Seen here at the wheel of Louis Chevrolet's new twin ohc straight-eight Frontenac. Milton went on to break Ralph de Palma's record on Daytona Beach at 156.03 mph (251.10 kph) in the ingenious 10-litre, twin-engined Duesenberg, but the AIACR predictably declined to accept the record.

Fred and Augie Duesenberg's principal driver, the ingenious Tommy Milton.

From 1909 to 1920, the gallant Blitzen Benz dominated the raceways across the United States. After setting the flying mile record with a two-way average of 131.72 mph (211.98 kph) at Daytona Beach in 1910, Barney Oldfield endured a season of 'barnstorming', often competing on the famed Empire City Raceway, New York.

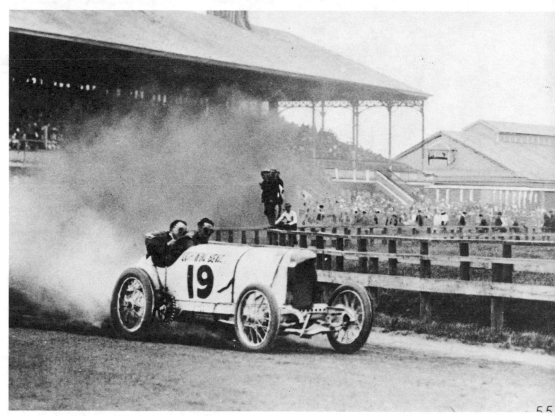

Tommy Milton broke de Palma's record at 156.03 mph (251.094 kph) in the 10-litre, Double Duesey at Daytona in 1920. The AIACR (Association Internationale des Automobiles Clubs Reconnus) predictably declined to accept it. The A.A.A. (American Automobile Association) did. Without further ado, the Sinclair Refining Company ran a full-page advertisement in the Chicago Times-Herald.

Veteran 'cigar-chewing' Barney Oldfield, who established a remarkable 131.275mph (211.256 kph) on 23 March 1910 at Daytona Beach, at the wheel of the 21.5-litre Blitzen-Benz.

In 1911, Barney Oldfield lost his coveted US national racing permit for competing in a non-AAA sanctioned meeting. In protest he sold his entire racing stock, including the 21.5-litre Blitzen Benz to Ed Moross. On 23 April 1911, American barnstormer, 'Wild Bob' Burman claimed to have eclipsed Oldfield's flying mile record by more than 10 mph with a one-way pass in 25.40 seconds (141.37 mph, 227.51 kph) at Daytona beach, The Americans accepted it ... the French predictably rejected it. For Benz however, it was sufficient to run an advertisement with worldwide syndication, extolling the virtues of Germanic engineering.

René Thomas broke the land speed record at 143.31 mph (230.634 kph) during the 1924 Arpajon sprint meeting in the V12, ohv 10.6-litre, 280 bhp engined Délage.

A prime example of an early corporate advertisement depicting the significance of automotive product association with land speed record vehicles, extolling the success of Ralph De Palma's record of 149.875 mph (241.189 kph) through the mile at Daytona in February 1919.

The Stanley brothers vowed then and there that they would never build another racing car. In Europe the news of this, the first serious accident in pursuit of the World Land Speed Record, and the subsequent destruction of the *Rocket,* was received with a sigh of relief, though it took no less than four years to reinstate the internal combustion engine as the dominant power.

At Daytona Beach on the morning of 23 March 1910, Barney Oldfield drove the 21½-litre *Blitzen Benz* to a new Land Speed Record of 131.724 mph (211.988 kph). Unfortunately, the European officials who at that time approved all world records did not recognize the attempt initially, but the lesson was perfectly clear: American drivers were just as fast as the French, English and Germans.

Oldfield's successful Land Speed Record attempt set the stage for the emergence of another American speed pioneer. On 23 April 1911, wild Bob Burman celebrated his twenty-seventh birthday by driving the same *Blitzen Benz* that Oldfield had raced, and Burman clearly proved he was faster on the Daytona sand, covering the flying mile at 141.370 mph (227.512 kph). The new international rules called for speed runs to be made in two directions to qualify as world records. Accordingly, Burman's great feat was never recognized, but in the United States he was suddenly a national hero. A month later, at the inaugural Indianapolis 500, entrepreneurial tyre manufacturer Harvey Firestone, placed a $10,000 crown on Burman's head, with the apt inscription 'The World's Speed King'.

It took an Englishman, L.G. 'Cupid' Hornsted, to become the first man on earth to set a two-way record when he achieved an average speed of

The intrepid Ralph De Palma, driver of the exquisite 9.9-litre, 240 bhp V12-engined Packard.

Major Henry Segrave thunders past the timing traps at Southport beach at the wheel of the 4-litre Sunbeam on 16 March 1926 to a new World Land Speed Record of 152.33 mph (245.149 kph).

124.100 mph (199.720 kph) with the aid of a 200 horsepower 'Blitzen'-engined Benz around the famed Brooklands track in Surrey on 24 June 1914. It was considerably slower than the existing record, but it satisfied the new two-way requirements and was declared 'official' by the newly formed FIA, a decision that outraged the Americans. Land speed records were entering a new golden era, but Hornsted's record was fated to last the duration of the First World War.

In Arpajon, France, René Thomas, the portly, French national champion and 1914 Indianapolis 500 winner, established a post-war 'official' record of 143.310 mph (230.634 kph) in the V12, 10.6-litre Delage on 6th July 1924, but it fell far short of the unrecognized one-way record. The great Indianapolis champion, Ralph De Palma, had travelled at 149.875 mph (241.199 kph) through the measured mile in a 12-cylinder Packard at Daytona on 12 February 1919. His unofficial record was broken on 27 April 1920, by Tommy Milton, who sped across the Daytona course at 156.030 mph (251.105 kph) in a Duesenberg, powered by two side-by-side 8-cylinder engines.

Thomas's record was the one that counted, not that of any of the Americans, but on the day the Frenchman set the record, Ernest Eldridge, an Englishman, was at Arpajon to challenge it. Eldridge was driving a highly modified Fiat, *Mephistopheles,* powered by an immense 6-cylinder, 24-valve, 300 horsepower A12 aviation engine of First World War vintage. Eldridge, with mechanic Jim Ames as a passenger, made his two-way run that day at 146.800 mph (236.251 kph). This annoyed Thomas, who strongly protested against the car on the grounds that it had no reverse gear, as called for by international rules. Officials ruled in favour of Thomas. His record was still the one that counted.

Across the Channel, the British were readying for the challenge with a new car. This was the famous 350 horsepower Sunbeam, which ushered in the era of aero-engined land speed record cars. The Sunbeam first appeared at Brooklands in 1920. Two years later, Kenelm Lee Guinness (founder of the famous KLG Sparking Plug Company) reached 144 mph (232 kph) around the Weybridge circuit.

On 17 May 1922, Guinness set a new World Land Speed Record of 133.75 mph (215.25 kph). It was the same car that Sir Malcolm Campbell later purchased to set the first in a series of nine records he was to hold.

On 27 April 1926, Parry Thomas made his début in the most famous of the behemoth cars, affectionately named Babs.

J.G. Parry Thomas in the cockpit of Babs *shortly before the fatal accident.*

Engines continuod to grow, as Sir Malcolm Campbell and Sir Henry Segrave embarked on their outstanding land speed record careers to set even faster speeds. Campbell and Segrave were soon joined by another challenger in the arena of speed, the Welshman, John Godfrey Parry Thomas.

Unlike Campbell and Segrave, Thomas did not have the resources to build a record car of modern racing specifications and standards. The Higham Special which he purchased for £125 from Count Louis Zboröwsky, was affectionately known as *Babs.* Thomas's car had an enormous 400-horsepower, 26.9-litre, 45-degree V12 American Liberty aero-engine, fitted into a long, sleek chassis made by Rubery Owen and sporting those longitudinal bracing stays designed to impart extra beam strength, and typical of the Brooklands racing cars of the twenties. After Thomas acquired the car, he streamlined it and fitted the engine with four Zenith carburettors and special pistons he designed himself.

On 27 April 1926, Thomas made six runs on the Pendine Sands in South Wales, setting a best two-way record of 169.30 mph (215.25 kph) through the flying mile. He returned the next day and raised the record to 171.02 mph (275.22 kph), the first man in history to set two World Land Speed Records in two consecutive days. Yet, he was far from satisfied.

Both Segrave and Campbell had set 180 mph – three miles a minute – as their goal, and Thomas knew his record wouldn't hold up for long with the aristocratic duo on his tail. It didn't. On 4 February 1927, Campbell averaged 174.88 mph (281.44 kph) and Parry Thomas was once again the challenger.

It was a cold, wet day when Thomas arrived at the Pendine Sands on 1st

Not unlike a beached whale, Babs after the crash at Pendine in which J.G. Parry Thomas lost his life. His was the first driver fatality in World Land Speed Record breaking in 29 years.

March 1927. It rained again the following day, but on 3 March the weather had improved enough to enable Thomas to roll *Babs* out onto the beach. On the first run he trailed black smoke, and blamed the trouble on his Zenith carburettors. Smoke was still billowing out of the exhausts when he started his sixth run close to the Beach Hotel. Thomas had just completed the measured mile on his return run when *Babs* was seen to slew. It suddenly

In quite remarkable condition after being buried for 42 years under the Pendine Sands, Carmarthenshire, J.G. Parry Thomas's Babs was exhumed from her watery grave by Owen Wyn Owen of Bangor. Apart from residual corrosion of the aluminium body panels, the car was almost as she fell on 3 March 1927, in the terrifying accident that killed her intrepid driver.

Sir Malcolm Campbell rolls out his new and costly 22.3-litre Lion-engined Napier-Campbell Bluebird in which he broke Parry Thomas's record at the Pendine Sands in February 1927, averaging 174.883 mph (281.446 kph) in two extremely wet and bumpy runs, which finally convinced Campbell a new venue for land speed record attempts was needed.

An advertisement celebrating Captain Malcolm Campbell's success in winning the 1925 90 mph Short Handicap in the Autumn BARC Meeting at Brooklands, at the wheel of his Chrysler Six. Campbell averaged a lap speed of 99.61 mph (160.30 kph).

went out of control, rolled, righting itself, then swathed a gigantic arc in the sand, ending up with the engine ablaze. Horrified spectators led by mechanic Jock Pullen rushed to the aid of the driver, but when they reached the wreckage they recoiled at the horrific sight. There sat Parry, upright in the seat of the car, with part of his head lying beside *Babs* in the sand. The drive chain to the rear wheels had broken at 2,000 rpm and slashed through its safety guard like a knife through butter, virtually decapitating Thomas. He never knew what hit him. Thomas was buried in the tranquil setting of Byfleet Church, Brooklands, the site of the race track where he made his name.

As to the speed in that final, fatal run, it was never known, for the timing wire had also been broken by the savage contortions of the car. So ended the career of a gallant speed pioneer. Parry Thomas was the first driver to be killed in pursuit of the World Land Speed Record, 29 years after its official beginnings.

Ab Jenkins and the 'Mormon Meteor'

Although in his late 60s, devout Mormon, Ab Jenkins embarked on a career with the sole objective of snatching the World Land Speed Record from under the very noses of the 'ruddy' Englishmen, who turned up on the Bonneville Salt Flats with their exotic streamliners to capture and retain the record over a span of 23 years. This was raised from a mere 146.16 mph (235.22 kph) to 394.20 mph (634.40 kph), broken only once for the United States by Ray Keech who established a record of 207.552 mph (334.021 kph) in the Liberty-powered *White Triplex*.

In 1933, driving a 12-cylinder Pierce-Arrow, equipped with a 200 horsepower engine with 488 cubic inch displacement, Jenkins set a 24-hour endurance record of 177.77 mph (286.09 kph), and covered some 3,000 miles

On 20 July 1951, at the age of sixty-eight, the pioneering Salt Lake City carpenter, Ab Jenkins, emerged from the salt-sprayed cockpit of the Mormon Meteor and announced his retirement from the Bonneville Speedway he founded in 1910 ... an encounter that launched a romance with Speed 'n' salt that had blossomed for more than forty years.

Ab Jenkins 12-cylinder, 750 bhp Mormon Meteor *stands sentinel on the Bonneville Salt Flats.*

in 25 hours 30 minutes 36.62 seconds. Although the Bonneville course became famous as a result of these records, it took the personal campaigning of Ab Jenkins at Daytona Beach to attract the top European competitors to Utah for their successful records.

The following year, Ab raised the 24-hour record to 127.229 mph (204.754 kph) driving a car with a similar chassis and equipped with a now-familiar streamline racing bodyshell. The 12-cylinder Pierce-Arrow engine was equipped with six carburettors, special manifolds and high compression heads. The car was christened the *Ab Jenkins Special.*

In 1935, the first Duesenberg Special to appear on the salt was designed and engineered for Ab Jenkins by Augie Duesenberg. The engine was a variation on a theme of an earlier design completed by the famous Duesenberg brothers, Fred and Augie, shortly before Fred's untimely death.

Built by Lycoming, the engine was a supercharged straight-8, developing 350 horsepower, with a 420 cubic inch displacement. A number of these chassis were built and sold 'off the shelf', at a cost of $11,000 each. The bodyshell was the first to be designed with the aid of a wind tunnel test facility, at the Ohio State University. Little did Ab know that, some 35 years later, this same, pioneering facility, would conduct the transonic and supersonic tests of the rocket-powered land speed record car *The Blue Flame.*

With this car, and with Tony Gulotta as relief driver, Jenkins established a new 24-hour record of 135.58 mph (218.19 kph) at Bonneville during the 1935 season.

*Romeo Palamides'
jet-powered* Infinity *is
rolled out onto the salt for
what LSR history has
recorded to be a reckless
foray in the quest for
speed. Glenn Leasher from
San Mateo, California lost
his life in pursuit of the
coveted title 'Fastest Man
on Earth', when the vehicle
exploded in a series of
rolls that scattered its
remains over two miles of
the hallowed Bonneville Salt
Flats.*

The first *Mormon Meteor* made its appearance in 1936. It was clearly designed from the ground up for speed.

The chassis was a specially-designed Duesenberg with wire wheels. The bodyshell was built at Indianapolis by Augie Duesenberg, Ab Jenkins and a select team of expert mechanics.

Successful British challenges to Jenkins' endurance records in 1935 had convinced the most famous man in Utah that aero-engines would be needed to power future vehicles. He found what he wanted in New Jersey, in the possession of the famous 'barnstormer' Clyde Pangborne.

Ab returned to Indianapolis with a complement of two Curtiss Wright Conquerors-V-type, 12-cylinder, water-cooled powerplants that developed 700 horsepower. One of these aero-engines was used by Pangborne and Hugh Herndon Jr in their famous round-the- world flight of 1931, also for the first non-stop crossing of the Pacific Ocean.

The car was completed in time to race in 1936 and, using Babe Stapp as relief driver, Jenkins once again rewrote the record books for endurance driving.

It was a hard year, with Capt George Eyston and John Cobb on hand to make the contest a three-cornered event for the endurance records. Eyston was first in the slot with his *Speed of the Wind.* He set a new 24-hour record of 149.096 mph (79.012 kph), then went on to establish a 48-hour record of 136.34 mph (219.41 kph).

Jenkins and Stapp, with the *Mormon Meteor,* made the next bid but were interrupted after the 500-kilometre (310 mile), and 500-mile (805 km) records had fallen.

A front universal joint burned out, and the *Meteor's* run was aborted for vital repair. New records, set before the race was ended by misfortune, included: 500-kilometres, 164.47 mph (264.68 kph); 500 miles, 152.34 mph (245.16 kph); 12-hours, 152.84 mph (245.97 kph).

Cobb then took to the circular track and replaced Eyston's 24-hour record with a speed of 150.163 mph (241.663 kph), but Jenkins and Stapp were far from finished.

Returning to Bonneville in late September of 1936, they captured for America every record from 50-miles to 48-hours inclusive. The times: 24-hours, 153.823 mph (247.55 kph); and for the 48-hours, 148.641 mph (239.213 kph).

At the close of the most colourful season so far on the salt, all parties

A few pieces of steel framework, the seat, safety harness, and a solitary boot were among the recognizable bits of wreckage that remained after Glenn Leasher, 26, of San Mateo, California, was killed on 10 September 1962, driving Romeo Palamides' General Electric J47 5,200 lb thrust jet-powered Infinity. *To this day the wreckage remains in the Utah Highway Maintenance Yard in Wendover.*

withdrew to their respective workshops to build or rebuild their cars.

The *Mormon Meteor II* saw only minor changes, including the installation of a revolutionary new design of a vertical fin at the rear of the car. The creation of a potential World Land Speed Record car was beginning to emerge from the chrysalis of time and experience.

Ab Jenkins, the carpenter from Salt Lake City, first saw the salt in 1910 when he drove his motorcycle to a speed of 60 mph.

The most spectacular event to promote the Bonneville Salt Flats as a potential land speed record speedway, took place in 1925, shortly after the completion of the Lincoln Highway, linking Salt Lake City with Wendover.

W.D. Rishel, life-long friend of Ab Jenkins and the first man to drive a car across the saline highway, in 1900, asked his old friend if he would race the special excursion train from Salt Lake City to Wendover, a distance of 125 miles. Ab Jenkins said he would – provided there was a purse of $250 riding on the outcome. The money was quickly raised and the race was on – the dawn of sponsorship had broken!

Streaking across the Salt Flats, Ab beat the train by no less than 4 minutes 29 seconds. That very run cemented the confidence of all associated with speed and record breaking; Bonneville became a household name in the workshops and garages from coast-to-coast.

At the age of 68, Ab returned to Bonneville for what many people thought would be his last appearance.

On 20 July 1951, just short of a year before the birth of the author, Ab Jenkins set 24 new International Class A and American records, the most notable being a 196.36 mph (361.01 kph) average for 100 miles.

In July 1952, Ab, tired of his desk in the Utah Capitol, where he had served as a safety engineer, was signed by the Firestone Tire and Rubber Company to appear on a strenuous tour of the United States. In addition to personal 'cameo' appearances, Ab's publicity routine consisted of driving at 80 mph, and purposely blowing out a front tyre to demonstrate the safety factors incorporated in his sponsor's supreme product, the first in the historical development of what has become known as 'the safety tyre'.

In August 1952, the *Mormon Meteor* was turned out to pasture for the last time, amid the stately surroundings of The Capitol Building in Salt Lake City.

At 69, Ab Jenkins embarked on a career to capture the most coveted prize of all – The World Land Speed Record. At an age when most of us would be well into retirement, and limiting our activities to tending the vegetable plot, the devout Mormon set about designing and building a jet-powered car capable of attaining a terminal velocity in excess of 500 mph. To power the LSR car – tentatively named the *American Meteor* – a J30 or the larger J34 turbo-jet, manufactured by Westinghouse, would be used. These powerful engines develop 3,000 to 4,000 horsepower a piece, at speeds of 375 mph and up. A vertical tail fin would again be incorporated in the design, for at such speeds, Jenkins observed the power-to-weight ratio of many of the early jet-powered research aircraft, and noted that without a substantial tail-fin the aircraft were left with great instability, with a subsequent tendency to yaw. This occurred when the thrust of an engine mounted at the rear of the craft exceeded the weight of the fuselage forward of the propulsion system, resulting in the very simple, although often tragic result, of the rear overtaking the front of the aircraft.

On 1 August, 1960, Salt Lake City garage owner Athol Graham fired up his $2,500 Allison-powered, Firestone-sponsored car, *City of Salt Lake*. Some two miles down range, the car veered slightly off course, it began to slide, turned, became airborne and crashed in a blazing inferno. Graham, 36, died three hours later in a Salt Lake City hospital.

Two years after the tragic death of Athol Graham, on the morning of 10 September 1962, Glenn Leasher had already completed what was to be the first in a series of runs in Romeo Palamides' jet car *Infinity*. On his second run into the mile the car (without a vertical tail fin) began to yaw and slide approaching 250 mph; the car rolled and exploded killing Leasher instantly. Some say this was due to the absence of a tail fin. Less learned LSR sceptics were quick to put the tragedy down to the inexperience of Leasher; a somewhat common practice when the victim is unable to reply to the scepticism of the 'armchair' experts of speed.

As far back as 1952, Ab Jenkins predicted the mandatory inclusion of a vertical tail fin in the design of any land bound vehicle or projectile, for both guidance and greater stability at speeds, in excess of 200 mph.

While his 12-cylinder, 750 bhp *Mormon Meteor* had a speed potential of 275 mph, Jenkins' proposed assault on the World Land Speed Record never came of age.

Ab Jenkins was born in 1883 and died in his sleep in 1956 at the age of 73. On the day of his death the plans for the *American Meteor* jet car were almost complete; only four days previously he accepted from Firestone, the delivery of four transonic tyres, tested at speeds in excess of 450 mph (725 kph). The Grand old man of speed had gone ...

Major Henry Segrave - The English Gentleman

Major Henry Segrave, the debonair test driver for the Wolverhampton-based Sunbeam Motor Company, was the obvious choice to drive the first in a new series of potential land speed record Sunbeams. He was a staunchly patriotic Englishman, winning for Sunbeam the 1923 French Grand Prix and no less than 14 other road and track races.

Powered by a V12, twin ohc, 4-litre, 306 bhp, supercharged engine, the Sunbeam was the latest racing machine to emerge from the stable of Louis Coatalen, chief engineer and racing team manager for the famous Sunbeam-Talbot-Darracq group.

The street machine that launched an industry: Camille Jenatzy's 1899 La Jamais Contente, a truly remarkable streamliner engineered and designed by the renowned Léon Auscher, Chief Engineer with the Paris based light-alloy manufacturing concern, Carrosserie Rothschild. In 1903 Jenatzy and Auscher donated their vehicle to the Musée National de la Voiture et du Tourisme, Château de Compiègne, Oise, France, where it still remains today.

The magnificent V12 Sunbeam Tiger was the last World Land Speed Record car to be raced on a circuit. Only two of these remarkable cars were built, based on the 1925 2-litre Grand Prix model. Major Henry Segrave took this car to a new record of 152.33 mph (245.140 kph), at Southport in 1926, and subsequently went on to race at Brooklands, Boulogne and San Sebastian. Its Brooklands career included victory in the Mountain Championship for Sir Malcolm Campbell in 1932. A second car, fitted with a Napier Lion engine, is currently raced in British Vintage events as the Sunbeam-Napier.

The 3976cc, V12 engine of the Sunbeam Tiger was based on two of the 1925, 2-litre, Grand Prix engines, mounted in a 75-degree vee on a common crankcase. The supercharged engine developed 306 bhp and was versatile enough to be used for both circuit racing and record breaking.

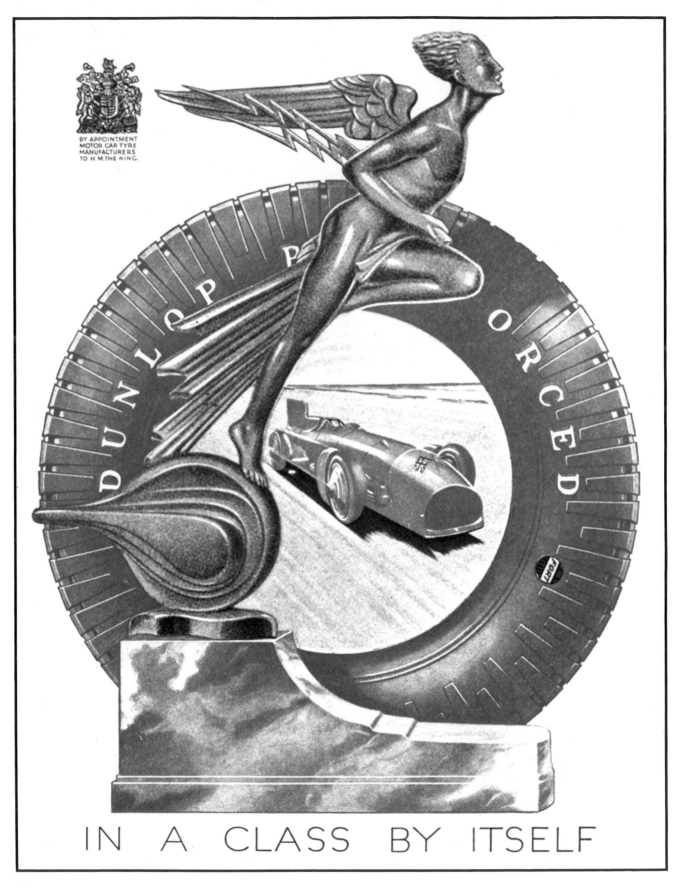

IN A CLASS BY ITSELF

Such was the decline of the English motor industry in the 1930's, automotive product association with projects such as Malcolm Campbell's 1931 Campbell-Napier-Railton Bluebird, prompted the Dunlop Rubber Co. Ltd to invest the princely sum of £13 17s 6d in a full-page advertisement in Punch magazine.

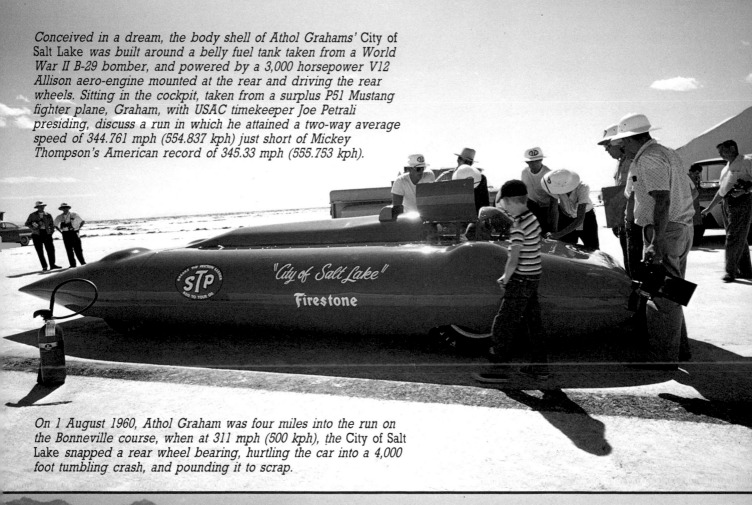

Conceived in a dream, the body shell of Athol Grahams' City of Salt Lake was built around a belly fuel tank taken from a World War II B-29 bomber, and powered by a 3,000 horsepower V12 Allison aero-engine mounted at the rear and driving the rear wheels. Sitting in the cockpit, taken from a surplus P51 Mustang fighter plane, Graham, with USAC timekeeper Joe Petrali presiding, discuss a run in which he attained a two-way average speed of 344.761 mph (554.837 kph) just short of Mickey Thompson's American record of 345.33 mph (555.753 kph).

On 1 August 1960, Athol Graham was four miles into the run on the Bonneville course, when at 311 mph (500 kph), the City of Salt Lake snapped a rear wheel bearing, hurtling the car into a 4,000 foot tumbling crash, and pounding it to scrap.

Designed by Monsieur Louis Coatalen, Major Henry Segrave's 1,000 hp Sunbeam was powered by two mighty V12, 22½-litre, Matabele aero-engines for the record-breaking Ormond-Daytona runs. Even on the test bed at Sunbeam's Wolverhampton works, the 1,000 hp vehicle was an awe-inspiring sight. 'When I stood in front of it I doubted human ability to control it,' Segrave confessed.

The exquisite 26.9-litre, Irving-Napier Golden Arrow, considered by many to be the pinnacle of land speed engineering by the British motor manufacturing industry.

Four posters produced by Castrol to show their involvement with Sir Malcolm Campbell and Sir Henry Segrave's achievements in record breaking. Shown here are Campbell's 1928 and 1931 Bluebirds and the 1000 hp Sunbeam and the Golden Arrow of Segrave.

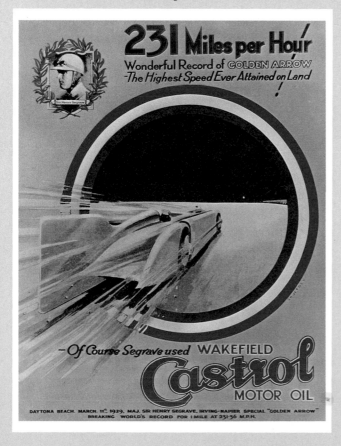

The beautiful lines of Donald Campbells Bluebird at Lake Eyre.

Corrosion from the salt had badly affected Bluebird's exterior and also the internal electrical connections, and the Proteus engine proved very difficult to start. Leo Villa and his team worked around the clock to prepare the 'Skipper's' car for the final run at Lake Eyre.

Mickey Thompson built Challenger *around four 6.7-litre Pontiac V8 engines, one pair driving the front wheels, the other the rear. In 1960 the enterprising Mickey Thompson supercharged the engines and on 9 September covered the measured mile on a one-way average speed at 406.60 mph (654.329 kph) beating John Cobb's record by over 12 mph. A driveshaft broke, preventing a return run and an official record, and subsequently bad weather, mechanical problems and eventually Thompson's health forced him to give up his attempt.*

Inset: Mickey Thompson and Challenger 1 *at Bonneville, the seemingly endless, glistening white, sterile salt flats in Western Utah — 3,000 square miles and 500 million tons of salt.*

By the time Mickey Thompson reached Bonneville on 30 October 1968, with his new Ford Autolite Special, *the salt was already wet from sporadic rains. Despite the threat of further rain approaching from the Stansbury Mountains to the east, Thompson hurtled his streamliner across the salt to 425 mph (683 kph). The rains came, robbing Thompson of a chance of a return run at the record.*

Bob Summers and Goldenrod.

THE 1,000 HP. SUNBEAM CAR

Built specially for an attempt
to attain a speed of

200 MILES PER HOUR

THE design and production of this remarkable British car is the latest achievement of the Sunbeam Company and its well known designer, Mr. Louis Coatalen. It has been built not merely in an endeavour to raise the present world's record for land speed, but with the avowed intention of reaching a speed of 200 miles per hour.

The car has been designed and built throughout at the Company's Works in Wolverhampton, and will be driven by Major H. O. D. Segrave. Apart from its phenomenal speed capabilities the design and lay-out are of unusual engineering interest.

The stresses and strains, enormous wind resistance and forces encountered at 200 m.p.h., represent an entirely new field for the designer, simply because the highest speeds hitherto attained on land have been far short of this figure. Sunbeam experience in the design and production of racing cars, and in building high powered aircraft is unique; and this experience has been brought thoroughly to bear in connection with the design of this car, together with the fullest use of wind tunnel experiments and aero-dynamical knowledge. By such means the Sunbeam Company have produced a car capable of safely accomplishing its object.

The car leaves for America on March 2nd, by the s.s. "Berengaria," and Major Segrave hopes to make his attempt at Daytona Beach, Florida, on or about March 20th, as there is no stretch of road or sands in this country where such a speed could be safely attempted.

The Sunbeam Motor Car Company, Ltd.   Moorfield Works, Wolverhampton.

Sir Henry O'Neale de Hane Segrave, the Baltimore-born son of an Anglo-Irish father and an American mother, was undoubtedly Britain's greatest Grand Prix star of the Golden Age of LSR attempts — the 1920s. Segrave broke the World Land Speed record three times, in 1926, and in 1929.

An advertisement, placed by the Sunbeam Motor Car Co. Ltd, that appeared in the 10 January 1927 issue of The Autocar.

Major Henry Segrave was the first European to use the hard sands of the famous Ormond-Daytona beach for a World Land Speed Record attempt, witnessed by some 125,000 spectators.

Segrave wasted no time in taking the new Sunbeam to Brooklands for trials in September 1925. Still unpainted in the now familiar red racing team colours, he was clocked at 145 mph (233 kph) through the half-mile. A number of predictable teething problems were overcome and the car, now painted red, was ready for an attempt on the record.

On 16 March 1926, Segrave and his team of eight mechanics arrived on the windswept Lancashire coastline. With very little pomp and even less publicity, the Sunbeam was rolled out onto the Southport beach. After walking the length of the course, still glistening from the retreat of the ebbing tide, Segrave was ready to go. Trailing a plume of spray, the Sunbeam hurtled down the beach to a new record of 152.33 mph (245.149 kph).

The following month J.G. Parry Thomas raised the record to 169.30 mph

This view of the incomplete chassis of Golden Arrow shows the massive frame construction and location of the 925 hp Napier Lion engine which drove the rear wheels from a position set low between the twin propeller shafts, located on each side of the driver's seat.

(272.458 kph) on the Pendine Sands. Not content with the speed, Thomas went on the sands again the following day, raising the record to 171.02 mph (275.229 kph). That very record however, cost the respected Welshman his life. The so-called experts and the boys in the bar at distant comfort, said the man was at fault, but without a question of doubt, the conditions on the beach were a major contributing factor to the tragedy. I have spent many hours, while researching this book, walking the sands at Pendine and other similar stretches of sand on Carmarthen Bay, and having spoken with observers of Thomas's tragic run, I am in a position to confirm the conditions at Pendine at the time were far from favourable; even today, this stretch of Carmarthen coastline is not at it's best until the end of Spring at the very earliest. As for the man ... his remarkable career speaks for itself!

The following year, Segrave set sail for the United States with a new car, the remarkable 1,000 hp Sunbeam, with the objective of raising the record of 174.883 mph (281.447 kph) set by Malcolm Campbell on 2 February 1927, driving the Campbell-Napier *Bluebird,* the first to adopt *Bluebird* livery, and also the first car to be specifically built as a record breaker.

Driven by two V12, twin ohc, 22.5-litre, 435 bhp, 48-valve Matabele engines, and weighing in at 3 tons 16 cwt, Segrave required a course nine miles long to attain its anticipated speed, and this factor alone ruled out most of the European beaches. Pendine, Saltburn, Southport, Perranporth and Fanöe were far too short and most certainly unpredictable. Segrave decided – and with his noted charm and diplomacy, convinced his sponsors – that the famous Ormond-Daytona beach, was the only suitable venue for the attempt.

Segrave's visit to Daytona was widely publicised, and for good reason. He was the first European of the post-war era to attempt an official World Land Speed Record on the Florida beach, and he was promoting that he intended to surpass the 200 mph mark.

On his inaugural run, a party of school children carelessly walked through the timing traps, making it impossible for the USAC officials to

The Golden Arrow being wheeled into Olympia for the Motor Show.

A rare photograph of Major Henry Segrave about to set out on the trial run of the Irving-Napier Golden Arrow at Daytona Beach, Florida. The vehicle is on record as having been the least-used Land Speed Record car. It was never driven on English soil before Segrave took it to Daytona in 1929. He made one practice run at the mile, then set a new Land Speed Record of 231.446 mph (372.340 kph). His car had been driven no more than 18.74 miles in all.

certify any speed higher than 163 mph, though with regret Segrave knew he had well surpassed that speed. There was a crowd of spectators estimated at between 30,000 and 35,000 on hand when, on 29 March 1927, Segrave made what was considered to be his 'last chance' at the record.

Buckled into his seat, Segrave fired the mighty V12 aircraft engines and

Major Henry Segrave was knighted for his achievement in setting the new land speed record at Daytona in March 1929, in the Irving-Napier Golden Arrow.

within seconds he was gone; manipulating the two three-speed gearboxes, he entered the speed traps at just short of 200 mph as a gust of wind caught the car, sliding him sideways. Segrave fought for control and was struggling hard to maintain his course as he left the measured mile. He thumped the brakes and literally incinerated them. With a stream crossing the beach dead ahead, he had no alternative other than to steer the car out into the shallow water to slow her down. When the car finally came to a halt, the brakes were quickly replaced during the turnaround, and with 11 minutes remaining within the hour, launched the 1,000 hp Sunbeam back down the beach to establish a new World Land Speed Record of 203.792 mph (327.981 kph). Segrave had beaten Campbell to both 180 and 200 miles an hour in a multiple stroke of speed, skill and determination. Moreover, in doing so he had made obsolete the expensive Napier-Campbell *Bluebird.*

Campbell set off on an aerial expedition to seek a more stable venue for his attempt to regain the record.

While Campbell was away, Segrave announced he was to have another crack at the record with an all-new vehicle designed by the renowned J.S.

After setting the new World Land Speed Record Golden Arrow, *in its packing case, is lifted onboard the SS Oramo at Tilbury Docks, London, on the first leg of a world tour, backed by the British section of the Society of Motor Manufacturers and Traders, as part of a campaign to attract overseas trade orders. Such was the prestige of record-breaking in the 1920s that the result of the venture attracted no less than £11.5 million in advance orders for product related components and lubricants.*

All British "GOLDEN ARROW"
WORLD'S SPEED RECORD 1929 - 231 M.P.H.

The Golden Arrow returns to England after Major Segrave set a new World Land Speed Record of 231.446 mph (372.475 kph) in March 1929. The road from Southampton to the KLG's Robin Hood works at Putney Vale was lined with jubilant onlookers, the car is seen here pausing briefly at Wandsworth Town Hall.

Irving. Both Campbell and Segrave had turned their back on Sunbeams by then, but Segrave had found corporate sponsorship and his new car was already well on the way to completion at the Robin Hood Works of K.L.G. at Putney Vale.

Segrave and Irving went to Napiers to hire a powerful engine, a Schneider Trophy unsupercharged racing unit, producing 925 bhp.

Irving designed a remarkable multi-plate clutch with servo assistance, the first in a concept that was subsequently adopted by both private and commercial vehicle manufacturers.

The car was to become a household name, the Irving-Napier, or popularly the *Golden Arrow.*

Major Henry Segrave drove the three-ton *Golden Arrow,* to a new World Land Speed Record of 231.446 mph (372.340 kph) at Daytona Beach on 11 March 1929; a record that once again proved to be far out of the reach of the Campbell-Napier *Bluebird.*

Segrave was convinced the *Golden Arrow* was capable of a greater speed, but soon after he set the new record he witnessed a horrifying

Henry Segrave receiving floral tribute to Golden Arrow *at the Robin Hood works.*

tragedy that was to turn him away from further attempts at the World Land Speed record. American Lee Bible, team mechanic for the famed *White Triplex* driven earlier by Ray Keech, wanted to shoot for the Englishman's record. In confidence, and as some onlookers explained, he was driving too fast in preliminary trials, and seemed oblivious of the danger of the sands. He worked the car rapidly up to 200 mph on practice runs. On a third, yet unofficial run, at the mile, the car veered out of control, skidding sideways at some 128 mph, the car then appeared to lunge into the sands, throwing debris over 300 feet of the course, hitting a Pathé newsreel cameraman who couldn't get out of the way of the rolling car. Both Bible and the cameraman, Chuck Wynn, were killed instantly.

Major Henry Segrave returned to England and was knighted shortly afterwards. Eager to return to some sort of record breaking, he turned to

Sir Henry Segrave's boat Miss England II *travelling at full throttle on Lake Windermere shortly before she capsized, killing her helmsman, Sir Henry, and his mechanic Victor Halliwell.*

The upturned hull of Miss England II *appeared remarkably intact after the fatal accident on the Westmorland Lake, there was no evidence pointing to the cause of the tragedy, although at the inquest, Ulverston coroner, Mr F.W. Poole, reported that twenty minutes after the disaster, a water-logged branch was seen 250 yards to the stern of the boat. The sole survivor was chief engineer Michael Willcocks.*

Lord Wakefield, founder of the Castrol Oil Company in Cheapside in the City of London, or as the company was then known, C.G. Wakefield & Co. Ltd. Such was Lord Wakefield's involvement in the fast-growing sport of power-boating, that in September 1930 he financed the building of a potential record-breaking boat *Miss England II,* and Sir Henry Segrave was chosen to drive her.

In common with tradition, Sir Henry went out on the second of what was to be three trial runs prior to an attempt at the World Water Speed Record, when at a staggering 98.76 mph (158.93 kph), he hit a submerged log from a fallen Rowan tree at the far end of Lake Windermere, the log catapulted Sir Henry and the boat across the glass-like surface of the lake, submerging the intrepid Sir Henry under the upturned hull of *Miss England II.* The crew rushed to the scene in a flotilla of craft, searching for Sir Henry. He had captured the World Water Speed record from the American, Garfield Wood in *Miss America VII,* but the attempt had cost him his life.

Sir Henry Segrave, who only one year before returned to England in triumph after smashing three World Land Speed Records in a span of less than five years, was to end his life in a watery grave. The English Gentleman had lost his life in the pursuit of speed.

Sir Malcolm Campbell ~ Ambassador of Speed

The First World War cast a shadow of despair over Europe. Motor racing and record breaking paled in to insignificance as men's thoughts were eclipsed by the winds of war. The famous Weybridge race track became a dust bowl in a field of desolate pastures in the Surrey countryside.

Col Lindsay-Lloyd, the ageing Brooklands Clerk of the Course, walked alone along the Outer Circuit recalling the sounds of speed that spawned a succession of champions. The most celebrated champion of all was the dashing Malcolm Campbell.

Campbell was born to set records. At the age of sixteen the young Malcolm was sent to school in Germany, where he won his first bicycle race. Even as a youngster, speed was his obsession: "When I drove my first, seven horsepower car, I craved for ten. I wanted to experience the

Conditions at the Pendine Sands were often treacherous for Sir Malcolm Campbell, seen here steering with one hand, and attempting to wipe the wind-shield with the other, during his successful record breaking run in the 12-cylinder, ohc 'broad arrow' 22.3-litre, Napier-Campbell Bluebird No 1 in February 1927, attaining a two-way average speed of 174.883 mph (281.447 kph).

A poster advertising Wakefield CASTROL lubricants used in Captain Malcolm Campbell's Napier-Campbell Bluebird, with which on 19 February 1928, he raised the World Land Speed Record to 206.956 mph (333.062 kph) at Daytona Beach, Florida.

The retiring Ray Keech, driver of J.M. White's 81-litre, 400 bhp Liberty-engined White Triplex, in which he snatched the land speed record from Malcolm Campbell, at a two-way average speed of 207.552 mph (334.022 kph) at Daytona Beach on 22 April 1928.

sensation of progressive speed", and he was once fined for riding his father's bicycle at 27 mph down Box Hill with his hands in his pockets.

At the age of twenty-four, he built his own aeroplane, but frequent crashes in the Kent orchards were too great a burden on his savings. And in 1910, at the age of twenty-five he entered and won his first automobile race on the Brooklands circuit, in the first car sporting the *Bluebird* livery.

At the outbreak of the First World War, Campbell became a dispatch rider, and soon after, was commissioned. Campbell transferred to the Royal Flying Corps. At the end of the Great War Campbell was discharged with the rank of captain.

No sooner had peace returned to Europe than Campbell re-entered the racing circuit, taking part in just about every meeting in Europe. Then, fired by the spectacular barnstorming American, 'Wild' Bob Burman, who claimed to have broken Barney Oldfield's flying mile with a one-way run in 25.40 seconds (or 141.37 mph) on the famed Ormond-Daytona Beach, Campbell began his campaign to capture the World Land Speed record for Britain.

Campbell's first assault on the record was made on the Saltburn sands, Yorkshire, a month after Kenelm Lee Guinness set a new record of 133.75 mph (215.25 kph) at Brooklands in the 350 hp Sunbeam.

Campbell, already an accomplished racing driver, persuaded Louis Coatalen, chief engineer of the Sunbeam racing team, to let him drive the car. He averaged 135 mph (217 kph) one way on the sands, but the speed wasn't accepted because the run had been timed by a hand-held Rolex stop watch instead of the electrical timing devices determined by the official ruling of the ACF (Automobile Club de France).

Less than a year later, Campbell purchased the Sunbeam, which he promptly entered in the international speed trials meeting on the Danish holiday island of Fanöe, and on 24 June 1923, attained a terminal speed of

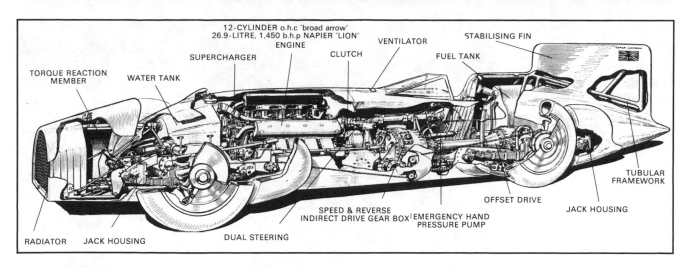

12-CYLINDER o.h.c 'broad arrow'
26.9-LITRE, 1,450 b.h.p NAPIER 'LION' ENGINE — SUPERCHARGER — CLUTCH — VENTILATOR — STABILISING FIN — FUEL TANK — TORQUE REACTION MEMBER — WATER TANK — TUBULAR FRAMEWORK — RADIATOR — JACK HOUSING — DUAL STEERING — SPEED & REVERSE INDIRECT DRIVE GEAR BOX — EMERGENCY HAND PRESSURE PUMP — OFFSET DRIVE — JACK HOUSING

A cutaway drawing of the 1031 Campbell-Napier-Railton Bluebird.

136.31 mph (219.32 kph) through the kilometre, and 137.72 mph (221.59 kph) through the mile. Again, Campbell failed to win recognition.

Twice, he had battered the existing record, but twice his efforts were rejected. Undaunted, Campbell took the car to the Pendine Sands. By this time he had been joined by three other contenders, including René Thomas (winner of the 1914 Indianapolis '500'), J.G. Parry Thomas, and Ernest A.D. Eldridge.

On 6 July, René Thomas clocked 143.31 mph (230.634 kph) at Arpajon in the V12, 10.6-litre Delage, setting a new World Land Speed Record. Four days later, Eldridge upped the mark to 145.2 mph. However, Thomas lodged a protest against the car, claiming that Eldridge's vehicle had no reverse gear fitted, as was required by the international rules.

Eldridge returned to Paris with the car, and, in a hired workshop devised a reverse gear after working round the clock for 48 hours.

This time, Thomas could only observe as Eldridge clocked an even faster 146.01 mph (234.986 kph) on the Arpajon road. There were no protests from the Frenchman ... the record yet again, returned to Britain.

In the Sunbeam car, named *Bluebird* after a successful play running at London's Whitehall Theatre, Campbell finally achieved his goal on 25 September 1924 on the Pendine Sands. In driving rain, Campbell hurtled to a record speed of 146.16 mph (235.217 kph). Malcolm Campbell and the *Bluebird* became a household name, and to the World Land Speed Record circuit, a force to be reckoned with.

By this time, however, there were numerous challengers preparing cars to attack the magical 150-mile-an-hour barrier, including Major Henry Segrave.

Campbell's mechanic, Leo Villa, and designer C. Amherst Villiers had begun work on a new car, the Napier-Campbell, with which they intended to raise the speed record to 200 mph, but the car was far from ready. The impatient Campbell immediately set Leo to work supertuning the old faithful Sunbeam *Bluebird* for one last assault on the 150 mph barrier.

After several unsuccessful runs on the Carmarthen beach, he returned on 4 February 1927 with his new 450 bhp Napier Lion-engined Napier-Campbell.

With his new car, Campbell made his first run at the mile, attaining just under 180 mph. On the return run, approaching the better 195 mph he hit a ripple in the sand left by the retreating tide; Campbell was jolted so

Sir Malcolm Campbell at the wheel of Bluebird, shortly after raising the World Land Speed Record to 276.82 mph (445.703 kph), taking the record for the eighth time, on the famed Daytona Beach.

Sir Malcolm Campbell taking the World Land Speed Record for the eighth time, in the supercharged Rolls-Royce 'R'-engined Bluebird.

violently his goggles slipped over his head, forcing him to drive with one hand and shield his eyes with the other. Despite the incident, Campbell attained a two-way average of 174.883 mph (281.447 kph); he had the record once again, but the speed was less than his goal.

Meanwhile, Major Henry Segrave was already ship-bound for the New World, where, in the mighty 1,000 bhp *Sunbeam* he was to set a new World Land Speed record of 203.792 mph (327.981 kph) on the Florida beach of Ormond-Daytona, beating Campbell to both 180 mph and 200 mph in a single stroke.

Without further ado, Campbell put *Bluebird* into the Vickers windtunnel to evaluate areas of improvement to the aerodynamics of the car. Campbell again consulted Reid A. Railton at Thomson & Taylor of Brooklands, and managed to secure a powerful Schneider Trophy Napier Sprint engine. The

Soon after Malcolm Campbell established a new record of 246.09 mph (396.04 kph) at Daytona Beach, he returned to England where he was informed that he was to be knighted. Civic receptions followed in both Southampton and London. The Great Southern Railway in recognition of his honour laid on a special train — The 'Bluebird' Special, to take Campbell and his working crew back to Waterloo.

A cutaway drawing of the 1935 Campbell-Railton, the last of Sir Malcolm's record breakers, with which he achieved 301.129 mph (484.818 kph) in a farewell performance at Bonneville on 3 September 1935.

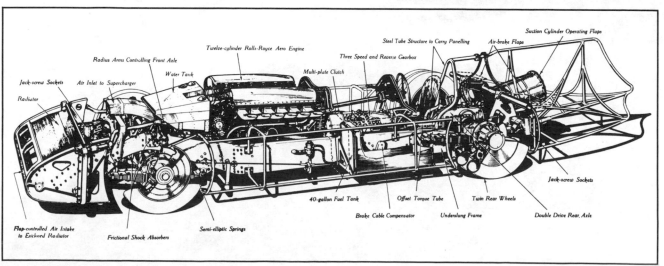

In 1935, the Campbell-Railton Bluebird *car was rebuilt yet again, at Sir Malcolm Campbell's own workshop behind the Brooklands track, under the learned supervision of Leo Villa. This, the final version of the* Bluebird *incorporated some of the original chassis, front axle and brake drums from the 1927 car. The new design had a completely new body shell with a driver-controlled air-intake slot in the nose, which could be closed for additional streamlining. Unlike the earlier cars, the wheel fairings now formed part of the main body.*

redesigned *Bluebird* made her debut during the Daytona Speed Week in February 1928.

It was 19 February when Campbell rolled out *Bluebird* for her first 200 mph dash. On the outward run the car developed a yaw, sending the car into a terrifying sideways slide as the indefatigable Campbell momentarily lost control. His return run was as rough as the first, as the speeding car was caught by a gust from an ocean breeze, but Campbell regained the record, attaining 206.956 mph (333.062 kph), but his triumph was short-lived, for Ray Keech increased the speed to 207.552 mph (334.022 kph) in the Liberty-engined *White Triplex*.

Campbell, having experienced extreme difficulties in driving on the sands of both Ormond-Daytona and Pendine, decided the time had come to seek a more stable venue for his next attempt at the record.

Campbell purchased an aircraft and left on an expedition to Africa, and the Middle East. In January 1929 he went to South Africa, where he had heard there was a vast dry lake bed, Verneuk Pan, some 400 miles from Cape Town.

Campbell stayed at the Verneuk Pan in early 1929, sending for his team of engineers, mechanics and fifty-six packing cases of spares. It was while Campbell was there that Segrave drove his three-ton *Golden Arrow* to a

On the morning of 3 September 1935, with the timing officials at their stations, Sir Malcolm Campbell at the wheel of 'Bluebird' exceeds the 300 mph barrier at Bonneville.

The Bluebird support team, with only minutes to spare, make a final inspection of the 2,300 bhp supercharged Rolls-Royce-engined car for the vital return run through the mile on the Bonneville course.

new World Land Speed record far out of the reach of *Bluebird*.

Reid Railton was commissioned to design a new *Bluebird* streamliner around a Napier Lion aircraft engine, capable of producing almost 1,500 horsepower.

Meanwhile, Campbell stayed in South Africa long enough to set a number of new British Empire speed records, but the best he could attain against the World Land Speed record was 218.50 mph (351.64 kph).

While in South Africa Campbell learnt of the death of Segrave on Lake Windermere. At a time when the record was in danger of being captured by the Americans, Campbell returned to Florida with the new *Bluebird* where, on 5 February 1931, he covered the flying mile at 246.153 mph (396.143 kph). England was in ecstasy. The returning hero was still on board ship, when as he approached Southampton water he was greeted by a flight of aircraft which dipped their wings in salute of the champion. On landing he was greeted by the news that he was to be knighted for his

As early as May 1934 Adolf Hilter hired Dr Ferdinand Porsche's design office to develop a land speed record car. The result was the outstanding Mercedes-Benz streamliner, seen here driven by Hermann Lang on the Avus track in Berlin, venue for the legendary Rüsselsheim rocket cars. Although the outbreak of World War II prevented a serious attempt on the record, Mercedes-Benz co-driver Rudolf Caracciola drove the car to numerous records on conventional race tracks. Until 1959 Caracciola held the highest average speed ever attained on a circuit.

achievements, and was taken to London in a special train dubbed the *Bluebird Special,* where he was welcomed with a Government reception at Westminster Hall.

Campbell still wasn't satisfied, and the *Bluebird* was altered yet again. Nine months later the car was completed, and by way of recognition, the only familiar aspect of the vehicle was the colour. The *Bluebird* was much heavier, and sporting a V12, ohc, 36.5-litre Rolls-Royce 'R' engine, was much more powerful. Campbell returned to Ormond, where, on 23 February 1933 he set a new World Land Speed record of 272.46 mph (438.123 kph). For Sir Malcolm however, the beach had far outlived its usefulness as a venue for attempts at the record, and he set out to find a far longer and harder course. His journey ended on the vast Bonneville Salt Flats in Western Utah. This was to be the setting of his new assault on the record, where, on 3 September 1935, he fulfilled his ambition with a 301.13 mph (484.51 kph) average. His first assault through the flying mile lasted exactly 11.63 seconds, the return run lasted 12.08 seconds, establishing a two-way average of 301.129 mph (484.818 kph).

For Sir Malcolm Campbell, this was indeed the pinnacle of his outstanding career. Having established just about every record he had set out to attain; he turned his attention to water, where he achieved no less than four World Water Speed Records in a period spanning no less than three years. The Ambassador of speed had well and truly established Great

Sir Malcolm Campbell and Captain George E.T. Eyston listening to each other's recorded accounts of the Land and Water Speed Records on the Castrol stand at the 1938 Earls Court Motor Show. Sir Malcolm (left) described his Water Speed Record on Lake Hallwil, Switzerland, where he attained a two-way average speed of 130.93 mph (210.710 kph) in the 2,500 hp Rolls-Royce R-type Bluebird *single-step hydroplane*, and Captain Eyston described his *World Land Speed Record* on the Bonneville Salt Flats, where, at the wheel of Thunderbolt he set a new record of 357.50 mph (575.33 kph).

Britain and, indeed, the *Bluebird* name, in just about every chapter of land and water speed record books.

Shortly before his death on New Year's Eve, 1948, Sir Malcolm Campbell had already made plans to raise the World Water Speed Record to 200 mph in the jet-powered *Bluebird* three-pointer.

Sir Malcolm Campbell was finally laid to rest in his birth-place town of Chislehurst, Kent, in the same grave as his mother and father.

In the years ahead Sir Malcolm's son Donald was to pick up the gauntlet left by his father in the pursuit of speed on land and water.

Eyston and Cobb and their Silver Leviathans

Between 1937 and 1939, the Bonneville speedway saw two gallant Englishmen, Captain George E.T. Eyston and the statuesque John R. Cobb, pick up the gauntlet left by Sir Malcolm in their dashing pursuit of the World Land Speed record.

Captain Eyston began his quest for the speed record on land as early as 1923 in the European road and track races, establishing numerous distance and endurance records in his car *Speed of the Wind*.

This was the first picture of Capt George E.T. Eyston's Thunderbolt *nearing completion at the Bean works at Tipton, Staffordshire. The mile-eater was twice the power of Sir Malcolm Campbell's* Bluebird *and was designed to reach a colossal, unheard of, speed of 400 mph (640 kph). In reality the car in this form attained a two-way average speed of 345.50 mph (555.93 kph) on the Bonneville Salt Flats.*

Shortly after dawn on 19 November 1937, the retiring Captain Eyston, with the help of a 'push start' from a car to save straining the transmission, hurtled his ten-wheeled, 7-ton *Thunderbolt* to a new World Land Speed Record of 312.00 mph (501.374 kph). Within half an hour, the unpredictable Utah weather broke, and Bonneville's first winter rains began to approach the salt from the north. Without further ado, Captain Eyston ordered his team to pack up and return to Britain.

Despite establishing a new record, the assault was not without its problems. During a series of trials with the *Thunderbolt,* the new 'electric eye' recording apparatus failed to register the car as it flashed through the mile. Calmly, Captain Eyston suggested that the combination of the blazing sun, the silver fuselage of the aluminium car, and the blinding whiteness of the salt were to blame.

Less than a year later, Captain Eyston returned to Bonneville with a modified *Thunderbolt,* sporting a matt black arrow painted each side of the 7-ton car to overcome the problem of visual recording, a new front cowling

The début for the leviathan Thunderbolt in which Capt George Eyston was to attempt to break Sir Malcolm Campbell's record of 301.129 mph (484.818 kph) set two years earlier. It had four wheels at the front (like the bogie of an express steam train), all of which were connected to the steering wheel. The rear wheels were twinned, not unlike those on a large lorry.

with a significantly smaller intake, a fully enclosed cockpit, and larger air scoops for the mighty centrifugal superchargers of the two Rolls-Royce 'R' engines.

On 27 August 1938, Eyston upped his record to 345.50 mph (555.93 kph), attaining 347.49 mph on the outward run and 343.41 mph on the return.

Two weeks later, John R. Cobb turned up on the salt with the remarkable turtle-shaped Railton. Cobb clocked several runs under the watchful eye of it's creator, Reid Railton, before attempting an assault on Eyston's record. Both Railton and Cobb ironed out a number of teething problems, and within days both the car and it's driver were ready for the assault.

On the morning of 15 September, Cobb shattered Eyston's record with a timed speed of 353.30 mph (568.57 kph) one way and a slower 347.20 mph (558.76 kph) on the return run through the mile, establishing an average speed of 350.20 mph (563.471 kph). ''An outstanding performance; John's got it,'' shouted Eyston watching the run with Reid Railton. Indeed, no sooner

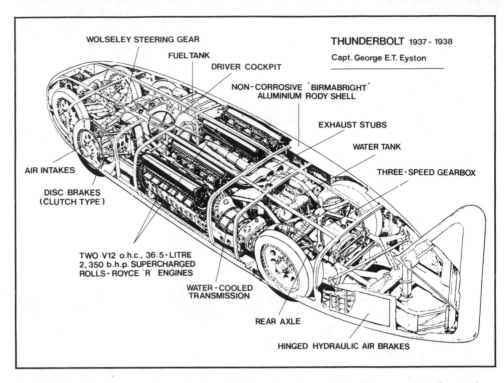

THUNDERBOLT 1937 - 1938

Capt. George E.T. Eyston

WOLSELEY STEERING GEAR
FUEL TANK
DRIVER COCKPIT
NON-CORROSIVE `BIRMABRIGHT`
ALUMINIUM RODY SHELL
EXHAUST STUBS
WATER TANK
THREE-SPEED GEARBOX
AIR INTAKES
DISC BRAKES
(CLUTCH TYPE)
TWO V12 o.h.c., 36.5-LITRE
2,350 b.h.p. SUPERCHARGED
ROLLS-ROYCE `R` ENGINES
WATER-COOLED
TRANSMISSION
REAR AXLE
HINGED HYDRAULIC AIR BRAKES

Under the hood. Capt George Eyston commenced his pursuit of speed in 1923 in European road races. On 19 November 1937, the modest Englishman piloted his 7-ton Thunderbolt *to a new World Land Speed Record of 311.42 mph (501.18 kph). Less than a year later, 27 August 1938, Eyston upped his speed to a staggering 345.50 mph (556.02 kph) in* Thunderbolt *now painted black to overcome the blinding glare of the sun at Bonneville.*

Portrait of a legend. Capt George E.T. Eyston, the most prolific Land Speed Record breaker of them all, was also the inventor of the Powerplus supercharger which was used on many of his racing and record-breaking cars, including Thunderbolt. *He was made an OBE in 1948.*

had Cobb begun to celebrate the fruits of victory, than Eyston rolled out the *Thunderbolt* to establish a higher record of 357.50 mph (575.217 kph). The World Land Speed Record had been broken twice by the duo, in less than twenty-four hours.

Captain Eyston held the record for a year, when John Cobb returned to Bonneville on 23 August 1939, to reclaim the record. Conditions on the salt could not have been better for Cobb; the salt was firm and there was no sign of winds. Without further hesitation Cobb roared from the starting line and the Railton streaked across the salt attaining a new record through the mile of 369.70 mph (593.56 kph). This was to be the last record to be established prior to the outbreak of the Second World War.

During the war Cobb was in service as a pilot with the British Air Transport Auxiliary, the civilian operation responsible for aircraft ferrying.

No sooner had peace in Europe been achieved, than Cobb and Railton went to work on a number of modifications to the Railton. Initially the car was not totally changed, but for a new auxiliary drive to prevent the possibility of the engine stalling during gear changing sequences on freewheel. Prior to the outbreak of war the Railton was without clutches and flywheels on the powerful engines. The gear ratios were also changed, raising them slightly for easier management at high speeds. In addition, the vehicle was fitted with new Dunlop tyres that were tested for speeds in excess of the low 400s. In recognition of the prestige that World Land Speed Record breaking developed, the Mobil Oil Company offered financial backing for the project in return for the publicity that a new record would offer. This was clearly the inauguration of realistic corporate sponsorship, by way of product and logistic support association. The car, in recognition of the support of Mobil, was renamed the 'Railton-Mobil-Special'.

On 16 September 1947, John Cobb began his shakedown runs with the new 'Special'. ''She handled like a dream,'' Cobb reported to Railton and confirmed both man and machine were ready to go.

Thunderbolt *is rolled out of the Bean works at Tipton, Staffs, in the spring of 1937, ready for the assault on the World Land Speed Record at Bonneville.*

Eyston's Thunderbolt *was push-started at Bonneville by a modified Ford Prefect, with a reinforced front bumper. The course on the southward run was far from satisfactory on the morning of 19 November 1937; this did not deter Eyston from breaking the indefatigable Sir Malcolm Campbell's record.*

In a passive mood, John Rhodes Cobb sits comfortably in position between the massive Dunlop tyres at Thomson & Taylor's works. Note the independent front suspension to the wheels.

The two 12-cylinder supercharged Napier 'Lion' engines of the Railton were located at an angle, one each side of the cranked backbone chassis. The rear wheel track was narrower than the front for both stability at high speed and for ease of housing within the turtle-shaped one-piece removable body shell.

For easier assembly and maintenance, the body shell of the Railton was built in one piece, contoured with a rounded front incorporating the driver's cockpit.

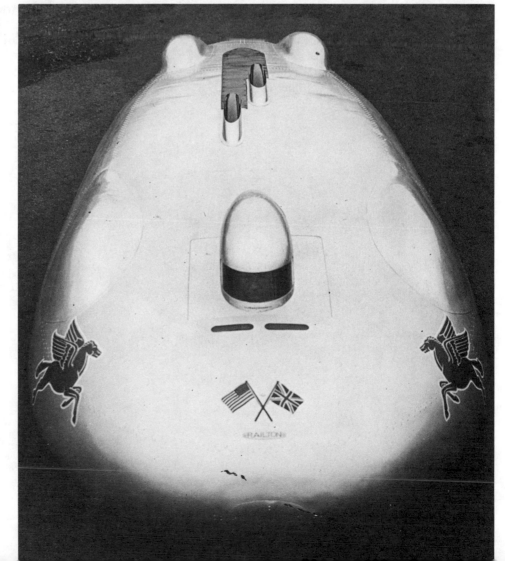

In 1936 John R. Cobb commissioned Reid A. Railton, designer of Campbell's 'Bluebirds' from 1931 to 1935, to design a new land speed record car. The result, the beautiful 'Railton Special', later renamed the 'Railton-Mobil Special' under backing from the Mobil Oil Company.

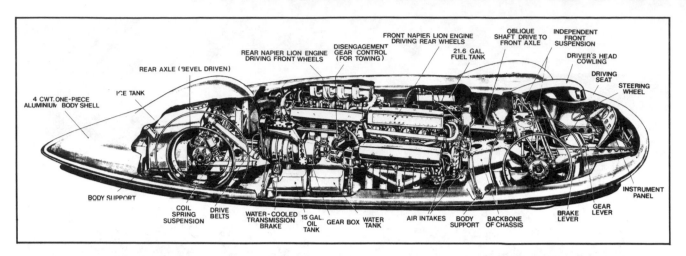

A cutaway view of the immensely complex Railton-Mobil Special.

REAR NAPIER LION ENGINE DRIVING FRONT WHEELS
DISENGAGEMENT GEAR CONTROL (FOR TOWING)
FRONT NAPIER LION ENGINE DRIVING REAR WHEELS
21.6 GAL. FUEL TANK
OBLIQUE SHAFT DRIVE TO FRONT AXLE
INDEPENDENT FRONT SUSPENSION
DRIVER'S HEAD COWLING
DRIVING SEAT
STEERING WHEEL
REAR AXLE (BEVEL DRIVEN)
ICE TANK
4 CWT.ONE-PIECE ALUMINIUM BODY SHELL
INSTRUMENT PANEL
BODY SUPPORT
COIL SPRING SUSPENSION
DRIVE BELTS
WATER-COOLED TRANSMISSION BRAKE
15 GAL. OIL TANK
GEAR BOX
WATER TANK
AIR INTAKES
BODY SUPPORT
BACKBONE OF CHASSIS
BRAKE LEVER
GEAR LEVER

Cobb fired both engines, working up slowly through the gears of the two 1250 horsepower engines, the car gaining rapid momentum. Cobb's outward run through the mile was clocked at 385.645 mph (620.50 kph). It was very fast, but still below the 400 mph mark Cobb had established as the goal.

Within the hour, the car was refuelled and John Cobb began his return, south-to-north run.

Within a span of less than nine seconds, he was already within the flying mile, attaining a mean speed of 415 mph, with an official timed recording of 403.135 mph (648.781 kph). Cobb had established a two-way average speed of 394.20 mph (634.267 kph). It had taken the intrepid fur broker from London seven weeks to better his pre-war record. Within days the Bonneville speedway became waterlogged and the season came to a rapid

John Cobb in the 'Railton-Mobil-Special' approaches the timing corridor at Bonneville at a velocity in excess of 400 mph (640 kph).

The very last photograph of John Rhodes Cobb, the London fur broker who exchanged his career for the pursuit of the World Land and Water Speed Records, is seen here at the helm of his jet-powered Crusader. *Approaching 240 mph on the south-to-north return run through the mile on Loch Ness, Scotland, he hit the wake of a spectator boat, bounced, and then disintegrated. On impact, Cobb was thrown 150 feet ahead of the burning wreckage and was killed instantly.*

halt, with a Briton yet again holding the World Land Speed Record.

Like Segrave before him John Cobb was not content with holding the World Land Speed Record alone, and turned his career path to water.

On 29 September 1952, John Cobb set out to regain the World Water Speed record for Britain, and the coveted Harmsworth Trophy, held by the Americans since the 1920s.

Cobb's assault on the record was to be in the behemoth, the jet-powered *Crusader* on Loch Ness, a loch that was not without it's own behemothic legend. On the outward run against the record, Cobb attained a particularly buffeting 206.89 mph (332.88 kph), some thirty miles an hour greater than the existing record. On the return run, the nose of *Crusader* appeared to lift, when, at a staggering 240 mph (390 kph) he entered the wake of a spectator boat, bouncing the boat even higher out of the water, Cobb was thrown fifty yards ahead of the *Crusader* which disintegrated in a blinding explosion.

Cobb, watched by his horrified wife, Vera, was killed instantly. At the age of 52, a pioneer of record speed on land and water was killed, pursuing yet another frontier of speed in the name of King and Country.

Donald Campbell's
Bluebird-Proteus CN7, in its
second incarnation
complete with vertical
stabilizer.

Chapter 2
Last of the Purists

Donald Campbell ~ In his Father's Shadow

Behind closed doors at the Coventry works of Motor Panels Limited, the birth of a legend in the form of Donald Campbell's Bluebird-Proteus CN7, is seen for the first time during the early stages of construction. It was designed by Kenneth and Lewis Norris at Norris Brothers Limited, consulting engineers and designers of the 3,750 lb thrust jet Bluebird three-pointer boat. Clearly visible are the four longitudinal members which form the basic structure of a light alloy foil formed into a honeycomb sandwich, three quarters of an inch thick, and faced on either side with alloy sheeting.

Donald Campbell grew up slight of stature, a victim of rheumatic fever as a child, and he seemed content to enjoy the country life at his home in Horley, Surrey and a passive career as head of a small engineering company.

He was only fifteen-years-old when his father, Sir Malcolm Campbell, broke the World Land Speed Record at Bonneville. He had always lived in the shadow of his father who by now was a national hero, and remained so until he died of a heart attack on 1 January 1949. As a boy, Campbell was reputed to have said he once regarded his father as a god.

The thrill of speed began to fascinate Donald, and after five years of setting and holding World Water Speed Records on Ullswater and Coniston Water in Westmorland, and on Lake Mead, Nevada, he entered the land speed record sphere with a new gas turbine-powered car bearing the famous *Bluebird* name.

It was following his second successful waterborne attempt in November 1955 on Lake Mead, that Donald Campbell conceived his ambition to try for the land speed record as well. From that moment, he was a man with a single dedicated purpose: to develop a turbine car faster and more stable than any other vehicle that had gone before, and at the same time to show to the world what could be achieved by a pooling of British industrial resources to design and build such a machine. As it transpired, the project could not have been more timely, for there were no less than five other contenders in the chase for the title 'Fastest man on earth', moreover all five were financed by corporate America. These included Craig Breedlove, Art

Arfons, Walt Arfons and Mickey Thompson. As this chapter will reveal, Thompson had very little time for the Englishman and was one of the loudest critics of the British initiative unlike Craig Breedlove who not only respected Campbell but became a great personal friend.

Five painstaking years went into the design and building of the new *Bluebird*, and the result would be all-British. Sixty-nine leading British companies, manufacturing everything from ball-bearings to the turbine engine itself, had to grapple with and overcome problems never before met in the field of engineering – for the car they were to build was venturing into the realms of the unknown. First the design, then research into hundreds of intricate details, then testing and more testing, until by the time the vehicle was completed, over 5,000 drawings had been made and nearly one million man-hours expended on the project. But the final test remained, and rested on the shoulders of the man whose vision had become a reality – Donald Campbell.

Work on the design of the new car began in January 1956, and was entrusted to Kenneth and Lewis Norris at Norris Brothers, Consulting Engineers, the designers of the *Bluebird* boat. The basic requirement was for a peak speed of 500 mph (800 kph). The immediate objective however, was a new World Land Speed Record of 400 mph plus, and Campbell had already decided that the engine he required was a Bristol-Siddeley Proteus free turbine. Four-wheel drive was considered essential for which the engine would require substantial modification.

From the earliest planning stage, the designers were governed by the regulations laid down by the Fédération Internationale de l'Automobile, which state that to qualify for a land speed record, a car must be 'a land vehicle, propelled by its own means, running on at least four wheels, not aligned, which must always be in contact with the ground; the steering must

The enormous Bristol-Siddeley Proteus 4,100 bhp gas turbine power unit undergoing extensive test runs at Bristol Siddeley's Patchway works near Bristol, prior to being fitted in Donald Campbell's 1964 Bluebird-Proteus car. Similar versions of the power plant were used in the Britannia airliner.

be assured by at least two of the wheels'. The last stipulation was most
important. It meant that there had to be direct drive from the engine to at
least two wheels. At the time this ruled out the use of a pure jet, or rocket
engine. And manufacturing transmission and reduction gear units to take the
power from the engine to the wheels was one of the most difficult problems
that had to be solved.

The finished car weighed 8,000 lb, giving it an unprecedented power to
weight ratio of approximately 2 lb for 1 bhp. The engine developed more
than 4,000 brake horsepower. The overall body dimensions were; length, 30
feet; width, 8 feet; height, 4 feet 9 inches; wheelbase, 13 feet 6 inches; and
track, 5 feet 6 inches. Suspension was fully independent, with wishbone and
oleo-pneumatic spring and damper units allowing plus or minus two inches
vertical wheel movement. The steering was of conventional pattern to give a
wheel deflection of five degrees each side of the centre line. Brakes
consisted of two systems; air brakes to slow the car from peak speed to 400
mph and disc brakes – acting inboard on each side of the front and rear
reduction gears – to be used to bring the car to a halt.

An essential consideration in the design concept was to achieve
maximum strength with minimum weight, and with this in mind, the frame
was constructed in a unique way. This involved the use of light alloy foil
formed into a 'honeycomb' sandwich, three-quarters of an inch thick, and
faced on each side with alloy sheeting. Four longitudinal members of the
honeycomb material formed the basic frame, joined together by four
cross-members forming separate compartments for the cockpit, engine,
transmission gear units, and wheels. Air from the air-intake at the front of
the car was ducted on each side of the cockpit to the engine. Two fuel
tanks, with a total capacity of 25 gallons, were mounted one each side of the
car, slightly forward of the rear wheels.

In view of the vital importance of the project to British prestige, Donald
Campbell felt that a Trustee Council should be formed of leading public

figures who would take over the project in the event of his illness or death. This council was formed in 1957, under the Chairmanship of the Duke of Richmond and Gordon, the members being The Duke of Argyll, Mr Charles Forte, Mr Eric Knight, Mr A.G.B. Owen, the Hon Greville Howard, Mr Cyril Lord, Mr R.W. Coley, Mr Victor Mischon and Mr P.J.P. Barker. In the event of Campbell's death or indisposition two reserve drivers were nominated – Sqn/Ldr Peter Carr, AFC, RAF, Rtd, who was also managing the project, and Sqn/Ldr Neville Duke, the celebrated Second World War fighter pilot and former holder of the World Air Speed Record. The fact that both of these men were distinguished pilots was no accident. It was felt that driving a record-breaking car involving huge power and turbine technique at speeds never before achieved by man was closer related to test flying than driving a Grand Prix racing car, which called for a very different skill and experience.

Sqn/Ldr Peter Carr retired from the Royal Air Force in 1959 to co-ordinate the land speed record project and also to act as first reserve driver. His release from the RAF was given special approval by the Air Council. He was no newcomer to high speeds. Before his release he commanded a Hunter Squadron and earlier was responsible for much secret ultra high-speed research flying. Prior to this, he was seconded to the United States Air Force, where, at Las Vegas, Nevada, he was directly concerned in the service development of the F100. It was, in fact, at Las Vegas that he met Donald Campbell, during the water speed record attempt on Lake Mead in 1955. Coincidentally, both men were decorated by Her Majesty the Queen at the same investiture in March 1957.

A steering committee was formed in the early stages of the project to advise on policy and planning. It comprised a senior executive member of each group concerned in a major role. It was made up of the following organisations: The Owen Organisation (Mr Alfred Owen, CBE); The British Petroleum Company Limited (Dr K.E.W. Ridler); Dunlop Rubber Company Limited (Mr Evan Price); Joseph Lucas Limited (Mr Nigel Breeze); Smiths Industrial Instruments Limited (Mr F.J. Hurn); Bristol-Siddeley Engines Limited (Sir Arnold Hall, FRSMA, ACGI, FRAeS.); Ferodo Limited (Mr G. Sutcliffe, OBE, TD); Norris Brothers (Mr Kenneth W. Norris); Tube Investments Limited, including The British Aluminium Company and Accles and Pollock Limited (Mr Leslie Hackett); and Sqn/Ldr Peter Carr, AFC. The committee guided an advisory council made up of a representative from each company concerned or associated with the endeavour.

The chassis and body of the vehicle were built by Motor Panels Limited of Coventry – a member of the Rubery Owen Organisation, where engineering co-ordination was conducted under the direction of Mr J.M. Phillips, the Managing Director. Installation was effected in the same factory under the supervision of Leo Villa with facilities provided by the Rubery Owen Organisation.

There was no clutch or conventional gearbox in the *Bluebird*. Power was transmitted by the gas stream between the primary and power turbines – there being no direct mechanical link between the two. In operation, air was induced at the air-intake and passed to a multi-stage compressor. Here it was compressed and fed into a series of combustion chambers. Fuel was injected into the air stream in each chamber, and burned, imparting additional energy to the incoming air. Some of this energy drove the first turbine which in turn drove the compressor. The excess power, governed by throttle opening, was automatically absorbed by the second, or power

In 1960 Donald Campbell, son of the illustrious speed king Sir Malcolm Campbell, entered the World Land Speed Record sphere with a new turbine-powered car bearing the famous 'Bluebird' name.

The shattered bulk of Donald Campbell's Bluebird *after the 1960 crash during a trial run at Bonneville.*

One of the shod wheels of Bluebird *torn off at over 300 mph.*

turbine, which was directly connected through the reduction gears to the drive shafts connected to the four wheels of the car.

Torque was smoothly transmitted to the wheels throughout the entire speed range without the necessity of clutch or gear change. In operation the engine was started and run up to a predetermined compressor speed with the car locked on the brakes. When this point was reached the brakes would be released allowing the car to accelerate at a rapid but progressive and controlled rate to the maximum speed. Full torque could not be applied until the car had reached 200 mph (320 kph); if applied at a lower speed it would result in drastic wheel spin.

Achieving sufficient power to break the land speed record was one problem for Campbell and his team. Stopping the car in the distance available was just as great a problem. The maximum length of the Bonneville Salt Flats straightway was 15 miles, and since, under the international regulations governing such attempts, two runs have to be

The modified
Bluebird-*Proteus* model in
the wind tunnel at the
Imperial College, London.
Note the build-up of shock
waves forward of the tail
fin.

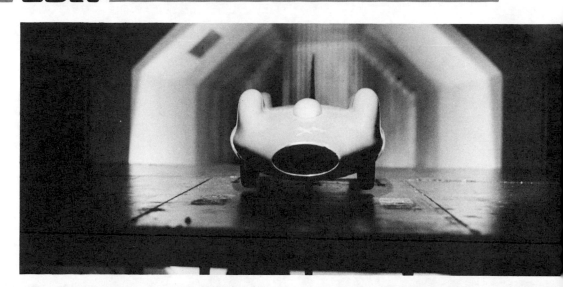

Bluebird, *bathed in BP
Comprox fuel, is prepared
for her first run at Lake
Eyre.*

The Bluebird *convoy moving on to the specially built road from Muloorina to Lake Eyre to prepare the car for the first test run on a desolate Salt.*

made, the final time being the average of these two runs, the measured mile is naturally in the centre. There is therefore a distance of seven miles in which the car has to stop after reaching anything up to the estimated speed potential of 500 mph (800 kph).

The disc brakes had a considerable task – to bring the car from 400 mph to a halt in 60 seconds. Because of the limitations of weight and space, the design, by Girling Limited, departed from normal practice. To economise on weight, the calipers which carried the linings were made of

Donald Campbell's view of Bluebird*'s open cockpit and instrument panel. Beyond, the vast expanse of the course at Lake Eyre.*

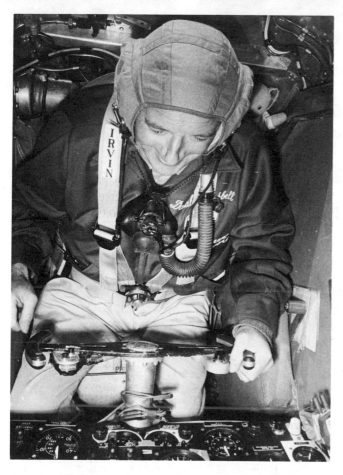

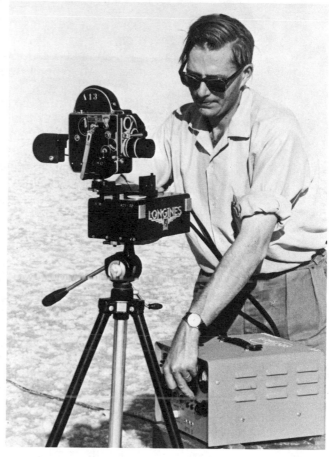

Donald Campbell sitting at the controls in the tiny cockpit of the Bluebird-Proteus, prior to making his return run through the mile at Lake Eyre. The instrumentation was by Smiths Industrial Instruments Limited; steering wheel by Bluemel Brothers Limited; and the safety harness was the 'flying' type, by Irvin Brothers. Donald Campbell was the first LSR driver to adopt the yoke type steering wheel.

At Lake Eyre, official time-keeper Bill Bates, prepares to clock Donald Campbell's attempt at the World Land Speed Record; the first and only attempt at the record on Australian soil.

magnesium alloys. There were two calipers each consisting of three pairs of brake linings, acting on each side of each of the rotating discs, making 24 pairs of linings in all. The discs were keyed into the driving hubs so that they could slide along towards the fixed linings as wear took place. The brakes were power operated with compressed air from 3,000 psi storage cylinders, the circuit being duplicated for the completion of safety. The total amount of energy to be dissipated during the 60 seconds of braking was an estimated 75 million foot pounds.

The Bluebird Project was not only a tremendous effort to further human knowledge and capability, but at the time was a major endeavour to keep Britain ahead. This was the first time such a project had been based on a turbine engine and the knowledge and experience gained with new materials, structures, braking systems, tyres, bearings and suspension, and indeed the vital lubricants, all helped to enhance Britain's ability to engineer and design a vehicle with the capability of regaining the World Land Speed Record from the American invaders with their jet-powered missiles.

During the inaugural trials at Goodwood, Campbell had been towed around in the car to get the feel of the cockpit and instrumentation, but had never driven *Bluebird* alone and under power until he arrived at Bonneville in August 1960.

His first glimpse of the blinding salt flats came on 4 September, when he watched Mickey Thompson turn 372 mph (598 kph) in his powerful *Challenger 1.* He later spoke with the American hot-rodder who went out of his way to play on Campbell's superstitions. Thompson shrugged his

Leo Villa, the engineering entrepreneur, companion, and devoted friend to both Sir Malcolm and Donald Campbell, who always referred to his famed employer as 'The Skipper'.

shoulders, ''I've seen the salt an awful lot better than it is right now''. The more he teased, the paler Campbell grew, and Thompson gleefully poured it on.

Campbell had always been a superstitious man and made sure his lucky mascot 'Mr Woppit' was with him during all his record attempts on land and water.

On arrival at Bonneville he viewed the salt with scepticism, which was justified in a near fatal crash which totally wrote off the costly *Bluebird* and left Campbell with a cracked skull, a pierced eardrum and divers cuts and bruises. Thus the *'Bluebird*-Proteus' saga at Bonneville ended. He immediately inaugurated a search of the globe for a better, longer track than Bonneville and eventually accepted the learned recommendation of his long-standing sponsors, BP: Lake Eyre in central Australia, some 400 miles north of Adelaide.

The nearest inhabited point to the selected course was Muloorina, a sheep station less than 30 miles away. The Southern Australian Government agreed to grade 65 miles of road from the railhead at Marree to Muloorina, and from there to the lake, and to construct a 400-yard causeway on to the vast expanse of Lake Eyre itself.

After several unsuccessful attempts, thwarted by severe weather conditions on the dead lake, Campbell eventually cemented the land speed record of 403.10 mph (648.58 kph) on 17 July 1964, breaking John Cobb's record of 394.20 mph (634.26 kph) set at the Bonneville Salt Flats in 1947.

Campbell was jubilant about his final success and was eager to reflect that he had actually forgotten to take 'Mr Woppit' along for the ride.

Campbell never did rid himself of the tormenting superstitions that haunted his life. On the evening of 3 January 1967, Campbell was playing solitaire in the room of his hotel overlooking Coniston Water, when he turned up two consecutive cards, the ace and the queen of spades.

''Mary, Queen of Scots, turned up the same combination of cards,'' he

On 15 October 1959, Donald Campbell received the Segrave Trophy for the second time ... like father, like son; Donald's distinguished father, Sir Malcolm Campbell, also received the trophy twice. After the presentation at the London Headquarters of the Royal Automobile Club in Pall Mall, Donald Campbell proudly stands by the trophy with his wife Tonia.

said "and from this she knew she was going to be beheaded. I know one of my family is going to get the chop. I pray it will not be me".

The following day he was aboard his jet boat *Bluebird*, making the return run on Coniston, of an attempt to raise the World Water Speed Record to over the 300 mph mark. His voice came calmly over the radio:

"She's doing 260 ... 280 ... 300 ... she's tramping! I can't see much ... She's going. She's going ..." The boat lifted in a high arc out of the still water, bounced off her wake, and did a somersault, When *Bluebird* hit the shimmering surface of the Westmorland lake, there was a blinding flash, amidst a plume of spray, and Donald was gone ..

The next day, Royal Navy frogmen searched the lake for Campbell's body but he was never found. At a depth of 140 feet, they found the main hull of *Bluebird*, Campbell's steering wheel, seat belt and even his lucky mascot 'Mr Woppit'. Thus the legend of the racing Campbells was over. Together, father and son established 21 land and water speed records over a period that covered more than four decades.

Donald Campbell suffered that particular comparison which any son of a famous father has to endure. The 'old boy' had broken the record nine times, and it was no doubt the driving force behind the obsession that sadly took him to a watery grave in the English Lake District.

Before his death, he was already working on plans for a rocket-powered car to break the sound barrier. Engineered and designed by Ken Norris, the 22ft long delta-shaped projectile, appropriately dubbed 'Bluebird Mach 1.1 (CMN-8)', would be powered by a complement of two 4,200lb thrust Bristol-Siddeley BS 605 rocket-assisted take-off (RATO) engines.

Indeed, such was the initial interest in the project, the Jamaican Government offered to construct a 14-mile track between Falmouth and St.

Donald Campbell and his faithful mascot Mr Woppit absorb the peace and tranquility of the English Lakes. Within three days he was to lose his life in pursuit of his own World Water Speed Record, a tragic end to a family tradition of speed with excellence.

Donald Campbell in the Bluebird jet-boat, about to make the fatal return run on Coniston Water. Campbell was barely four minutes into the run when, at 250 mph (402 kph), the boat soared into the air, somersaulted and crashed to the glass-like surface of the lake. Despite stupendous efforts by Naval divers, under the command of Lieutenant-Commander Futcher, Campbell's body was never found.

Ann's Bay, on which Campbell could run the vehicle.

Despite several attempts to revive the project it would seem the rocket car died with him.

In the 1930s, waiting crowds had to be held back by the police when the boat train from Southampton arrived in London, bearing the latest hero to have broken or brought back the World Land Speed Record to Britain. The names of Campbell, Cobb, Segrave and Eyston were commonplace. In those days, speeds of 300 and 400 mph were almost unimaginable. Today we can all cross the Atlantic in Concorde at twice the speed of sound, while spacecraft travel at speeds measured in tens of thousands of miles an hour.

Despite this, a new breed of British land speed record challenger has emerged to bring back the World Land Speed Record to Britain after an absence of eighteen years. The publicity-conscious, former salesman from Twickenham, Richard Noble and his Rolls-Royce Avon 302 jet-powered *Thrust 2*.

But *Thrust 2* wasn't the first of the jet-powered leviathans to enter for the quest for record speed on land.

Mickey Thompson ~ A Chapter for the 'Challenger'

On 11 March 1969, Senator M. Kennick ordered the Senate of the California Legislature to honour its native son for 'becoming the first man to travel on the ground at a speed in excess of 400 miles per hour, and for his many contributions to the automobile industry of the United States of America, and to the youth of the State of California and the Nation'.

His outstanding record of accomplishments included 485 national and international speed and endurance records. Mickey Thompson had international fame and recognition, and his ability to turn a passion for speed into a multi-million dollar industry, made him a highly respected and wealthy entrepreneur; a feat almost without precedent in the field of World Land Speed Record breaking. Yet, despite this acclaim, the one thing he has

The face of speed. From the cockpit of his *Challenger* car, Mickey Thompson scans the Bonneville Salt Flats where he will attempt to break the World Land Speed Record. Thompson drove to 406.60 mph (654.43 kph) over the flats in September 1960, but mechanical trouble prevented the return run and an official record. Helmet, goggles, oxygen mask and plastic face shield give him an unworldly appearance.

Pop goes the record — Mickey Thompson pops the braking chute on his dash car Attempt at March Air Force Base, California, after topping a 23-year-old record established by a German car. In his vehicle, equipped with a 550-horsepower engine and experimental racing slicks made by The Goodyear Tire & Rubber Company, Thompson averaged 112.088 mph (180.387 kph) on a two-way kilometer run on 15 July 1961 in the International Class D competition. The old record of 110.20 mph (177.34 kph) was set by Rudy Caracciola in the Hitler-sponsored Mercedes in 1939.

always wanted above all else has eluded him for more than a decade: breaking the speed record for wheel-driven cars. A purist record of 409.277 mph (658.52 kph) set on 12 November 1965, by fellow Californian, Bob Summers in the *Goldenrod*, a record that has remained unbroken for 20 years.

Sadly, however, Thompson's principal sponsors throughout his record breaking years, the Ford Motor Company, pulled out of the land speed record business in 1968, shortly after Mickey Thompson at the wheel of the *Autolite Special* failed in his attempt to capture the elusive record from the Summers Brothers.

Unlike his rivals, Mickey Thompson was a purist, a true crusader of the first order. Despite the appearance on the salt in 1960 of the early jet-powered driving machines, Thompson, not unlike his fellow Californian,

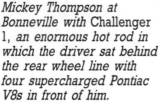

the late Frank Lockhart, refused to increase the power of his car with the assistance of jet-turbines. Thompson insisted that the record should remain within the realm of wheel-driven cars, by protesting that the jet-cars were simply aircraft without wings.

The season of 1969 saw for the last time, Mickey Thompson at the wheel of the *Autolite Special*. After a few dry runs Thompson was ready to attack the record, but the water table on the Bonneville Salt Flats had risen to a level that thwarted an attempt at full power.

Mickey Thompson decided to seek sponsorship for a new LSR car that was to become the last in a series of wheel-driven cars from the stable of the Californian hot-rodder – *Challenger I*.

The *Challenger I* made its inaugural run on the sun-baked surface of Rosamund Dry Lake at the legendary Edwards Air Force Base, adjacent to Rogers Dry Lake, where, some nineteen years later, Stan Barrett was to become the first man to exceed the speed of sound in the land-bound 48,000 horsepower rocket car, the *Budweiser Rocket*.

Challenger I was comparatively small by land speed standards, being some eight feet shorter and three feet narrower than the late John Cobb's 'Railton Mobil Special', and was powered by four V8, ohv 6.7-litre, 700 bhp Pontiac engines with four General Motors Rootes-type superchargers with fuel injection.

On 9 September 1970, Thompson and *Challenger I* roared across the Bonneville Salt Flats attaining a terminal velocity of 406.60 mph (654.329 kph). During the return run it soon became obvious the car was in trouble as it approached the timing traps; he was about to cement a new record,

Mickey Thompson at Bonneville with Challenger 1, *an enormous hot rod in which the driver sat behind the rear wheel line with four supercharged Pontiac V8s in front of him.*

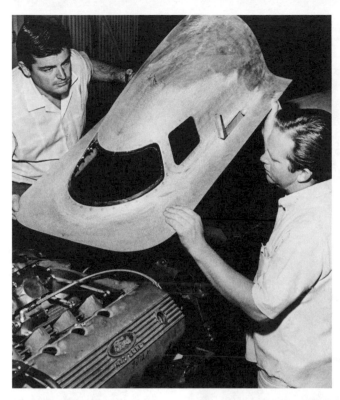

Mickey Thompson (left) and assistant Pat Foster fit the aluminium cockpit canopy into place on Thompson's land speed record car Autolite Special. In the foreground is one of the two 427 cu in Ford single overhead cam engines that powered the car.

Mickey Thompson's Challenger 1 takes shape in his Long Beach, engineering shop. The four-engined car burned fuel at the rate of a gallon-a-mile when Thompson approached the 400 mph barrier at Bonneville.

Mickey Thompson slides into the snug cockpit of the Autolite Special for what was to be his last run in the remarkable vehicle. Already flooding can clearly be seen to the north of the carefully prepared Bonneville course line.

Weather had always been a problem for Mickey Thompson's record attempts in the Autolite Special, *seen here shortly after an unofficial test run of 425 mph (683 kph), within an hour torrential rain was to close the 1968 season at Bonneville.*

The Ford Autolite Special was powered by two Ford engines; one drove the front wheels, and a second, supercharged, engine turned the rear wheels. 29 feet 7 inches in length, the chassis was of tubular steel, space frame construction, covered with a lightweight aluminium body shell. all four wheels were fitted with 23³/₄ inch diameter Goodyear tyres; 19 inch tread on rear, 24 inch tread on the front.

when, at a speed approaching 210 mph, the driveshaft snapped when he shifted into third gear. He was so near, yet so far, when he dejectedly vowed "We'll be back in a week". Mickey Thompson was never to be seen at the wheel of *Challenger I* again. It was the end of Mickey Thompson's pursuit of the World Land Speed Record for wheel-driven cars.

Thompson had planned to return to Bonneville, but that was before he fractured his back driving a twin-engined dragster accross Lake Mead, Nevada.

Despite his injury, Thompson did drive again, on 9 July 1971, on the runway of March Air Force Base in Riverside, California, establishing 14 international and national speed records, during a five-hour automobile spectacular, with a team of four different vehicles, including the Class C special, *Assault I.*

Thompson did try for the World Land Speed Record once again, but the acute pain of his back and awful ground conditions robbed him of the opportunity to grasp the record. For Mickey this attempt was to be the last in a golden era of wheel-driven cars, before the mighty jet-powered projectiles scorched their way into the record books. It was to be the exit of the piston engine for the man and the final chapter for *Challenger I.*

Autolite Special

Power:	Two 427 cubic-inch Ford single overhead cam engines. Front engine – normally aspirated; 810 horsepower. Rear engine – supercharged; 1,260 horsepower
Length:	29 feet 7 inches
Height:	27 inches; 37³/₈ inches at canopy
Width:	34⁷/₈ inches
Weight:	5,400 pounds
Transmission:	Two three-speed modified automatics
Chassis:	Tubular steel; space frame construction
Shell:	Lightweight aluminium
Tyres:	23³/₄ inch diameter; 19 inch tread on rear, 24 inch tread on front
Brakes:	Ventilated disc brakes on all four wheels
Parachutes:	Three plus one set of safety chutes; a 2-foot pilot chute, a 7-foot high speed chute and a 16-foot final brake chute.

The Summers Brothers - The Forgotten Heroes

The Summers Brothers' *Goldenrod*, now on tour for special showings at car shows and exhibitions throughout the world, holds a very special place in automotive history, shared by only the most innovative creations built since the beginning of the century.

In simplest terms, *Goldenrod* is the fastest automobile of all time. With

Bob Summers inspects one of the four ohv 6.9-litre 608 bhp Chrysler Hemi engines that power Goldenrod.

an official World Land Speed Record of 409.277 mph (658.526 kph) set on 12 November 1965, *Goldenrod* has travelled faster than any other wheel-driven vehicle before or since. While faster times have been recorded by free-wheeling jet and rocket-propelled designs they have never been recognized as automotive records by the purist, since the power was not driven through the wheels.

The *Goldenrod* represents the culmination of the combined racing and mechanical engineering efforts of Bill and Bob Summers, which began in the middle of the nineteen-fifties. Also playing a major role in the project were such sponsors as the Champion Spark Plug Co., the Chrysler Corp., Firestone Tire & Rubber Co., Hurst Performance Products and the giant Mobil Oil Co.

They were all attracted to the Summers Brothers' plans of recapturing the land speed record for the United States on the basis of their progressively successful showings at the annual Bonneville Nationals held at the Bonneville salt flats in Western Utah.

Goldenrod *without body panels, is prepared for a run on the salt. The vehicle was push-started at Bonneville by Bill Summers in the family station wagon.*

The bright golden streamliner was rolled off its trailer onto the hard, bleached white surface of Bonneville at 2.30 on 1 September 1965. Two hours later Bob 'Butch' Summers squeezed into the cramped cockpit, while crewmen fastened down the rear quarter panel that enclosed him.

After getting their feet wet with a 1936 Ford coupé (which Bill Summers characterized as a flop), the Summers Brothers became perennial winners with every new machine they put together. From 1955 until they began the *Goldenrod* project in 1963, the Summers Brothers always took first place in their respective category, and almost always established a new national class record.

Their initial success came with a 1929 Ford Model A roadster that achieved 175 mph, and they eventually worked their way up to a front-engine streamliner, nicknamed the *Pollywog*, that hit a very impressive 323 mph on the Bonneville speedway.

At that time, Britain's Donald Campbell held the officially-recognized

Shielded from the glare of salt 'n' sun, Bob Summers prepares for the first of two runs through the timing beam that would secure a record that still stands today, over 20 years later.

The form-fitting cockpit of Goldenrod. Instrumentation is dominated by four, independent gauges, enabling Bob Summers to monitor the oil pressure of each of the four Chrysler 6.9-litre, 'hemi-head' V8 engines at a glance.

World Land Speed Record of 403.10 mph (648.72 kph) set at Lake Eyre, and Bill and Bob concluded that they might as well use the momentum of their past efforts to go for the big one and bring the prized record back to America.

While they were confident that they possessed the technical knowledge and operating skills, there was always the matter of the vast financial support required for such an ambitious project. They accordingly directed their energy to acquiring such resources, and soon came up with a healthy financial package and some very valuable support. Firestone Tire & Rubber Co. agreed to provide a portion of the funds along with developing the special tyres required to ensure safety at speeds in excess of 400 mph. Financial assistance also came from the Mobil Oil Co., who had a long history of underwriting past land speed record efforts, as well as George Hurst, President of Hurst Performance Products. Hurst also furnished the complicated gear changing mechanism needed for the sleek, four-engined, four-wheel drive *Goldenrod*, and the special wheels. Adding credibility to the project was the much needed support of Ray Brock, then publisher of the Los Angeles based *Hot Rod* Magazine, now part of the Petersen Publishing Company. The basic package was rounded out with the all-important contributions of the Chrysler Corporation in the form of four brand new 426 cubic inch Hemi engines. The Summer Brothers had always relied upon the early-style Chrysler Hemis for their previous record-setting efforts at Bonneville, and the afternoon that the big truck came to their shop

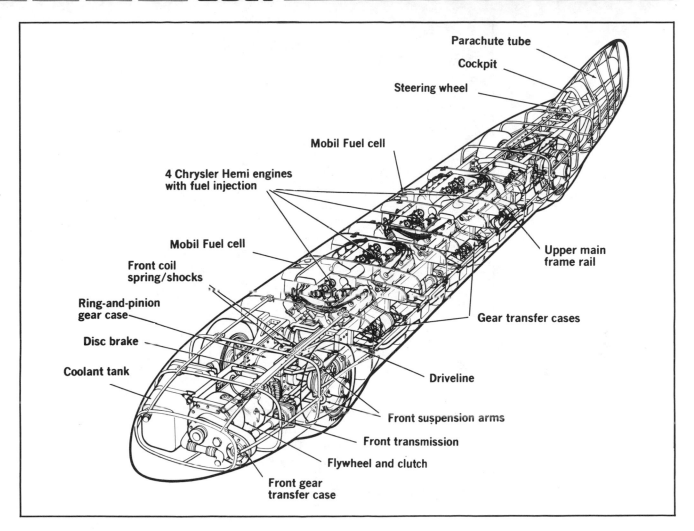

Parachute tube
Cockpit
Steering wheel

Mobil Fuel cell

4 Chrysler Hemi engines
with fuel injection

Mobil Fuel cell

Front coil
spring/shocks

Ring-and-pinion
gear case

Disc brake

Coolant tank

Upper main
frame rail

Gear transfer cases

Driveline

Front suspension arms

Front transmission

Flywheel and clutch

Front gear
transfer case

A line drawing showing how Goldenrod's *four Chrysler Hemi engines, and two four-speed gearboxes driving all four wheels, were accommodated in the streamlined vehicle.*

in Ontario, California to unload four crated brand new engines was one that they still remember vividly.

After exhaustive wind-tunnel tests had been completed at Cal Tech, it was determined that the lowest, narrowest shape possible would offer the best chances of breaking Campbell's 403 mph record. Accordingly, the four Chrysler Hemi engines were mounted in-line, and a fuel injection system was utilized instead of conventional carburettors. Driver Bob was placed right behind these powerful engines, and a lightweight aluminium body was formed around this long and streamline shape for maximum aerodynamic efficiency.

Construction of the car began on 1 January 1965 at the Summers Brothers' shop. Just seven months later, the completed *Goldenrod* moved under its own power for the first time during a series of shakedown tests at the nearby Riverside Raceway.

After making the final necessary adjustments, the Summers Brothers trailered *Goldenrod* to Bonneville in September, and made four successful runs. Instructed by all involved to 'take it easy' on the first pass (in other words, not to exceed 100 mph), Bob Summers more than slightly exceeded this limitation with a clocking of 250 mph on the *Goldenrod's* first voyage across the salt. 'It felt so good that I just didn't see any reason to lift the throttle', Bob later explained to newsmen.

Goldenrod

Chassis and Body

Length overall:	32 feet
Wheelbase:	207 inches
Tread, front and rear:	36 and 24 inches
Overall height	(to top of tailfin) 42 inches; (to top of engine hood) 28 inches
Overall width:	48 inches
Ground clearance:	5 inches
Frame:	Mild steel. Lower rails: 2 in dia. x $^1/8$ in wall. Upper rails: 2 x 6 in rectangular tubes. $^3/6$ in wall, tubes mounted vertically for maximum rigidity
Body material:	Harvey aluminium; alloy 3003, 0.064 in thick
Wheels:	Aluminium. Hurst designed, forged by Harvey Aluminium. 16 in dia. x $6^1/2$ in rim width. Demountable rim
Tyres:	6.50 x 16 Firestone tubeless Nylons; special low-profile treadless design. Width of tread contact area: 4 in. Static dia: 23 in. Inflation: 150 psi. Design speed: 600 mph
Braking systems:	Airheart triple spots mounted on front and rear pinion gear coupler flanges for use at 100 mph and below. Deist parachutes for high speeds: pilot chute; 8 foot dia. first stage for maximum speeds; 24 foot final chute for 250 mph and below; plus emergency 8 foot chute. Automatic systems with manual override.

Engines and Drive Train:

Engines:	4 Chrysler Hemi V-8s, mounted in-line and coupled in pairs, back to back, front pair driving front wheels, rear pair driving rear wheels. Engine rpms synchronized between pairs by mechanical coupling. Except for dry sump, lubrication and fuel injection (required for low overall height) engines are to stock specifications throughout
Bore and stroke:	4.25 x 3.75 in.
Displacement:	426 Cu in each engine
Estimated horsepower:	600 @ 6600–6800 rpm, each engine
Fuel:	Racing gasoline, 105 research octane, supplied by Mobil Oil Co
Lubricants	Mobil Oil Co products
Fuel supply:	5 gallons per engine in 4 tanks
Transmissions:	2, 5-speed Spicer units, utilizing top 4 gears
Ratios:	2nd – 2.6:1
	3rd – 1.5:1
	4th – 1.19:1
	5th – 1:1
	Simultaneous synchronized shifting via special Hurst Shifter

Clutches:	2 Schiefer double-disc, hydraulically actuated
Ring-and-pinion ratios:	1:1, locked rear ends
Final drive ratios:	May be varied. Anticipated: 0.95:1 to 1.05:1
Steering:	Chrysler, hydraulically actuated, 10 degrees limit
Suspension:	Fully independent, all 4 wheels via upper and lower A-arms. Upper arms pivot on frame, act on 4 special Monroe coil spring/shock units mounted inboard

Performance Data:

Frontal area:	9 sq ft. Coefficient of drag: 0.117
Total Weight:	5500–6000 lb (estimated)
Speed Capability:	450 – 500 mph

Three more runs were made, the best of which was 390 mph (on petrol!) and it was a pair of encouraged brothers who took their racing machine back to their Ontario workshop to prepare for the final record breaking assault.

It was back to Bonneville in October, and things looked especially good as Bob pushed *Goldenrod* past the 400 mph barrier on his first run at the record. With a chance to break the record now well within their grasp, the Summers Brothers experienced what was to be the first in a series of frustrations as one of the engines separated from the drivechain, causing it to over-rev and produce internal component damage. By the time that the wounded motor was replaced, rainstorms had soaked the salt to the point where record run attempts could not be made.

Making matters worse was the fact that the Summers Brothers were alloted a limited number of days on the Bonneville course. Before the conditions could improve, their course reservation had run out.

With all hopes of setting the record now apparently postponed until next season, they reluctantly towed *Goldenrod* back to Ontario. But on 7 November, an unexpected phone call from Wendover, close to Bonneville, gave hopes of yet just one more shot. Land speed jet veteran Art Arfons had the salt booked for that week, but after setting his own record for jets in the *Green Monster* on the first day, a factory rep from Firestone, who was also working with Arfons, told the Summers Brothers to get back to Bonneville to use the remaining track time.

Conditions were still somewhat damp on the course, and it took two 'push cars', one right behind the other, to get *Goldenrod* fired. But if the salt wasn't perfect, *Goldenrod* certainly was, as Bob Summers hit 417 mph on his first run and then produced another successful effort on the return, back-up pass, netting a new official World Land Speed Record of 409.277 mph (658.665 kph). That record was set on Friday, 12 November. The following day, an unofficial one-way run was made, and this produced for the Summers Brothers a clocking of 425 mph, the fastest speed ever attained by a wheel-driven vehicle.

It has now been close to 20 years since this achievement was recorded at Bonneville, and the passage of time certainly makes for an interesting perspective. According to Bill Summers, the cash contributions from the associated sponsors totalled about $108,000, and product development costs boosted the overall tab to over $250,000. To reproduce that effort in today's inflationary times would result in costs that would stagger the imagination.

On the other hand, the still well-preserved *Goldenrod* is certainly capable of making another attempt today, and subtle implementation of current 'state of the art' engine technology and weight reduction could easily result in speeds approaching 500 mph. Hard as it may be to believe, *Goldenrod* produced the record with engines that were factory standard except for the induction system and exhaust.

Even more interesting is the fact that the Summers Brothers received absolutely no financial rewards or endorsements for their outstanding efforts. "We were able to support ourselves during the construction of the vehicle and hire some additional help with the sponsorship money, but we took home only $150 a week each, and there was nothing to come after we set the record. All we ever wanted was the recognition. Looking back now, we probably should have worked out something for additional financial incentives, performance fees, bonuses for breaking the record, and all that. These things are so commonplace now in most forms of automotive competition and the big contracts that you see in professional sports.

"But it did give us a national reputation for our technology and expertise, and with that as a springboard, we founded Summers Brothers, Inc., now a major manufacturing enterprise specializing in drivetrain components for high performance applications. We have a lot of customers that first started getting interested in racing when *Goldenrod* set the record for wheel-driven cars and a lot of other clients heard about it from their older friends. The reputation that we established with that one project is very much with us today."

And so *Goldenrod*, having moved under its own power for almost two decades, now tours the globe as a great attraction to the world's motorsports enthusiasts. Luring large crowds wherever it goes, *Goldenrod* has been just as successful as a showpiece as it was in its original competition assignment on the Bonneville Salt Flats. But one can only speculate as to just what might happen if a big truck were to pull up at the Summers Brothers shop and start unloading four new aluminium 426 Hemi engines ...

Nothing is permanent in the land speed business. New efforts were mounted to break the Summers Brothers record. Mickey Thompson tried in 1969 with a twin-engine streamliner utilizing narrow, low profile lines similar

On 12 November 1965 the tranquil-looking hills of western Utah became alive with the sound of music when the Goldenrod, *the longest, narrowest and lowest package of piston-horsepower ever to run on the Bonneville Salt Flats, roared through the measured mile.*

to *Goldenrod's*. Bonneville Speed Weeks veteran Bob McGrath, in partnership with Jack Lufkin of Ak Miller Garage fame and drag racer Bill Hielscher, was preparing his twin-Chevrolet streamliner *Olympian*, an even lower and narrower car, to slice through the thin Utah air in an attempt to top the 500 mph barrier.

Craig Breedlove also explored the possibility of taking Donald Campbell's *Bluebird* out of mothballs for an attempt at the Summers Brothers' wheel-driven record. Britain's Richard Noble has even toyed with the idea ... but to date it has been little more than talk!

One thing is certain, should the record be taken away from Bob and Bill Summers, they have more than enough technical knowledge and experience to snatch it right back. The Summers Brothers welcome the challenges and invite others to go ahead and set a new record. And besides, unless somebody breaks Bob's record, it is doubtful whether we will ever see the sleek golden lines of their *Goldenrod* on the Bonneville Salt Flats again.

Although not always recognized by the purist, unlimited-class World Land Speed Records, that is to say records established by land-bound vehicles or projectiles powered by jet or rocket engines, are recognized by the FIA (Fédération Internationale de l'Automobile) the world governing body for motor sport and record-breaking since the Second World War.

With the sound barrier undoubtedly being the ultimate objective of many land speed record drivers in this category, one man, a Briton, recently realized a life-long dream of becoming the fastest man on wheels, when he drove his all-British sponsored, Rolls-Royce Avon 302 jet-powered car *Thrust 2*, to a speed in excess of 630 mph, regaining the World Land Speed Record for the United Kingdom after nearly twenty years.

Chapter 3

The Quest for Power

The Opel Rak 2 *rocket car.*

In 1927 an innocent letter arrived at the Rüsselsheim works of Opel; innocent in that the mere slip of paper led to one of the most bizarre episodes in the history of any of the world's automobile companies. The letter was written by Herr Max Valier, an Austrian-born author, university lecturer and enthusiastic advocate of the development of rocket propulsion for flights into space. Then thirty-two, Valier addressed his letter to Fritz von Opel at the suggestion of his wife, Hedwig, who thought that the indefatigable von Opel would be just the man to provide the financial backing, sought in vain by her husband for years, to support a programme of rocket research and development proposed by Valier. Not long after the letter arrived in Rüsselsheim, so did Valier.

In their meeting at the Opel works in the late Autumn of 1927, Valier learned that the von Opel heir was interested in aviation and at that time was taking flying lessons at Rebstock near Frankfurt. Von Opel learned something of Valier's background: early study of physics and astronomy, experience as a test pilot in the first World War, and an association of several years with Professor Hermann Julius Oberth, the Rumanian-born rocket pioneer from Hermannstadt who did so much to stimulate European interest in reactive flight. Studying the sharp-featured Valier through his horn-rimmed glasses, von Opel realised that the demonstration of a rocket-powered car – which Valier was willing to help build – would be a fantastic publicity coup for Opel, and without precedent in the automobile industry, and of far greater value than its modest cost. Von Opel agreed to finance a series of tests.

Valier had to find a source for ready-made rockets. He turned to Freidrich Sander of Wesermünde, a respected manufacturer of compressed-powder rockets for marine use in signalling and line-throwing.

Valier devised a simple thrust-measure and in January, 1928 he and Sander started experimenting with different versions of his largest rocket.

The 'honour' of taking the wheel of the first rocket car, Rak 1, was given by Fritz von Opel to Kurt Volkhart, a former Dürkopp designer who was also active throughout the 1920s as a racing driver.

On 11 April 1928, Kurt C. Volkhart depressed the accolorator of Rak 1, electrically igniting seven of the twelve rockets to launch him down the almost-one-mile Opelbahn at a terminal speed of more than 60 mph (96 kph).

By mid-February the two men had prepared a report which they posted to von Opel. Von Opel reacted fast to the receipt of this information. He wired Sander and Valier that he wanted a meeting and demonstration at Rüsselsheim on March 11, surprisingly soon. Not wanting to risk the possibility of failure in front of their sponsor, Valier urged Sander to contribute his little Opel sedan to the cause for static firing tests. Sander, however, fearing his learned association and respectability as a founder member of the VfR (Verein für Raumschiffahrt), was not willing to go quite that far in the interest of advancing rocket-propulsion in land-bound vehicles.

They arrived at the Opel plant on the specified day, shipping their rockets there by road because the Deutsche Bundesbahn railway refused to carry them. Opel had begun the conversion of an old racing car to serve as a test facility for the rockets, but the vehicle wasn't ready, so a simple passenger car chassis was fitted with a wooden frame, not unlike a wine rack, to hold the rockets, and a steel bulkhead to offer the driver some protection.

The 'honour' of taking the wheel of the first rocket car was delegated by Fritz von Opel to Ing. Kurt C. Volkhart, thirty-seven. Then employed by Opel. Volkhart was a former Dürkopp designer who was also active throughout the 1920s as a racing driver, owning three Bugattis during the period.

With the brave young Volkhart at the controls, Opel mechanic Carl Lutzmeyer lit the fuses hanging from the rockets and then ran for cover. In seconds the rear of the car was enveloped in a cloud of hissing smoke, and it was seen to lurch forward at a walking pace, no more.

This pathetic performance subjected the two pioneers to a barrage of derisive remarks. Their reply, a further series of tests culminating in the development of a special Opel rocket car, or *Rak* for *Rakete*.

The first moment of truth for the Opel Rak came on April 10. Only six rockets were used in the first test, in which the car reached 44 mph (71 kph) from a standing start. In a second test with eight rockets the Opel went

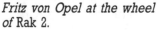

Fritz von Opel at the wheel of Rak 2.

The Rak 2, *was deservedly the most famous of the Rüsselsheim rocket cars. It had an ultra-low chassis with semi-elliptic springing, a bullet-shaped body and large down-thrusting side wings, whose angle of attack could be adjusted by a hand lever inside the cockpit.*

6 mph faster in spite of a misfire by one closely bunched compliment of rockets. This was encouraging enough for Fritz von Opel to invite the press to a public demonstration the following day, 11 April 1928. For the first time the vehicle was equipped with twelve of the high-thrust rockets, which were wired so that the accelerator lit a pair of them with each downward thrust. Von Opel hoped this would be enough to drive Rak all the way round the almost-one-mile Opelbahn.

Fritz von Opel in white coat and Friedrich Sander of Wesermünde, without hat, pose behind Rak 3, *the last of their landbound experimental rocket vehicles.*

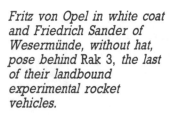

Sadly, the rockets did not produce sufficient thrust, propelling the car to no more than 60 mph (100 kph), however, the rumbling progress of the car down the track was sensational enough to warrant headlines in the papers the following day, even if they did offend the serious German rocket researchers who considered the Valier-Opel-Sander venture to be no more than a promotional stunt; a problem that also faced Bill Fredrick's remarkable 'Project Speed of Sound' in 1979, as explained later in the book.

Still more attention was accorded the next Opel demonstration, which took place on 23 May 1928, before a crowd of some 2,000 reporters, photographers and invited guests, including a young, and relatively unknown graduate from the Berlin Institute of Technology called Wernher von Braun.

Fritz von Opel and the cat who was to travel in Rak 3 *at speeds in excess of 150 mph (240 kph). Contrary to humanitarian considerations, animals were later used in experimental orbital rockets by both the United States and USSR.*

Rak 3, although unmanned, achieved a speed of 155 mph (250 kph) on rails at Rebstock near Frankfurt.

The driver, Fritz von Opel, and the car a completely new vehicle, the Opel Rak 2. This fabulous looking device was deservedly the most famous of the Rüsselsheim rocket cars. It had an ultra-low chassis with semi-elliptical springing, a bullet-shaped, black bodyshell with room at the rear to accommodate twenty-four rockets, two extremely large down-thrusting canard fins were fitted to both sides of the fuselage, forward of the driver, whose angle of attack could be adjusted by hand lever inside the cockpit. There was some thought of using *Rak 2* for an attack by Volkhart on the Land Speed Record, which at that time was held by the American, Ray Keech and stood at 207.552 mph (334.022 kph); and if looks alone could do it, *Rak 2* had the record in the bag.

It was a thrilling sight for those who lined the AVUS test track in Berlin's

Grunewald. A report in the Berliner Zeitung detailed the event: "The car started with a terrific roar, emitting a ball of flame and a billowing cloud of yellow, acrid smoke as the rockets ignited. The mighty machine gradually gained momentum as one rocket after another, all of uniform power, were fired – the car taking a lunge forward every time one ignited".

All twenty-four of the special 550-pound-thrust rockets fired properly, and von Opel is said to have reached speeds of 130 to 145 mph while covering a distance of 1^1/4 miles. Over one section of the track he was *alleged* to have attained an unheard of speed of 420 mph (676 kph) for a few seconds, although the speed was not timed. At the highest speeds the nose of *Rak 2* started to lift menacingly; the canard fins weren't angled sufficiently but von Opel was too busy keeping the car under control to spare a hand to operate the adjusting lever. It must have been quite a ride, even for an experienced driver like von Opel, and as the illustrations show, *Rak 2* had no windshield, in any shape or form!

Von Opel went on to develop yet another vehicle, but this time he wasn't so eager to sit behind the wheel, and was to experiment with an unmanned rocket vehicle on a section of disused railway line at Rebstock near Frankfurt, with a far from willing cat as passenger. The *Rak 3* was far from successful, attaining a terminal velocity of only 155 mph (250 kph).

Despite the ultimate failure of *Rak 3,* von Opel felt there was practically no limit to the speed that could have been reached by his earlier rocket car. However, the brilliant inventor never pursued the land speed record, and turned his efforts to flight, eventually realising his dream of building and flying a rocket-powered aircraft.

It wasn't until 1965 that a rocket-powered car took aim at the World Land Speed Record. However, Walt Arfon's *Wingfoot Express II,* propelled by 25 rockets and driven by Bobby Tatroe, lacked the sustained thrust to shatter the record. Despite the failure, the land speed rocket era had come of age.

Five years later, another rocket-propelled car attempted to succeed where the *Wingfoot Express II* had failed. *The Blue Flame,* driven by Gary Gabelich, was the culmination of five years of dreams, sweat and tears by Reaction Dynamics Inc., of Milwaukee, Wisconsin.

The second generation of the quest for speed on land had begun. With the emergence of the high-velocity thrust and rocket-powered landbound vehicle, the sound barrier was no longer an unattainable target, but an objective. Shortly before the worldwide economic recession started to bite, potential sponsors throughout the world were staking all on this objective.

Broken Barriers

Man has been faced by a series of barriers throughout his history. Columbus, for instance, lived in a time when men thought the earth was flat, and that he and his small fleet would tumble into an abyss once they reached the edge of the world.

The Wright Brothers proved that man could fly. Another barrier had been broken. On the morning of 14 October 1947, United States Air Force Captain Charles 'Chuck' Yeager established aviation history by piloting the rocket-powered Bell X-1 through the 'sound barrier'. Dropped from the belly of a B-29 bomber at an altitude of 35,000 feet Yeager relied totally on his four rocket engines developing 6,000 pounds of thrust to push the Bell X-1 *Glamorous Glennis* to a speed of 1,200 mph (1931 kph) across the sky, high above the Edwards Air Force Base. Today, supersonic aircraft travel at more than three times the speed of sound on regular training flights.

On 19 March 1954, U.S. Air Force Colonel John Paul Stapp, a veteran of aviation medical research, rode a rocket sled to a record of 632 mph. The 2,000 pound sled, propelled by nine rockets unleashing 40,000 pounds of thrust, required just five seconds to complete its run down the 35,000 foot test track at the United States Air Force Missile Development Centre, Holloman Air Force Base, New Mexico. Three years later, a driverless sled attained 2075 mph (3339 kph) over a two-mile track. A monorail sled has reached 2850 mph (4586 kph) again unmanned.

But could a car or wheeled projectile hold the ground at high subsonic to low supersonic speeds? Land speed record drivers, technicians and leading NASA telemetry experts, as well as an automobile wind-tunnel testing scientist at the Ford Motor Company in Dearborn, Michigan, had varied opinions.

First, the driver:

''A lot of aerodynamists think the pressure will blow the vehicle off the ground. Some think the pressure will crush the car. The sound barrier presents a whole new set of problems,'' said Gary Gabelich.

''When a plane breaks the sound barrier the shock wave is dispersed through the air. We don't know what the shock wave will do to a car.'' Conceivably, it could bounce off the ground and flip the vehicle. Breaking the sound barrier is only the beginning, according to Stan Barrett, the only man to have surpassed the speed of sound on land.

Bill Fredrick, engineer and designer of the *Budweiser Rocket* believes, ''Someday they'll be running on light rays, laser beams, or something like that, ... the amount of distance could have a lot to do with the ultimate speed limit. Under the right conditions at the Edwards Air Force Base, or a similar venue, it's possible a car could travel to 1,000 mph. The British 'Project Lionheart' is based on such a concept; with their vehicle they plan to surpass the speed of sound and attain a terminal velocity in excess of 1,000 mph.''

To understand the problem, the nature of air itself must be understood. Although invisible, the air is composed of countless numbers of extremely small atoms and molecules of nitrogen, oxygen and other gases. Each atom or molecule is so tiny that some 400 billion of them can be found in every cubic inch of the air at sea level.

Sound waves can be likened to the ripples created by the dropping of a stone or pebble into a void of still water. Travelling outward, the sound waves eventually pulsate against the ear drums, much as water pulsates when agitated.

The speed of sound is the rate at which the sound travels from its source to the receiver, which, in turn, depends upon the speed at which the atom molecules 'carrying' the pressure waves are moving.

Generally speaking, sound travels at 1,100 feet per second, but this varies with altitude, air density and temperature. At normal temperature at sea level, sound travels at a speed of about 760 miles per hour. Because of the lower air temperature at higher altitudes, however, sound travels slower. At an altitude of 20,000 feet, for example, the speed of sound is only about 700 mph; and at 36,000 feet it's 660 mph.

At subsonic speeds the airflow ahead of a plane or car is relatively stable, but when the vehicle travels faster than the speed of sound, a different airflow pattern results, much like a small boat tossed in a raging storm. At such speeds, the air is compressed into a cone-like pattern called a shock wave. This extreme disturbance accumulates in a narrow region just ahead of the travelling vehicle or craft. The shock wave travels to the ground at the speed of sound, follows the path of the craft, and becomes audible as a sonic boom.

A symetrically-shaped aircraft, travelling in free air, has fewer problems travelling faster than sound, due to the equalizing of the pressure exerted on all parts.

This is not the case, however, with a land-bound vehicle. The shock waves created at supersonic speeds are also cone-shaped. But because of the land obstruction beneath, the pressure exerted on the car is uneven. The top half of the car body produces a negative or suction-like pressure. The bottom wave creates a positive or lifting pressure. After slamming against the ground the shock wave has only one place to travel – up! This upward pressure could possibly disintegrate the land-bound vehicle or turn it into a wingless plane. Without the proper body design, a vehicle might alternately fly and touch down.

Another major problem is heat. Air flowing around an aircraft is heated to a high temperature. For example, the local air temperature in low altitude flights at Mach 3 (three times the speed of sound) would be about 940°F. Heat holds the speed of a plane down and tends to weaken and even melt its parts; this is particularly evident in the re-entry of the NASA Space Shuttles, the leading edge of the craft, in this case the underside of the nose, is heated to intense temperatures through such a process, necessitating the use of those famous tiles that caused such anxiety in the early missions.

In a land-bound vehicle the body shell must be constructed sturdily enough so that it can resist the pressures exerted on the front end: this can approach 1,500 pounds per square foot on Mach 1.

In attempting to exceed the speed of sound, the main problem that faced the aircraft industry was one of designing for the airflow encountered at transonic speeds, and in providing sufficient thrust for the aircraft to accelerate through the transonic region, with its attendant drag rise. The horsepower produced by a rocket varies with the speed. Power is thrust times velocity. At 1000 mph (1690 kph), 80,000 horsepower would be produced by a rocket engine having a thrust ratio of 30,000 lb.

They finally overcame the problems through improved aerodynamic design and better engines. Wind tunnel tests would be mandatory to the design concept of a successful sound barrier-breaking, land bound vehicle, as was the case with Bill Fredrick's *Budweiser Rocket*. The speed limit for such a car would probably be the rotational speed limit of the wheels. The vehicle would without any question of doubt, have to have a vertical tail fin, like an aircraft, and might also have to have control surfaces like an aircraft for control of pitch attitude; both the *Budweiser Rocket* and the earlier Success Motivation Institute-sponsored *SMI Motivator* had variations of these components.

Clyde Hayes of NASA's Langley Research Centre at Hampton, Virginia, maintains, "Theoretically, there is no reason why a landbound vehicle could not be engineered and designed to travel faster than the *Budweiser Rocket* and beyond the speed of sound'.

Generally, the rules used to define a landbound vehicle for setting a record beyond the speed of sound would require engineering skills that are normally applied to vehicles leaving the ground, such as aircraft and high velocity experimental rockets and missiles.

In 1887 Dr. Ernest Mach, an Austrian scientist, wrote a lengthy scientific paper entitled 'Photographic Registration of the Phenomena in the Air Produced by a Projectile'. This paper described experiments with artillery shells travelling at supersonic speeds through the air. The photographic registration system was called 'Schieren apparatus' (Schieren in German meaning 'shadow') hence the birth of the wind tunnel. Little did Dr Ernest Mach envisage then that the wind tunnel he developed would play a vital role in preparing the first landbound vehicle to exceed the speed of sound almost 100 years later. The 'Project Speed of Sound' team subjected the *Budweiser Rocket* to rigorous wind tunnel tests prior to the sound barrier success at the Edwards Air Force Base. This, too, happened to many of the earlier World Land Speed Record cars, including Donald Campbell's *Bluebird* and more recently Britains' *Thrust 2* , driven by Richard Noble.

Information gained from wind tunnel testing and through telemetry has proved invaluable in the attainment of new World Land Speed Records and will almost certainly continue to do so, as landbound vehicles are designed to achieve ever increasing speeds in pursuit of a new record or scientific objective. Who knows, in the not too distant future, Mach 1 racing may be commonplace, only time will tell ...

'Barriers' as such exist more in the minds of journalists than in fact. No physical barriers exist to impede the passage of an aircraft or landbound vehicle through the air, and today supersonic transport is a commonplace, experienced not only by highly-trained professionals but by passengers in the new generation of supersonic transport like the Concorde. But what physiological forces would the human body encounter during the periods of sustained transverse acceleration that the new era of thrust and rocket-powered vehicles would impose upon their drivers?

Escape Systems

The controlled application of high but brief accelerations in a precisely ordered sequence lies at the heart of the escape systems used in present military aircraft. In the days of low-speed flight and of open cockpits it was possible for an aviator simply to climb from his seat, jump clear of the structure and to pull the rip-cord of his parachute. But at speeds in excess of 200 mph (322 kph) 'bailing out' becomes impossible, because the would-be escaper does not have the strength to clamber out in the teeth of the wind. Moreover, a manually operated parachute cannot be used safely below 300 – 400 feet (91 – 122m) because there is no time for it to open fully and begin to retard the descent before the subject hits the ground. But in land-bound (ground-effect) vehicles, there is no margin of altitude for a driver to escape the car and its highly explosive payload. Bill Fredrick had explored the possibility of engineering a gyro-controlled ejection capsule for the *Budweiser Rocket*. Present-day automatic escape systems have been successfully used at supersonic speed at high altitudes and at zero speeds on the ground. Indeed, at the White Sands Missile Range, Holloman Air Force Base, New Mexico, a full-scale mockup of a land-bound vehicle was attached to a 35,000 horsepower rocket-propelled sled, and used for

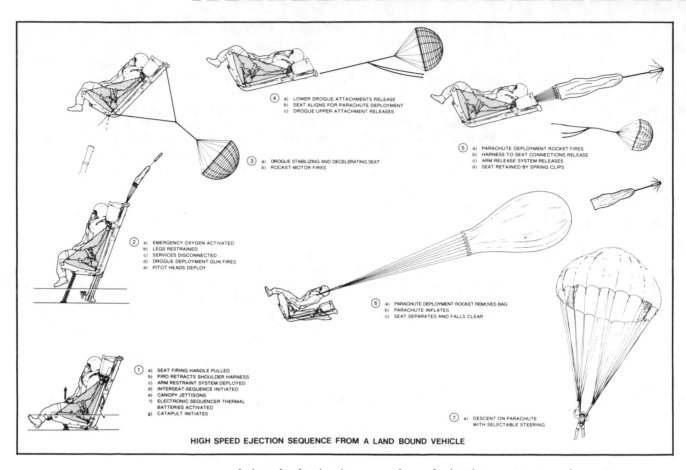

4 a) LOWER DROGUE ATTACHMENTS RELEASE
b) SEAT ALIGNS FOR PARACHUTE DEPLOYMENT
c) DROGUE UPPER ATTACHMENT RELEASES

3 a) DROGUE STABILIZING AND DECELERATING SEAT
b) ROCKET MOTOR FIRES

5 a) PARACHUTE DEPLOYMENT ROCKET FIRES
b) HARNESS TO SEAT CONNECTIONS RELEASE
c) ARM RELEASE SYSTEM RELEASES
d) SEAT RETAINED BY SPRING CLIPS

2 a) EMERGENCY OXYGEN ACTIVATED
b) LEGS RESTRAINED
c) SERVICES DISCONNECTED
d) DROGUE DEPLOYMENT GUN FIRES
e) PITOT HEADS DEPLOY

6 a) PARACHUTE DEPLOYMENT ROCKET REMOVES BAG
b) PARACHUTE INFLATES
c) SEAT SEPARATES AND FALLS CLEAR

1 a) SEAT FIRING HANDLE PULLED
b) PIRD RETRACTS SHOULDER HARNESS
c) ARM RESTRAINT SYSTEM DEPLOYED
d) INTERSEAT-SEQUENCE INITIATED
e) CANOPY JETTISONS
f) ELECTRONIC SEQUENCER THERMAL
BATTERIES ACTIVATED
g) CATAPULT INITIATES

7 a) DESCENT ON PARACHUTE
WITH SELECTABLE STEERING

HIGH SPEED EJECTION SEQUENCE FROM A LAND BOUND VEHICLE

research into both ejection capsule and ejection seat tests using an anthropomorphic dummy as test subject. The only reaction required of the driver is to pull a handle mounted on his seat. The cockpit canopy is jettisoned to clear the path for the subsequent ejection and an explosive charge then propels the seat up guide rails attached to the vehicle structure. A rocket motor then ignites, to sustain guided thrust and so to increase upward velocity of the seat or ejection capsule. (It is this added velocity which makes escape possible from a land-bound vehicle). After a brief delay, the seat or capsule is stabilized by the deployment of a small drogue parachute, not unlike the braking chutes used on the majority of land speed record vehicles; this in turn draws the main canopy from its capsule. The harness is released and the seat falls away separately, leaving the driver to descend on his now fully-opened parachute.

Each phase of the escape from the vehicle (including the landing) involves acceleration and deceleration, but the greatest force is applied in the first tenth of a second, during which the capsule reaches a vertical velocity of about 80 fps (24.4 mps). A properly restrained man can withstand an acceleration of 25 g in the spinal axis, but the ejection force comes very close to the limit of human tolerance. In fact, transient backache is an almost inevitable consequence of ejection and a crushed vertebra is a not uncommon complication, although it is rarely a serious injury, and is a small price to pay for the preservation of life.

The shock forces of parachute deployment are normally less than the 20 g or so which can be tolerated by an unsupported body, but in ejections at very high speeds deployment of the main canopy must be delayed so that

Safety at speeds in excess of Mach 1 on land would be complete with the addition of a gyro controlled ejection capsule. In this test from the cockpit of a Northrop T-38 aircraft, an anthropomorphic dummy is used as a test subject.

A sophisticated ejection seat that has the capability of sensing airspeed and adjusting its mode of operation accordingly, the Martin-Baker Mk.12 high performance escape system would serve admirably in a land bound vehicle. The only action required of the driver is to initiate the firing sequence — everything else is operated automatically in this remarkable 'zero-zero' system.

the abrupt deceleration of the system does not break both the parachute and the man. A g-sensitive device therefore inhibits the sequence until most of the forward momentum has been lost.

Another avenue of escape systems suitable for land-bound vehicles that has been explored is a horizontal separation capsule, or 'second stage' unit that could be jettisoned from the main fuselage of the vehicle by an explosive charge, not unlike the method of escape discussed earlier, although as an alternative to upward velocity produced by a rocket propulsion element, the separation capsule, by the very force of the explosive charge, would be fired backward at a velocity equal to the forward acceleration of the vehicle, leaving the capsule and its occupant free to coast or roll to a halt. However, one of the most significant factors to emerge from the study of this method of escape, is that while the jettisoned capsule would be free from the 'mother' vehicle, as a unit, it would be without control, and the only way to ensure safety of the driver would be the incorporation of a reinforced 'roll bar' into the overall design concept of the vehicle and the separation capsule, this in itself would present an enormous increase in the power to weight ratio, at a stage when the vehicle's peformance is based entirely on transverse acceleration on the calculus of power – thrust times velocity.

A feasibility study is currently under preparation on this form of escape system by Robert C. Truax of the Saratoga, California-based Truax Engineering Inc., who also engineered Evel Knievel's 1974 rocket-propelled 'Sky Cycle', in which he attempted to jump Snake River Canyon, Idaho, but it will be some time before the feasibility study is completed, and indeed the system put to the test. So for the time being, the only feasible escape system that would be suitable for a land-bound vehicle is that of the gyro-controlled ejection capsule favoured by Bill Fredrick.

But where would man attempt to exceed the speed of sound on land? The search for a natural race-strip with Mach 1 capabilities would not be easy, and the logistics of such a project would be greater still.

The Search for a Supersonic Raceway

There are few places in the world where one can drive a vehicle faster than a speeding bullet. With but four exceptions, all land speed record attempts since the mid-1930s have taken place at the desolate Bonneville Salt Flats in Western Utah – 3,000 square miles and 500 million tons of salt.

Popularity came to Bonneville when Sir Malcolm Campbell sought a faster, safer and considerably longer speedway than the drifting sands of Ormond Beach in Florida. The strain of a car streaking across the sands at terminal speeds approaching 300 mph forced the dry crust to crack and thus ended a golden era of racing. In 1935, Campbell took his Bluebird to Bonneville and became the first man to reach 300 mph. His two-way average speed across the glistening white salt flats was 301.13 mph (484.89 kph).

Thirty years later, Craig Breedlove shattered the 600 mph barrier in his powerful jet-powered *Spirit of America – Sonic 1.*

On 12 January 1904, Henry Ford in the Arrow, completed the first assualt on the World Land Speed Record on American soil. Hot cinders were spread along a course measured to the mile across the wastes of Lake St-Clair, Michigan.

The flats, seemingly limitless and with a grim backdrop of the Wasatch mountains, not unlike a lunar landscape, were first traversed mechanically by railway in 1909. To ensure a water supply for the locomotives they ran a pipeline some 35 miles from the mountains to a point on the western edge of the vast salt flats near the Nevada border, and there a settlement called Wendover grew around the pipe. Then the Lincoln Highway was built, linking Salt Lake City with Wendover and far to the west, the great city of San Francisco.

So immense are the Bonneville Salt Flats that the curvature of the earth is clearly visible. In summer they are parched, glaringly white, and were lethal in the early pioneering days to travellers on foot, lured on by tempting mirages and a desperate need for the water they never found. In the winter when it rains, fed by the flow of the three main tributaries of the Bear, Weber and Jordan Rivers, the water remains on top of the salt, never drains, and takes days to evaporate; a problem that has fallen upon many land speed record contenders, in particular Britain's Richard Noble, who in 1981 and 1982 was forced to abandon his costly attempts at the record and seek an alternative venue on a dry lake bed in the Nevada Desert.

To the east of Wendover, twentieth-century alchemy converts the salt into metal at the Amax Magnesium Corporation, who have been quarrying the salt for some years during the dry season, but when the winter rains return the salt naturally finds a new level under the water table. Thus, over a period of years, sedimentary rock has breached the surface of the crystalline salt. At high speeds, the subsequent effect of the erosion is certain disaster. Carefully selected sections of the salt flats are still combed for regular drag-racing meets during the annual 'Bonneville Nationals', organised by the San Diego-based Southern California Timing Association and, more recently, the abortive attempts of Richard Noble and the Project

Despite protests from local inhabitants. Campbell hit upon the idea of ploughing two deep furrows some 50 yards apart along the length of the 7-mile Pendine course, to drain the sea water away. This exercise however, made matters considerably worse. It certainly dried up the section close to the ploughed furrows, but appeared to make the course condition midway between the furrows perilous. The idea was later abandoned.

Laying down the line. This photograph shows the sighting strip being marked on the salt at Bonneville in the 1950s.

Thrust team to regain the World Land Speed Record for the United Kingdom.

Bruce N. Kaliser of the Utah Geological Survey told me, "Never, ever, in historic times has Bonneville been so waterlogged." He continued, "The ground is so saturated that the slide hazard will persist for at least ten years".

While the surface of the salt is near perfect for speeds up to 600 mph, on dry sections, the new era of rocket-powered vehicles like *The Blue Flame* and the *Budweiser Rocket* find the crystalline surface too rough for the car to stay on the ground.

One of the most significant factors to emerge from this is the fickle nature of salt lakes and playas that are subject to annual flooding. Both the amount of rainfall and the evaporation process, together with prevailing winds and dust storms, all contribute to the final nature of the dry sun-baked surface year after year. One may not assume, therefore, that because a certain lake bed was ideal during 1980, it will again be suitable in 1981. In fact, abnormal cloud cover and late rains have made the flats almost unusable since 1981.

In the case of the alkali type lake bed, parts of the surface are soft and friable. These spots are virtually incompactable in certain places and a considerable amount of top soil needs to be graded or combed away to reach the hard, stable surface underneath.

Bill Fredrick, the entrepreneurial designer-builder of the *Budweiser Rocket,* had been searching for many years for a suitable alternative venue to Bonneville for his 1979 Project Speed of Sound team. The legendary Chuck Yeager, pioneer test pilot of the historical Bell X-1 rocket plane – first man to break the sound barrier upstairs – paved the way for Fredrick and Chief Engineer Kirk Swanson to get their rocket car on to the Edwards Air Force Base, at Rogers Dry Lake, high in the Mojave desert.

Like Bonneville, the three main dry lakes within the base, Rogers, Rosamund and Buckhorn are also seasonal. When the wind sweeps the few inches of rainwater back and forth across the lake beds, they become absolutely smooth and level. Then, when the waters evaporate in the Spring and the sun bakes the ground hard, the immense lake beds become the greatest natural landing fields ever discovered – and also the biggest, with miles of room for error.

That was highly desirable in the selection of Edwards by NASA as the

Fritz von Opel's 1928 Rak 2 takes pride of place alongside the 1912 Maffei S 3/6 Bavarian express locomotive in the Deutsches Museum, Museumsinsel 1, Munich, West Germany.

1. Salt buckling, one of many seasonal problems that face BLM Outdoor Recreation Planner, Gregg Morgan and his team prior to any land speed record attempt at Bonneville.

2. Cracking due to dessication of the top layer of mud and mineral residue can result in distinct polygons varying in size from a few inches to ten feet across and more. Not unlike a coral reef, an extreme example is seen here on the vast Laguna Salada dry lake, Mexico.

3. Although sections of El Mirage dry lake in the Sierra Nevada region of Southern California are graded for regular racing, the rapid evaporation of the watershed in recent years, has resulted in a rock-hard, incompactable surface that does not lend itself too easily to regular grading.

4. The Etosha Pan in Namibia, is probably the closest in prehistoric resemblance to the Bonneville Salt Flats, but Etosha Pan is a wildlife refuge and a sanctuary for game, and the Etosha National Parks Board would certainly not permit grading of the arid soil for a land speed record attempt.

Main picture: A BLM survey truck with a 12 foot x 40 foot land plane in tow, prepares to smooth the growing salt flats. Planing begins in the early summer the surface being dragged and skimmed until a smooth hard speedway is carved out of the salt.

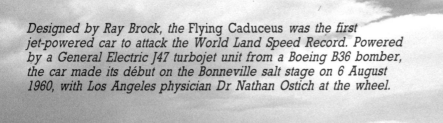

Designed by Ray Brock, the Flying Caduceus *was the first jet-powered car to attack the World Land Speed Record. Powered by a General Electric J47 turbojet unit from a Boeing B36 bomber, the car made its début on the Bonneville salt stage on 6 August 1960, with Los Angeles physician Dr Nathan Ostich at the wheel.*

Dr Nathan Ostich prepares the Flying Caduceus *for its inaugural run at Bonneville. With a sharply pointed proboscis, the vehicle took its name from the herald's wand or staff, winged, with two serpents twined around it, carried by the messenger-god Hermes of Greek Mythology. The staff is used as the symbol of the medical profession, and served as the emblem of the car proudly displayed between the flags of the United States of America and the 'chequered flag' of the winning post of motorsport.*

Art Arfons' powerful Green Monster *after cementing his third World Land Speed Record on the morning of 7 November 1965 at Bonneville. This was the second of three wild runs, the third ending in a near fatal crash when the* Green Monster *blew a right-hand rear tyre approaching the 500 mph mark.*

Art Arfons' Green Monster *hurtles through the measured mile at Bonneville to shatter Tom Green's record set three days earlier in the jet-powered* Wingfoot Express.

The Westinghouse J46
10,000 bhp triple-jet
powered Wingfoot Express
driven by Tom Green
during the record breaking
run at Bonneville. Green
averaged 413.20 mph
(664.95 kph) through the
mile at Bonneville on 2
October 1964.

Unlike Walt Arfons'
free-wheeling,
rocket-powered Wingfoot
Express II, the jet-powered
Wingfoot Express was
driven to a new World
Land Speed Record at
Bonneville. Walt Arfons
kneels before his creation,
exposing the great maw of
the business end of the jet,
prior to the fitting of the
vertical tail-fin.

Designed and built by Walt
Arfons, the Wingfoot
Express II by all accounts,
should have exceeded the
speed of sound at
Bonneville. The final
version had a total of
twenty-five 1,000 lb thrust,
Aerojet (JATO) solid fuel
rockets; fifteen mounted in
the tail, supplemented by
five more bolted on each
side of the fuselage. Driver
Bobby Tatroe approached
580 mph (933 kph) but
again was robbed of

sufficient thrust to surpass the official mile and indeed the sound barrier.

A striking rear view of the Wingfoot Express II *shows Walt Arfons endeavours to increase high-speed stability of the car. The rear wheels extend beyond the rear of the vehicle, and have a wide track for roll stability.*

Craig Breedlove and his Spirit of America jet car which set the World Land Speed Record of 526.38 mph (847.12 kph) on the 15 October 1964.

Following the black sighting strip marked in the salt, Craig Breedlove roars into the start of the measured mile, marked by timing equipment each side of the course.

GOOD☰YEAR   SHELL   SPIR

The beautiful Spirit of America - Sonic I *at Bonneville.*

Shoehorned into a marvel of motion engineering Gary Gabelich, alone in The Blue Flame, prepares to ignite the awesome 35,000 horsepower rocket motor that will launch him into history.

In a split ear-shattering second, the 35,000 horsepower, rocket-powered The Blue Flame disappeared in a stream of white smoke as it streaked toward the deep-blue horizon and the target, almost two miles away.

Not unlike a frozen Arctic waste, the hard crystalline surface of Lake Eyre. The sun-baked salt lake in Australia posed many problems for Donald Campbell and his team.

Cutting the salt islands on the track for the Bluebird-Proteus's first trial run on Lake Eyre. Here one of the two salt cutters, which were specially equipped for this purpose, is shown in grinding action. In the background are (left) the BP film unit vehicle, and the Bluebird chase car.

recovery test centre for the landing of the earlier *Columbia* Space Shuttle missions.

The clay playas or pans are reputed to be a more stable soil type and produce a hard consistent surface year after year. This type of surface can also vary across the lake bed as a close inspection of Rogers Dry Lake will bear witness. Cracking due to desiccation of the top layer of mud can result in distinct polygons forming, varying in size from a few inches to ten feet across and more. Loose, shale-type fragments are also to be found in certain parts of the lake bed, particularly on the smaller Buckhorn Dry Lake. In the case of salt lakes one has a surface that is consistently hard and lends itself to grading if flooding has occurred. A suitable track may be prepared whilst the salt is still in the process of drying out, without removing a great amount of top surface. However, if insufficient flooding occurs and the salt remains dry from one year to the next, the subsequent result is a rock hard surface that could not be graded or prepared for racing by conventional equipment.

The United States Air Force were very co-operative with the Project Speed of Sound team and recently made public their willingness to assist future World Land Speed Record attempts, with a particular emphasis on the availability of the Holloman Air Force Base, New Mexico. The 35,588 ft high-speed test track facility, Holloman is situated on the eastern edge of the White Sands Missile Testing Range. Long periods of acceleration are possible with the present track with sufficient track length remaining to allow low-g recovery and deceleration. The track can be readily extended should longer acceleration periods be required.

Bill Fredrick had also talked to Jim Neal of NASA who advised him to try the Upper Alkali Lake for the sound barrier attempt in 1979. Fredrick's attempts to prepare a suitable track on Upper Alkali were abandoned however.

The Alvord Desert, Oregon was the selected venue for Kitty O'Neil to capture the highest land speed recorded by a woman – 524.016 mph (843.319 kph) in the prototype of the *Budweiser Rocket*, the 48,000 hp rocket-powered three-wheeled *SMI Motivator* on 6 December 1976. Her official two-way average record was 512.710 mph (825.124 kph) and she probably touched 600 mpm (965 kph) momentarily.

Further south, Laguna Colorada, near the border of Salar de Atacama in Chile, is situated at an altitude of 4,800 metres in the Andes. The dry lake is salty and – as its name suggests – red, being coloured by algae.

In the internal drainage region of the Kgalagadi in central Botswana, there are something over 9,000 pans, including the largest 'dry lake' in the world, the immense Makarikari Salt Pan. Another prolific area is a belt, some 95 miles wide, of arid low-relief country running north-north-east across the veldt for nearly 600 miles from Calvinia in the Cape across the Karoo to the Transvaal. Few of these pans contain permanent water. For most of the time they are dry, their floors level, hard, encrusted with saline and rich mineral residue, shimmering with heat, glaringly white and full of mirages and tribal legend.

There are some famous pans in this belt, such as Verneuk (Deception) Pan, used by Sir Malcolm Campbell as a speedway during his attempt on the World Land Speed Record in 1929, and several others, notably the vast Grootvioer Pan, would serve admirably as potential land speed record venues if they were not so remote from centres of human habitation.

Such was the case with Donald Campbell. Following a near fatal crash at Bonneville and under mounting pressure from his sponsors, BP, Campbell went to Australia and explored a number of dry lakes, including Lake Eyre and Lake Carnegie. The former, was more suitable in soil stability, but the latter, less suitable but with relatively easy access, was the selected site for the attempt on the record. In his global search for an alternative venue to Bonneville, Donald Campbell happened upon the immense salt flats of Lake Deborah East, a vast, saline plain adjacent to Lake Seabrook in Western Australia.

George Lister who has a Salt Mining Lease on a small section of the Lake, claims that Campbell considered Lake Deborah East to be the finest

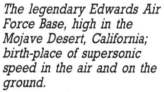

The legendary Edwards Air Force Base, high in the Mojave Desert, California; birth-place of supersonic speed in the air and on the ground.

land speed venue in the world. Sadly for Campbell however, he was already heavily committed to Lake Eyre and indeed the South Australia Government who had prepared both an access road and a course on the dead lake.

An ironic preamble to Campbell's discovery of Lake Deborah East, is that today, some 23 years later, Australian Rosco McGlashan plans an assault on Campbell's record on the lake in a Westinghouse J-34 12,500 lb thrust turbo-jet powered car *'Aussie Invader'*.

In an otherwise barren land, the shallow pans rank among the natural wonders of the world. Moving water is the most powerful erosive tool of nature. Set to work on a landscape, like the broom in the tale of the sorcerer's apprentice, it has to be sharply watched and tightly controlled by nature, otherwise its ceaseless labours will result in the ultimate of erosion, the production of what is known as a 'peneplain' (almost a plain). In this gently rolling almost perfectly flat landscape, the water is made captive by its own exertions and is unable to go anywhere at all other than straight up or down. Sideways, it just flounders, for there is no run-off on a level terrain.

In such a peneplain, rainwater will collect in any hollow and wait to evaporate or soak down into the earth. If the hollow is large, then a lake will be formed. But lakes are more generally geological accidents caused by landfalls or other natural obstructions blocking the flow of a river. On a peneplain, the rainwater is more likely to find its way into a shallow depression (oasis), leaving the level to form the peneplain or playa.

Undoubtedly the most supreme example of a peneplain is to be found at Lake Abbé, in Djibouti, although the current hostilities and political unrest in neighbouring Ethiopia, would prevent any land speed record attempt on the dry lake. Additionally the logistics of mounting such a project in the region would prove difficult.

Further south, the Etosha Pan in Namibia, has probably the closest prehistoric resemblance to the Bonneville Salt Flats, but my arduous research of the region would suggest that apart from poor accessibility, Etosha Pan is a wildlife refuge and a sanctuary for game, and the Etosha National Parks Board would certainly not permit grading of the arid soil for a land speed record attempt.

An old Heiqum Hottentot legend tells of a party of strangers that strayed into Heiqum territory. A band of hunters surrounded the intruders and killed the men and children but allowed the women to live. One young mother was inconsolable. She sat under a flame tree and rocked her dead infant in her arms, weeping so bitterly that her tears formed a huge lake. The sun dried the tears, leaving the ground covered in salt. That, say the Heiqum, was the origin of Etosha Pan – lake of a mother's tears.

Closer to Europe, in fact a relatively short flight across the Mediterranean, lie the dry lake beds of Chott Melrhir and Chott el Hodna in Algeria. Already a number of small drag racing meetings have been held on the larger, Chott Melrhir, but there can be very strong cross-winds, and the area is noted for its sandstorms. Sammy Miller of *Vanishing Point* and *Oxygen* fame had seriously considered the possibility of attempting to capture the World Land Speed Record on the Chott's in his new rocket-car, although as yet, no decision has been made on the venue for his attempt.

The typical 'sabkhah' territories in the Asir region of Saudi Arabia could easily be graded for land speed record attempts. The heat is often forbidding, the face of the landscape often cruelly dry. And yet

The immense salt lake of Daryácheh ye Namak, near Quom in central Iran. This vast region of Dasht-E Kavir (Great Salt Desert), was the chosen venue for Bill Fredrick's 1979 Project Speed of Sound, but increased tension between the United States and Iran following the deposing of the late Shah, not to mention the American hostage crisis, presented too many obstacles for Fredrick and his team.

temperatures and seasons vary greatly, and parts of the Kingdom's vast area enjoy dependable rains. The only regions condemned to barrenness are the great deserts of the Nafud in the north, and the Rub al-Khali, or Empty Quarter in the south.

The Saudi Arabians have shown a great interest in motorsport. HRH Prince Majid bin Abdul Aziz, former Minister for Municipal and Rural Affairs and now the Emir of the Mecca Region, has shown interest in the possibility of mounting a World Land Speed Record attempt within the Kingdom, although he is naturally most concerned about the safety aspect of such a venture.

To the east, the arid terrain north of Salalah in the Sultanate of Oman, is a further possibility.

HM King Hussein of Jordan has expressed a very personal interest in the quest for speed on land, and Brigadier General Hratch Etyemezian at the Royal Automobile Club of Jordan has confirmed that various forms of official co-operation and liaison could easily be arranged, and a suitable site could be prepared on the vast Wadi Rum desert south of Petra, in the southern Jordanian desert region, although my own experience of the site is recalled by memories of very strong winds.

In his search for an alternative site to Bonneville, Donald Campbell discovered a suitable dry lake bed at Karacheyevsk in the Caucasus Mountains of the USSR, but was reluctant to pursue this venue because of his staunch patriotism.

Bill Fredrick also explored the possibility of taking the *Budweiser Rocket* to the salt lakes of the vast Dasht-E Kavir (Great Salt Desert) in Central Iran, but increased tension between the United States and Iran following the revolution that deposed the late Shah, not to mention the American hostage crisis, presented too many obstacles for Fredrick and his team. Shortly after the death of the Shah while in exile in Cairo, it was discovered that among the very few personal possessions he was able to gather after he was deposed from his beloved Persia, was a scale model of the *Budweiser Rocket*, presented to him by the Project Speed of Sound team during the conceptual stages of the project. This may well be a reflection of the very great interest that is generated by a state-of-the-art project such as the *Budweiser Rocket*.

In 1982, Britain's Richard Noble was forced to seek a more stable soil type for his third assault on the World Land Speed Record. No sooner had the Project Thrust entourage arrived at Bonneville, than the Salt Flats disappeared under four feet of water. With no positive fall-back plan for the attempt and their dwindling sponsorship budget being eaten away, they had very little time for choosing an alternative choice.

With the numerous dry lakes along the high Sierra Nevada region on the California/Nevada borders to choose from, well known to all involved in drag racing and land speed ... El Mirage, China Lake, Lucerne, Carson Sink, Mud Lake, Tonopah, Searles, Winnemucca and even the immense Laguna Salada, albeit a short hop across the Mexican border, they were forced to settle for the relatively unknown alkali playa, once part of prehistoric Lake Lahontan, near Gerlach on the far edge of the Black Rock Desert, Nevada, some 600 miles west of Bonneville. Unfortunately, earlier attempts on the Black Rock Desert did not allow *Thrust 2* to be taken far enough back for a proper run-in to the measured mile, mostly due to the very poor surface conditions and now familiar watershed at the far end of the course. A later attempt at the World Land Speed Record on the desert finally secured the record for Britain, when Richard Noble hurtled his massive jet-car to an official two-way average speed of 633,468 mph (1019.465 kph). Through the determination of Noble and the excellence of his design team led by John Ackroyd, the record is now back in Britain.

There are no doubt many sites around the world suitable for World Land Speed Record attempts, but with the development and utilisation of 'reaction' rocket power in land bound vehicles or projectiles, has the time come for tighter controls against the exploitation of man and machine? In the United States today, Craig Breedlove is developing a new rocket powered car, *Spirit of America III – Sonic II,* in which he plans to become the first man to exceed 1,000 mph, moreover, he intends to organize the first Mach 1 – Supersonic Drag Race. Already, Breedlove has received several challenges including a serious contender from the United Kingdom 'Project Lionheart', of which the overall design concept is based on a design similar to the outstandingly successful 1979 *Budweiser Rocket*, although the British car will be sporting a mighty 48,000 horsepower, hybrid rocket engine. The funding of the £2.5 million project is expected to come from a Middle Eastern consortium.

The Spirit of America roars through the measured mile at Bonneville in 1964.

Chapter 4
Jets and Rockets

Dr Nathan Ostich ~ The Flying Doctor

The first man to race a jet car successfully at Bonneville will not be familiar to most readers and lay disciples of Land Speed Record, breaking for the name of Dr Nathan Ostich, a physician from the east Los Angeles barrio, doesn't appear in the record books, but certainly not for the want of trying.

For three years, the Los Angeles physician waged a battle with the elusive record on the great salt stage, in his 28ft jet car, the *Flying Caduceus.*

Powered by a General Electric J47 turbojet unit from a surplus Boeing B36 bomber, the *Flying Caduceus,* boasting a 7,000 horsepower punch, was some two years in the making 'between patients' in the garage behind the Doc's surgery.

Designed by Ray Brock, publisher of *Hot Rod* magazine and Allen Bradshaw, the car was built by a team of no less than twenty-one volunteers, including five patients, a lawyer, and three reporters from the designer's editorial team, at a cost of $100,000 dollars and 10,000 man-hours.

GM truck suspension, A-arms, torsion bars and steering units comprised the running gear, and as the driving force was thrust only, there was no transmission or differential. The almost spherical body cross-section tested

Dr Nathan Ostich, the Los Angeles physician who introduced the jet era to land speed racing with his $100,000 Firestone-sponsored Flying Caduceus.

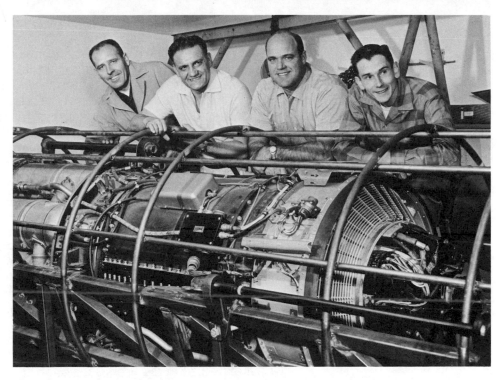

Pausing for a moment from their work constructing the world's first jet-powered land speed record car Flying Caduceus, are, left to right; Ak Miller, Dr Nathan Ostich, Ray Brock and Allan Bradshaw. Before them is the General Electric J47, 7,000 lb thrust turbojet power unit already in situ within the tubular steel framework of the car.

well in the wind tunnel facility at California Poly Tech. Overall chassis strength was achieved by combining heavy horizontal members of rectangular tubing with machine-bent hoops of heavy-gauge round tubing. The frame was of chrome moly, electrically welded, and the outer skin of the body shell was finished in aluminium. Shod with special high-speed Firestone tyres inflated to 200 psi, the wheels were outrigged and unstreamlined. Halibrand spot brakes on all four wheels supplemented a double-action speed-retarding chute which was fired from a tube in the vehicle's tail, just above the jet 'stove-pipe'. The chute first opened to a diameter of four feet, then a delayed action fuse in the reefing shroud lines exploded six to eight seconds after the initial deployment and allowed the chute to expand to eight feet in diameter.

Ostich caught the land speed bug in 1949, and was no stranger to the Bonneville Salt Flats, he had raced there for 10 years in a wide variety of exotic propulsion systems, and clocked a mean 189.90 mph (305.54 kph) in a modified road car.

Poor salt conditions in 1961 virtually eliminated all attempts to break John Cobb's record of 394.20 mph (634.26 kph), established in 1947; thus all efforts to regain the World Land Speed Record for the United States were shelved until the following year.

Pre-season publicity by the Southern California Timing Association heralded 1962 as a banner year, with no less than 10 contenders – including seven jet cars. The cast of competitors included Mickey Thompson, Art Arfons, Bill Johnson, Bob McGrath, Bill Fredrick, Dr Nathan Ostich, Glenn Leasher, Ermie Immerso, Craig Breedlove, Bob Knapp and Bob Funk. In addition, the car that carried Athol Graham to his death in 1960 had been rebuilt by Otto Anzjon, a 19-year-old mechanic from Salt Lake City. Athol's wife Zeldine, however, was never to see her husband's creation return to the salt, for the young Anzjon was robbed of his opportunity to drive the car by his sudden death in the winter of 1962 of leukemia.

No sooner had Ostich and his team arrived at Bonneville on 5 August, than things began to go wrong.

Air supply for the vehicle's jet engine was ducted from slots on each side of the cockpit proboscis. While the split ducting system was engineered and designed from recommendations made by General Electric, the engine's manufacturer, the laminated fibreglass, reinforced with square mesh steel was not strong enough to stand the air pressure differential between supply the demand at near full power settings, and the intake ducts, not packed out as normal by ram air, collapsed. A hasty all-night repair job did not prove to be strong enough and the *Flying Caduceus* was returned to Los Angeles where the crew constructed new ducts of honeycomb-section fibreglass.

On 5 September the *Flying Caduceus* returned to Bonneville and had progressively increased its speed from the low 200s to 324 mph. Ostich was ready to attack the record.

Approaching a speed of 331 mph, seven miles down range, the car suddenly veered to the left in a terrifying slide. The left-hand front wheel buckled, and snapped from its bearing. Fighting to regain control the 52-year-old driver fired his Deist safety chute and the *Flying Caduceus* remained stable until finally coming to a shuddering halt at the end of the salt.

Although Ostich wasn't injured, the car had suffered considerable damage, and the doctor and his crew returned to Los Angeles.

Ostich explained to the Press soon after his return to LA, "At high speed it is impossible to steer the car with wheels, at speeds between 319 and 324 mph, it handled perfectly. But if you get the least little bit out of line, say only two to three degrees, there's 19,000 pounds of pressure pushing on one side of the fuselage. There's simply no way to hold it, the wheels develop a form of gyroscopic co-efficiency. At such speeds the only thing you can do is control it with the rudder".

Then why the spin? "The left front wheel spindle had broken off, causing the wheel to come loose. As a result, the excessive transfer to the left front of the car when it began slipping sideways caused the break," he explained.

Ostich returned to Bonneville for a third crack at the record in 1963, and on one 324 miles an hour run into the mile, spun the car out of the timing trap while decelerating. He was travelling at only 75 mph when he finally lost control, relying on friction alone to halt the car.

Wind tunnel tests of the car prior to his attempts at the record, showed the *Flying Caduceus* had a speed potential of 500 mph, but in practice the vehicle never surpassed a terminal velocity in excess of 331 mph (532.57 kph).

While the car failed in its attempt to capture the record for the United States, the jet era had been officially launched.

Art Arfons and 'The Green Monster'

Art Arfons was an established drag racing celebrity when, in 1960, he learned that there was a slightly damaged $250,000 J79 jet engine for sale for $5,000 in Florida. The manufacturers, General Electric, would just as soon have broken it down for scrap, because a large wedge of steel had been run through the impeller blades, and the engine was believed to be worthless. What they hadn't considered was the mechanical genius of racing veteran/inventor Art Arfons.

He hung the enormous engine aloft in his workshop in Akron, Ohio, painstakingly removed the blades, one by one shaping them with a hand file. Those blades damaged beyond repair he discarded, respacing the remainder to compensate for those removed.

Without the co-operation of the manufacturer to supply spare parts, Arfons worked around the clock and, to the embarrassment of the United States Air Force who discarded it as scrap metal, rebuilt the engine to fine working order.

The Sunday afternoon in South Akron when Arfons first ignited his new engine is still talked about today. Art had put the engine in his *Green Monster* car upside down, and anchored the car to a three ton block of concrete he had buried in his backyard. Directing the exhaust toward the swamp behind his workshop, he ignited the 17,500 hp engine. His chicken shed was incinerated in a blinding flash, trees, shrubs and a freshly painted ranch fence were disintegrated. The roar of the potent engine rattled windows for over half a mile. The police and fire department responded to emergency calls from the neighbourhood; converging on Arfons' yard expecting to find a house destroyed by a mysterious explosion, they discovered a smiling Art Arfons testing his latest racing machine.

Having designed a jet car around his new engine, Arfons went to his local tyre dealer, which by way of coincidence just happened to be Firestone, asking them to sponsor the wheels. With initial reluctance, Bill McCrary, head of Firestone's race tyre sales, agreed to provide the wheels and tyres, inaugurating one of the largest single engineering projects in the company's history. Upon completion, Arfons had a $10,000 jet car sitting on half-million dollar's worth of tyres and wheels.

Within months his latest *Green Monster* was ready for the Utah speedway where he was always in his true element ... Bonneville.

The Green Monster, *it's afterburner blazing, scorches a path toward the timing traps at Bonneville.*

Arfons drove his 17,500 hp streamliner to an average speed of 576.553 mph (927.869 kph) in two consecutive runs at Bonneville on 7 November 1965.

His faster time during the mile run was a fantastic 577.386 mph (929.210 kph) in the second run. His first run averaged 575.72 mph (926.529 kph) through the measured mile. Art went on to establish three World Land Speed Records.

On his return to Bonneville on 17 November 1966, Arfons made a further run at the speed trap with full afterburn. He was clocked through the measured mile at 589.597 mph (948.862 kph), with a terminal speed of more than 615 mph. Coming out of the flying mile, wheel failure took Arfon's fate beyond his control. The forged-aluminium right-hand rear wheel held up, but the right front spindle snapped, and that wheel flew away from the car. *Green Monster* listed to the right, dug into the salt, and catapulted down the course for more than a mile. One wheel off the car bounced high in the air and miraculously passed directly through the blades of a press helicopter hovering overhead without hitting anything. Another wheel flew over the United States Automobile Club timing shack. It was later found four miles from the scene of the crash. The crew, time-keepers, indeed every man of the Bonneville contingent, jumped into available cars and trucks and converged on the wreckage of the jet car strewn over three miles of the course.

Arfon's right-hand man and project associate, Ed Snyder, wandering aimlessly through the carnage of twisted metal, weeping for his friend, 'Art, Art!'.

Green Monster

Engine:	General Electric J79 turbo-jet power unit with multi-stage afterburner
Fuel:	Kerosene
Fuel Tank:	110-gallon capacity. Consumption: circa 68 gallons a minute
Horsepower:	17,500 at sea level with afterburner, at 7,800 rpm
Length:	21 feet
Width:	74 inches
Height:	7 feet 2 inches (from ground to top of tail fin)
Weight:	6,500 pounds
Frame:	Chromoly steel tubing, spaced-tubed frame
Wheels:	Forged aluminium manufactured by Firestone Steel Products Company
Tyres:	Firestone 7.00-18 'Bonneville' tyres. Inflation: 200 lb + psi. Design speed: 750 mph
Brakes:	Disc brakes, two 16 foot diameter drogue parachutes for added drag at braking phase
Suspension:	Oleo-pneumatic (air over oil) front suspension, unsprung rear axle
Wheel base:	170 inches
Track:	(front) 65 inches (rear) 68 inches
Speed Capability:	650 mph + with afterburner
Cost:	$100,000

From amidst a pile of tangled wreckage, a blood-stained head emerged and answered, 'Ed, I'm all right!' With that Art Arfons lapsed into a state of unconsciousness. He was found strapped snugly in the seat of the driver's cockpit and today, credits the central location of the seat for saving him because he rotated with the turning car and was not snapped around.

Arfons was rushed to St. Mark's Hospital in Salt Lake City, 110 miles from Bonneville.

'It's amazing,' said Dr Albert Martin who treated Arfons, 'He's not as bad off as an average driver in a rear-ender'. The Doctor said there were no major fractures, although he might have cracked a cheek bone. Nursing supervisor Jalene Green said he had two small cuts on his face, plus bruises and salt burns. Within an hour of arrival at the hospital Art was taking a shower in his private room. Twenty-four hours later Art Arfons, having survived the most violent crash in automobile history was on an airliner flying back home to his family in Akron.

Nine years later, Arfons was just as determined to beat his land speed nemesis, Craig Breedlove, as ever.

Everybody wanted Arfons to quit – his wife June, his mother, his sponsor, and even a former land speed adversary, Dr Nathan Ostich, the man who first introduced jets to land speed racing with his $100,000 *Flying Caduceus* – but Arfons wouldn't hear of it.

No sooner, it seems, had Arfons returned home to recuperate than he began making plans for a new *Green Monster!* He even contemplated an assault on the World Water Speed Record. He wasn't at home on water, and admitted 'I don't like boats really. But I want to prove my theory'. He built an 0,000-horsepower jet boat *Green Submarine*. After a relatively short period of water trials on a chemical lake behind Firestone's Akron plant, and failure to attract a sponsor, he called it a day.

Arfons went on to build yet another *Green Monster* land speed record

The 17,500 hp Green Monster *with braking chute deployed, roars out of the speed trap on the Bonneville course, cementing a new record of 577.386 mph (897.023 kph).*

car , a name picked up in his early drag racing days when a radio announcer named his green, jet-powered dragster the *Monster*.

On 15 January, 1969, Arfons triggered his latest *Green Monster* to a new world quarter-mile record from a standing start of 267.050 mph (429.774 kph) at Firestone's seven-mile high-speed test track facility in Fort Stockton, Texas. In November of the same year, Arfons hit 273.55 mph (440.23 kph) at the Rockingham Speedway, North Carolina.

Arfons never returned to Bonneville, but in 1975 the land speed record 'grapevine' took note that Arfons was working on a revolutionary new concept of high speed racing. This is a three-wheeled 5,000lb thrust rocket car, *Firestone Mach I* which he believes will carry him past the 1,000 mph barrier. For the moment however, like its well-known creator, the project is temporarily grounded. With the ever increasing costs of high-technology state-of-the-art components and logistics, it is very doubtful whether Art Arfons will attract substantial sponsorship from United States based commercial backers, although now Britain has regained the World Land Speed Record after an absence of eighteen years, the field lies open for an American to take it back.

Art Arfons' contribution to the World Land Speed Record evolution did not pass without recognition. On 8 November, 1965, Arfons was presented with Utah's first Distinguished Service Medal by Governor Calvin L. Rampton. In making the presentation, Governor Rampton explained that the medal had been created for presentation to out-of-staters who had contributed significantly to Utah's prestige and recognition.

Since leaving the land speed record sphere, Arfons has concentrated

The Green Monster *'s shape is characterized by the demands of a large jet engine and its insatiable appetite for huge quantities of air. In essence the driver becomes an 'outrider' placed in an aerodynamically inconvenient position either side of the main 'tube'.*

his efforts on drag racing and competition 'tractor pulling', a very popular spectator sport in the United States, now gaining ground in Europe and Australasia.

His jet-powered tractor, also called the *Green Monster,* has become a featured attraction as well as an extremely potent competitor at tractor pulls across the United States. Like his land speed record cars and dragsters, the tractor utilizes Firestone tyres, in this case, monstrous 30.5-32 Firestone All Traction Field & Road Puller tyres on the rear, and Firestone Champion Guide Grip tyres on the front.

In addition to ranking among the nation's top ten tractor pullers in recent years, he and the *Green Monster* won the 12,000 lb unlimited class at the 1978 Indianapolis Grand National Pull, considered by many to be the national championship meet of tractor pulling.

Unlike fellow competitors, Arfons' inventive mind coupled with his flair and initiative, was a contributing factor in his decision to select a jet engine for his tractor: on this occasion, a 2,000 horsepower, Lycoming T-55 jet-engine, taken from a surplus Hughey helicopter, reminiscent of his earlier success in the repair and adaption of Government surplus propulsion systems.

In 1978 Arfons, now heavily committed to competition 'tractor pulling', sold the rebuilt *Green Monster* to Slick Gardner of Santa Ines Valley, California.

Gardner made a number of modifications to the vehicle, including the emplacement of two horizontal canard fins mounted either side of the fuselage, forward of the driver cockpit. In addition, the vehicle was

The tangled wreckage of the Green Monster, *shortly after Art Arfons survived a terrifying crash at over 600 mph (950 kph).*

equipped with Cragar solid forged aluminium wheels.

For sponsorship, Slick approached the Los Angeles-based Andersen Company, who by way of marketing procedure insisted the vehicle should bear their corporate identity. This Gardner conceded and the famed *Green Monster* was renamed *Andersen's Pea Soup Monster*.

Following a series of trials at El Mirage, Gardner took the vehicle to Bonneville with high hopes of eclipsing Gabelich's record of 622.407 mph (1001.664 kph) set in 1970. Sadly, however, neither man nor machine were up to their full potential, and a disappointed Gardner returned to California with the vehicle in tow.

In 1985 Australian speedster Rosco McGlashan and Loyd Coleman of Mullaloo, Western Australia, approached Gardner, as they were contemplating hiring the *Andersen's Pea Soup Monster* for an all-out assault on Australia's official land speed record of 403.100 mph (648.724 kph) set by Donald Campbell at Lake Eyre in July 1964, but the $500,000 rental Gardner was asking left the duo ''gasping for air'', McGlashan told me.

Walt Arfons - The Force Behind the 'Wingfoot' Cars

The transparent bullet-nosed 'Wingfoot Express', with ice cool Tom Green of Wheaton, Illinois, at the throttle, roared to a new World Land Speed Record of 413.20 mph (664.95 kph) on the afternoon of Friday, 2 October 1964, on the desolate Bonneville speedway.

It was a tremendous triumph for Green and the car's owner, Walt Arfons, and it came as the lowering sun warned that time was running out for the duo.

The Friday was the last day alloted to the crew of the *Wingfoot Express* to wrest the record from Craig Breedlove, who achieved 407.45 mph (655.696 kph) on the same course the previous year in the General Electric J47, thrust, jet-powered *Spirit of America*.

''We had to do it Friday because it was our last day on the salt,'' – a jubilant member of the working crew explained, ''And we did it. The runs on Friday were the fifteenth and sixteenth of the series. What a victory!''

Under instructions from Walt Arfons, at exactly 4.06 pm Green started on his south to north run through that measured mile that had dashed so many hopes in the past.

The four-wheeled, jet-powered vehicle gradually increased speed and then roared into the measured mile and timing traps. It was clocked on the fifteenth run at 406.55 mph (654.27 kph) but the record still hung in the balance.

But Green, Arfons and the crew swiftly wheeled the machine around and started back on the showdown run at exactly 4.47 pm.

And this time there was no doubt. Veteran observers at the flats sensed that the record had fallen and this was indeed verified by the official USAC timers with a clocking of 420.07 mph (676.03 kph). The average speed for the two runs was then computed at 413.20 mph (664.83 kph).

''Don't try to arrive at that figure by taking an average of the times on both runs, ''Clyde Schetter, public relations manager for the project, explained. ''It won't work out. It's a complicated mathematical telemetry formula the timers use to arrive at the official record speed.''

Walt Arfons inspects the jet-pipe of the 6,200 lb thrust Westinghouse J46 triple-jet engine on the Wingfoot Express, in between runs at Bonneville.

Walt Arfons' jet car also set a kilometer record of 415.00 mph (667.87 kph) based on runs of 415.63 and 414.55 mph (668.35 and 667.15 kph) through the measured kilometer.

"We don't intend to argue structural design or other engineering matters," Schetter said. "It's a 'jet-job' but as of right now it's the fastest vehicle in the world."

Green had made four runs over the course prior to the record dash, all of which were without the additional thrust of the jet-car's afterburner. But he couldn't produce enough power, for his fastest clocking was 297.72 mph (479.13 kph). With this factor in mind, and knowing time was running out, Arfons ordered the use of the afterburner, and the result ... a new World Record.

Green's wife, Patricia, and Walt Arfons were the first to greet the triumphant driver as the *Wingfoot Express* rolled to a halt at the far end of the north to south run.

"Everyone was yelling and crying," Schetter reported. They had a right to yell, for the success was the culmination of three years of research and development, construction and numerous trials on the salt. The previous year, they had tried for the record and failed because of a fault in the design that allowed the crystalline salt to enter the engine, a factor that was solved by the emplacement of a light alloy filter forward of the air intake chamber.

Wingfoot Express was powered by a 10,000 bhp Westinghouse J46 triple-jet power unit with additional power from the afterburner. With

Bobby Tatroe (left) and Walt Arfons working on the chassis of the Wingfoot Express II.

The tyres on Walt Arfons' rocket-powered Wingfoot Express II *were similar to those on Breedlove's* Spirit of America — Sonic I. *These were hand made 8 x 35in Goodyears of bias-belted construction, with wafer-thin treads, inflated with compressed dry air to 350l psi.*

oleo-pneumatic suspension on all four wheels, the vehicle skimmed across the salt with a clearance of only three inches.

Twenty-four feet long and weighing in at 24³/₄ cwt, it was a true streamliner, with a partly transparent, tapering nose for maximum observation of the course, and located at the rear, high above the power unit, was a now familiar sight on the Bonneville Salt Flats – a vertical tail-fin.

Turning to a new and revolutionary source of propulsion, Walt Arfons went on to design a massive five-ton projectile in the form of the *Wingfoot Express II,* with which he intended to exceed the speed of sound. In the span of less than 23 seconds, Walt said, ''the rocket-propelled car would unleash it's full 28,000 horsepower to demolish the existing record, held by Craig Breedlove in the new *Spirit of America – Sonic 1,* a massive jet with twice the power of his badly damaged three-wheeler. The new 'Spirit' boasted 15,000 horsepower from its General Electric J79 thrust jet engine with a three-stage afterburner.

The *Wingfoot Express II* was undoubtedly the world's first rocket-powered Land Speed Record car.

The 28 foot, sky blue car was built under sponsorship of the Goodyear Tire and Rubber Company and Arfons announced that the car would be driven by Bobby Tatroe, 28, of Grand Rapids, Michigan, who had driven many of Walt's earlier jet and steam powered dragsters, including *Neptune* and *Avenger,* on the drag racing circuits across the Nation.

Although the *Wingfoot Express II* was designed to break the sound barrier, Arfons said the immediate project objective would be to top the new World Land Speed Record of 536.71 mph (863.710 kph) posted the previous year by Walt's brother, Art, in the 17,500 horsepower *Green Monster.*

International rules demand that a record must be exceeded by at least

Last-minute instructions are given by owner Walt Arfons to driver Bobby Tatroe as he prepares to pilot the rocket-powered Wingfoot Express II en-route to history.

one per cent, in this race 5.367 mph (8.365 kph), which meant the *Wingfoot Express II* would have to average a speed in excess of 542 mph within two runs through the measured mile. The two runs must be made in opposite directions within the hour.

The earliest Arfons could run on the salt was 19 September in the 1965 season. He reserved the saline track for three separate weeks: 19-25 September, 17-23 October and 31 October – 6 November.

The previous October Walt Arfons' jet-powered *Wingfoot Express* established a new world's record, a record that stood for only three days before a new high was set by his brother. Walt was determined to snatch the record back and was convinced rocket-power was the answer to compete successfully with the mighty jet-powered cars of Breedlove and brother Art.

Ultimately, Walt Arfons disclosed, the new *Wingfoot Express II* would attempt to break the sound barrier, which, at Bonneville's altitude would be approximately 750 mph. The speed of sound varies according to altitude and atmospheric conditions.

Powered by a complement of 15 JATO (Jet Assisted Take-Off) solid fuel rocket 'bottles' the car had a potential power of 28,800 horsepower. The combined thrust of the rockets totalled 15,000 pounds, which, it was hoped, would guarantee rapid acceleration at high speeds, from transonic to low supersonic.

The 35-inch high tyres had been designed by skilled engineers at the Goodyear laboratories in Akron, Ohio, to perform safely at supersonic speeds, although the reputation of Goodyear was on the line; no one really knew what would happen to conventional rubber tyres at such speeds. As the book will reveal, no one ever put the concept to the test, it being believed that conventional tyres would simply disintegrate; thus followed the development of solid-forged aluminium tyres in the late Seventies by Bill Fredrick of Chatsworth, California. Goodyear also designed the wheels, brakes and braking parachute system for the new rocket car.

From the tip of the air speed pitot tube on the nose to the top of its bold, vertical tail fin, which towered nine feet in the air, the car was an outstanding example of modern aerodynamic design of the day.

Although it had four wheels, the sleek projectile had a definite triangular appearance. The two front wheels were paired very close together, and the covered rear wheels were set thirteen feet apart.

During the record runs of the *Wingfoot Express II*, Arfons planned to have Tatroe ignite the solid fuel rockets in five stages, with one stage being ignited every two seconds. Arfons estimated that firing the rockets in his car would take no more than 23 seconds for each run.

The car was steered through the front wheels, and a canard fin placed on the nose would add to the stability at high speeds. Most of the bodyshell was constructed in tempered aluminium, although the frontal area, forward of the cockpit, was covered in glass fibre, fitting over a robust frame of welded steel.

The new rocket-powered car was tailor-made for Tatroe. To preserve its aerodynamics, the cockpit was built with the interior shaped to Tatroe's own body dimensions (clearly evident in the photographs). Even the reclining seat was form-fitting to the broad-shouldered driver.

Alex Tremulis of Ann Arbor, Michigan, the brilliant designer and aerodynamicist, served as consultant to Walt Arfons during the construction of the car, and it was Tremulis who later rigged the extra rockets on the outside of the vehicle.

On 15 September 1965, the world's first rocket-powered Land Speed Record car made its debut in a publicity run down the Akron-Canton Airport runway. Leaving a tail of fire, and blanketing the runway with billowing smoke, the car attained a disappointing speed of 120 mph (193 kph) propelled by just two of its 15 rockets. Arfons predicted the unlimited World Land Speed Record was within his grasp. Sadly, he was far from success as the following sequence of events will show.

The *Wingfoot Express II* arrived at Bonneville with its team of specialists, Walt Arfons and driver Bobby Tatroe, and within two hours the car was ready for the assault.

Tatroe unleashed all 15 rockets, but only managed a terminal velocity of

Walt Arfons (standing) offers last minute advice to Bobby Tatroe before the record attempt in the Wingfoot Express II.

247.59 mph (398.45 kph) from a standing start, clocking a speed for the last 2,000 feet of the mile of 406.40 mph (653.89 kph).

Down, but not out, Arfons conceded, "We'll break the sound barrier yet" he vowed, and returned to Akron to consult with Alex Tremulis.

Within weeks Arfons returned to Bonneville with 10 additional JATO rockets bolted in position either side of the car, igniting at a 30-degree angle. Because the rockets had a short firing life, it was decided not to ignite them all at the same time. Tatroe was instructed to fire the side rockets first, with an interval of eight seconds before igniting the rockets at the rear of the car. Bobby Tatroe was literally surrounded by rockets in the tiny cockpit, packing some 50,000 horsepower.

After a delay of 35 minutes caused by heavy rain and high winds, the *Wingfoot Express II* roared from the starting line. To the horror of Alex Tremulis and Walt Arfons, one of the rockets fell out of the car, prematurely igniting seven rockets within the fuselage, Tremulis had expected to see rockets fire out of the rear, instead, the *Wingfoot Express II* was trailing a plume of fire from the top and underneath, turning the projectile into a potential fire-ball.

Inside the vehicle Tatroe looked out in disbelief to see he was surrounded by a blazing inferno. The air-speed indicator showed he was travelling in excess of 400 mph, timing equipment inside the flying mile recorded a terminal velocity of 510 mph. Tatroe managed to maintain control of the car until he fired the braking chutes. The car came to a halt some 38 feet short of the course, looking like it had been scorched by re-entry into the earth's atmosphere; but this rocket was launched horizontally. Tatroe emerged from the charred projectile visibly shaken, but unharmed. It was thought by many, that the *Wingfoot Express II* saga would see the end of rocket propulsion systems at Bonneville, but while Walt Arfons was counting the cost, a team of three young engineers were already working on another Land Speed rocket car in downtown Chicago. This was the Institute of Gas Technology-sponsored *The Blue Flame*.

Craig Breedlove - The King of All Cars

The story of Breedlove's achievements actually began in 1950, when he started working on automobile engines. Two years later, when he was only 16, he began driving racing cars, and he garnered his first record-breaking trophy at 17 by driving a hot rod to a staggering 103.84 mph (167.11 kph) ... a considerable feat for the young Californian. In the next nine years Breedlove turned in seven more record-breaking performances across the country.

From his early teens, building cars and racing them came first in his thoughts and activities. His chief studies in high school in Venice, California, were drafting and machine shop – 'so I could built parts for my racing machines', he later said.

To earn his livelihood, and to learn more about his beloved racing, he worked at such jobs as welding for a builder of custom racing cars and in the engineering department of a west coast aircraft manufacturer.

Meanwhile, his plans for a vehicle to establish a World Land Speed Record were gradually forming. His first thoughts were about a

Seconds before the cockpit canopy is sealed, Craig Breedlove checks his oxygen feed from the Spirit of America's life support pack.

piston-engined, conventional, streamlined racing automobile. But he soon found he could buy lots more horsepower for more or less the same price in a jet-engine. Further, a jet-powered car would be simpler and far more efficient at the high speeds he had in mind.

Breedlove drew up plans for such a car but realizing his limitations as a designer, he turned to experts for help. Through his enthusiasm, he enlisted the technical aid of an aerodynamicist, a jet-propulsion engineer, a model builder and a mechanical engineer. More than 100 wind tunnel tests were carried out for specific design improvement.

At this point, two years after the start of the project, Breedlove's meagre resources ran out.

Casting about for potential sponsors, he walked into the Santa Monica, California, marketing district office of the Shell Oil Company, one day in October, 1961, and asked to see the manager. Under one arm he carried a brochure, under the other was a box containing a scale model of his unique racer.

Thinking he was a Shell dealer with the same surname, the manager agreed to see him. But when he learned his error, the manager asked Breedlove to limit his call to 10 minutes. Two hours later, Breedlove was still talking – and the manager, fascinated by the prospects and the young man's enthusiasm, was hooked.

Within three months, Shell had agreed to become a sponsor, and the Goodyear Tire and Rubber Company were enlisted as co-sponsor and builders of the tyres for the vehicle.

Breedlove's partly-completed machine was moved from the garage behind his home to the shop of a leading builder of custom racing cars. For months the work went on ...

In August, 1962, the *Spirit of America* was loaded on a trailer and brought to the desolate Bonneville Salt Flats. Accompanying the vehicle was an expert working crew of more than 20 men, equipped with everything from a complete machine shop to spare parts.

Here, on this table-flat, dried-up bed of Lake Bonneville, the *Spirit of America* was given its first low speed test trials. Breedlove drove it at an estimated 300 mph but, as could be expected, numerous bugs showed up. Light crosswinds caused the car to veer from the marked course, and the differential braking on the rear wheels, used instead of a steerable front wheel to maintain the car on course, was unable to correct the veering.

The only recourse was to go 'back to the drawing board'. New technical engineering expertise was called in. The *Spirit of America* was modified in various ways: The front wheel was made steerable through two degrees in each direction; a six-foot-high vertical tail fin was added to increase stability and move the centre of pressure to the rear, this also helped to counteract yaw tendencies; the Goodyear industrial-type disc brakes were rigged to work from a single brake pedal; the throttle linkage was arranged for either hand or foot operation, where formerly it was operated only by hand, thus leaving Breedlove to steer the massive jet-car with only one hand during operation.

Late in July, 1963, the *Spirit of America* and her crew were back at the

Final preparations. The crew of the Spirit of America *make a final check before the record-breaking run on the Bonneville Salt Flats, Utah. Riggers double-check the drag chute installation above the jet exhaust, and Goodyear tyre engineers make sure the four-foot-tall tyres have exactly 250 psi inflation.*

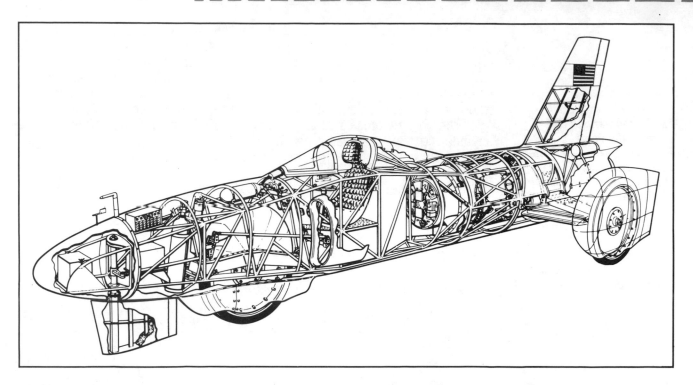

A schematic view of Craig Breedlove's three-wheeled Spirit of America, *showing the aft location of the J47 jet power unit, resembling an aircraft without wings.*

Salt Flats. Numerous test runs and minor adjustments were made. Early on the morning of 5 August 1963, Breedlove climbed into the cramped cockpit, closed the canopy, depressed the throttle to a setting that represented approximately 90 per cent of power, and moved down the carefully graded track on the salt.

At that moment, he had driven the car no less than 200 miles in a grand total of 22 separate runs.

That first run through the measured mile was made at an official speed – timed by the United Stated Auto Club (USAC) – of 388.47 mph (625.18 kph). Quickly the car was turned around, refuelled and started on its return run. For a record, two runs must be made in opposite directions through the measured mile within 60 minutes.

This time Breedlove set the throttle at 95 per cent of power. He roared through the measured mile at an unbelievable 428.37 mph (689.39 kph). The average for the two runs, calculated from the elapsed time of the two, was 407.45 mph (655.72 kph).

The young Craig Breedlove had broken the World Land Speed Record, set 16 years before by John Cobb ... He was the fastest man on wheels!

But Breedlove was not satisfied. He had his eyes firmly set on that magical mark of 500 mph. And he convinced Shell and Goodyear that such a speed was attainable with the *Spirit of America*.

So, late in 1963, after the furore over his achievement had subsided, the team of experts went back to work on their creation. The *Spirit* was given a new J47 jet engine with 5,700 pounds of thrust instead of the 5,200 pounds produced by the previous engine. The nose was given a more streamlined configuration. A new set of wheels and tyres was installed though not because of wear, for the previous set was used throughout all his 1963 runs. They were taken out of service for historical and exhibition purposes.

In the meantime, others had their sights set on the Breedlove record. Walt Arfons of Akron, Ohio, prepared to run his Goodyear sponsored

Wingfoot Express. His brother Art was ready again with his *Green Monster.*

Heavy rains on the Bonneville Salt Flats delayed the 1964 speed attempts for months ... A problem all too familiar with land speed record contenders. Not until late September was the Bonneville track in shape for trials.

First to attack the record was Walt Arfons and his *Wingfoot Express,* driven by Tom Green of Chicago, who raised the record to 413.2 mph (664.97 kph) on 2 October. Three days later, Art piloted his famous *Green Monster* twice through the measured mile at 434.02 mph.

His 1963 record exceeded twice in three days, Breedlove arrived back on the Salt Flats with his working crew on 11 October.

Around-the-clock testing and tuning made the *Spirit of America* ready for its initial time trials on 13 October. Repeating his procedure of 14 months before, Breedlove climbed into the cockpit, fastened his helmet and safety harness; watching as the cockpit canopy was closed above him. Alone he sat, waiting to regain his cherished record.

This year he had one more factor working in his favour. The hydraulic pressure on the Goodyear brakes had been increased so he could hold the car motionless while he primed its mighty jet-engine to the required acceleration speed.

With the brakes released, the *Spirit of America* hurtled down the 10-mile course toward the distant measured mile, 4¹/₂ miles away. Through the timing traps it roared at ever-increasing speed. Once past the second

A parking problem for Craig Breedlove at his home in Costa Mesa, California, shortly before setting off for Bonneville to regain his title as the fastest man on earth in the Spirit of America.

marker in the measured mile, Breedlove released the drag chute, which pulled his speed down to around the 150 mph point where he could begin to apply his foot brake by means of a slow pumping action until the car came to a gentle halt at the end of the glistening salt. His speed: 442.59 mph (712.27 kph).

While the Shell special turbine fuel was poured in for the return run, Breedlove made a number of minor adjustments to the car, in particular the throttle setting. This time he launched the *Spirit of America* through the timing traps at 498.13 mph (801.66 kph). His average speed – again calculated on the time required to make the two runs – 468.72 mph (754.29 kph) Breedlove was once again the fastest man on wheels!

But neither he nor his crew were satisfied. He hadn't used the full power available from his jet engine. The track was very rough and needing additional grading. With several minor adjustments, and given the right track and weather conditions, the project team were certain Breedlove would top the elusive 500 mph barrier.

For 48 hours, almost without pause, the team of experts and mechanics laboured over the *Spirit*. It was tuned to absolute micrometric fineness.

Early on 15 October, Breedlove's all-out effort was made. Down the course he raced toward the electronic timing equipment each side of the measured mile. Faster than man had ever gone before he sped past the markers. His speed: 513.33 mph (826.12 kph). Again came the fast

On 15 October 1964, Craig Breedlove broke his own record at 526.28 mph (846.96 kph), only to lose his braking parachutes, robbing the car of its essential braking power. Spirit of America demolished two telegraph poles in a six-mile skid, leapt into the air and finished up in a brine ditch at the end of the salt flats.

Inset: the path cleared by Spirit of America before it finally came to a halt.

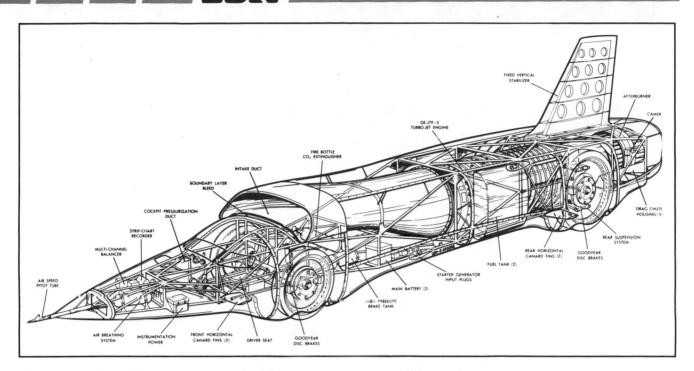

A schematic view of the powerful J79 turbojet-powered Spirit of America - Sonic I.

turnaround, the refuelling, and the resetting of the throttle to an even greater speed level. This was surely it! Equal or exceed his timed speed on the first run, and he would be the first man ever to establish a 500 mph record in a landbound vehicle.

To the spectators and project working crew, posted far back from the race course, it appeared he was 'in the groove', speeding faster than any man before him.

As he rocketed past the marker at the end of the measured mile, they watched for his drag chute to billow out behind the hurtling jet-car. But it didn't. Breedlove was reducing speed when, at 500 mph (800 kph), the braking parachutes broke away, robbing the hurtling car of its essential braking power. The *Spirit of America* demolished two telegraph poles in a six-mile (9.6 km) skid. Breedlove opened the cockpit canopy seconds before the car nose-dived into a brine ditch at the end of the vast salt flats, and swam to the shore unhurt.

Whether Breedlove had set a new World Land Speed Record or not, was forgotten. The brave young man and his safety was the only concern ...

What happened? Let Craig Breedlove tell you in his own words:

'I felt the car start to slide in the measured mile and knew that I had to stop as soon as possible. When I saw the sign at the end of the mile, I hit the drag chute button.

'The chute ripped right off and I immediately hit the emergency chute button. This chute came loose just as fast. My first reaction was to hit the brakes. At 500 mph they didn't begin to slow the car.

[Those brakes were designed to stop the car after it had been slowed down to a velocity of 150 mph (240 kph) by the drag chutes; they burned out in seconds at 500 mph (800 kph)]

'I knew I was in serious trouble. Then I saw a telegraph post right in front of me ... I was running out of track ... I *knew* I couldn't miss it. That pole shattered like a toothpick.'

'When I didn't flip then, I said to myself, "I've got another chance".

Then I ploughed through a quarter mile of shallow water and through an eight-foot-high dirt bank at the end of the salt flats.'

The car hurtled through the air and into an 18-foot-deep pool of water on the other side of the dike.

'To go through all of this and then drown really scared me,' he recalled. 'I pushed hard on the car's cockpit canopy. It flipped off and I was able to swim out of the cockpit, now filling with water, to safety. Thank God the car and its tyres held up through all that, or I'd have been a goner for sure.'

And how did Breedlove react?

To Bill Neely of Goodyear, one of the first to reach the crash scene, he calmly said, 'I'm all right, baby; what's the speed?'

The speed through the measured mile on that return run was an incredible 539.89 mph (868.86 kph). The official speed for the required twin runs was 526.28 mph (846.96 kph) equal to the cruising speeds of the newest, most sophisticated jet airliners.

But in the autumn of 1965, Breedlove showed up again on the salt, with a new car; a four-and-a-half-ton monster named *Spirit of America – Sonic 1,* at first thought to be capable of travelling faster than the speed of sound. It's rocket-like configuration, Breedlove explained, was designed to slice through the shock waves that build up as a car approaches the sound barrier (720 mph, 1158 kph at Bonneville's altitude). The new *Spirit of America* was powered by a General Electric J79 turbojet engine, the same as that used in the US F-104 fighter plane. Breedlove picked it up as government surplus in Charlotte, North Carolina, for $7,500. New, it cost the US Government a staggering $175,000.

With the help of some friends, Breedlove had designed the car and supervised its construction in six months. But once again, confident of his success, Goodyear agreed to foot most of the bill, which was close to $200,000. Before the 1965 season drew to a close, however, the costs to

Flame blasts from the afterburner of the General Electric J79 15,000 lb thrust jet power unit of the Spirit of America - Sonic I, *at full power on a test bed.*

Goodyear had risen beyond half a million dollars. The car had bugs in it from the start. At speeds over 500 mph (800 kph) hour, the aluminium panels rippled as if they wanted to tear off. Wheel wells twisted and buckled, once nearly blowing out a rear tyre.

'We're just going to have to bullet-proof the whole car,' Breedlove announced when a 534 mph run put a man-sized dent in the front cowling. And it was all Breedlove could do to keep the car on the ground. Once on a record run, the front of the car went airborne at more than 600 mph, and the new *Spirit of America – Sonic 1* veered off the Bonneville speedway out of control. Both braking parachutes were torn off the car, but Breedlove managed to pump his brakes and bring the car to a stop just 300 feet from the brine ditch where he had dunked the first *Spirit of America* in 1964. Unnerved by his second hair-raising experience, Breedlove fastened two large aerodynamic spoilers on the nose of the car to keep it on the ground at high speeds. Back on the salt on 2 November 1965, Breedlove raced to a two-way average of 555.127 mph (893.388 kph). He had got his record back!

But the record didn't stand long. Art Arfons, an incredible daredevil, hurried back to the salt flats, set up camp on the morning of 7 November, and before one o'clock in the afternoon, had upped the speed to 576.553 mph (927.869 kph) in two wild death-defying runs through the measured mile (two runs within an hour are required to break the record under the international rules). Coming out of the measured mile on the last run, Arfons car, the *Green Monster,* blew a right rear tyre. The explosion was heard for miles across the Bonneville Salt Flats. Some spectators at first thought Arfons had broken the sound barrier. The blow-out ripped out a huge chunk of the right rear cowling, much of the wheel well, blasted loose the entire parachute braking system on the right-hand side – casing and all – and embarrassed Arfon's sponsors, Firestone Tire and Rubber Co., who had earlier said in a public announcement that the tyres were good up to 800 mph (1287 kph). It was the third blow-out for the *Green Monster* in three

Spirit of America - Sonic I *thunders across the Salt Flats at Bonneville, with Craig Breedlove at the controls. In two runs through the measured mile, Breedlove established a new World Land Speed Record of 600.601 mph (966.528 kph).*

Craig Breedlove and his crew worked around the clock after his jet-powered Spirit of America - Sonic I *was damaged at the Bonneville Salt Flats. Breedlove is applying fibre-glass to the damaged air-duct that leads to the intake of the jet engine.*

Craig Breedlove and a technician from the Aviation Products Division of the Goodyear Tire & Rubber Company, discuss the single-disc, caliper-type braking system of the Spirit of America - Sonic I. *The disc brakes were of forged steel, 5/8 inch thick and 18 inches in diameter. There were two calipers per brake, each with two friction surfaces. In the background, the fibre-glass air intake duct to the General Electric J79, jet power unit takes shape.*

record runs in 1964 and 1965. Each time it was the right-hand rear tyre.

'It sounded like a bomb going off,' said Arfons. 'I knew that it was all right. I've heard that sound before'. Now on three wheels and a rim, the *Green Monster* careered down the speedway, crashed into a steel-pipe track marker, popped its emergency chute, and rolled to a stop. Arfons climbed out of the cockpit and walked in a daze around his car. He swore. Crew and spectators arrived. 'How are you, how do you feel?' asked a visibly shaken reporter. 'I feel fine' Arfons said, 'But I seem to have broken my car.'

He had the record once again, but this time his supremacy lasted exactly eight days. With winter storms already pushing across the Rocky Mountain region, Craig Breedlove and his crew were back with the *Spirit of America – Sonic I,* this time with just about every panel in the car reinforced with structural aluminium. Breedlove set up camp in a drizzling rain and then waited for a break in the weather. It came on 15 November. At 8.10 am the United States Auto Club gave Breedlove track clearance. He fired up the powerful jet engine, closed the canopy over his now familiar star-spangled helmet, and roared down the carefully graded track, leaving behind the eye-burning orange and red flame of his afterburner and a ghostly spray of white salt. The car screamed through the measured mile in just over six seconds at an average speed of 593 mph (954 kph) in the mile and 597 mph (960 kph) in the kilometre – faster than Arfons' record, but a little shy of the 600 mph (965 kph) goal that Breedlove had set for himself.

Coming out of the mile, Breedlove popped his braking chute. It held momentarily, then filled up with salt water on the wet north end of the salt flats and collapsed. But the driver once again was able to stop, with his brakes, just short of the red flag marking the end of the salt and the

Craig Breedlove explains the controls of the jet-powered Spirit of America - Sonic I *to his wife, Lee, in the cockpit. Lee Breedlove drove the car to the women's World Land Speed Record with a two-way average of 308.56 mph (496.57 kph) through the measured mile at Bonneville. the record is now held by Kitty O'Neil, who drove the 48,000 hp rocket-powered 3-wheeled* SMI Motivator *over the Alvord Desert, Oregon on 6 December 1976 attaining 524.016 mph (813.319 kph).*

beginning of the soft, crusted mud flats of Lake Bonneville.

With 20 minutes left in the hour time limit, Breedlove and crew refuelled the *Spirit of America*, turned it round, and towed it to the 11$\frac{1}{2}$ mile mark on the speedway. This would give him a 5$\frac{1}{2}$ mile speed build-up before the first timing light, a half mile more than on the first run. Once Breedlove fired up the jet was gone down the track trailing a plume of salt behind. This time he streaked through the mile in just under six seconds at an amazing 608 mph (978.478 kph) in the mile and 604 mph in the kilometre. The two-way average, 600.601 mph (966.528 kph) in both the mile and the kilo, made him the first man in the world to crack the 600 mark. He was also the first over 400 and 500 mph. The early 'Beach Boys' album *Little Duece Coupe* immortalised Craig Breedlove in the song 'Spirit of America', in which the lyrics of Brian Wilson crowned him the 'King of all cars'.

When asked what the ultimate speed would be, Breedlove said that by using maximum afterburner his car could go in the high 600s, 'But it'll never break the sound barrier,' he admitted. 'We're a long way from that. It's going to take something entirely different in the basic design and overall configuration of the car to go that fast.'

Within three days, Lee, the 28-year-old wife of Breedlove set a new women's World Land Speed Record of 308.56 mph (496.57 kph) at the Bonneville Salt Flats.

Lee Breedlove drove the *Spirit of America – Sonic 1* to the record during runs of 288.02 mph (463.52 kph) and 332.26 mph (534.71 kph) through the measured mile on 4 November. The run, marking the first time a woman travelled faster than 300 mph in an official measured mile, eclipsed the previous timed record of 277.15 mph (446.02 kph) set earlier the same year by Betty Skelton.

From Akron, Arfons conceded that the 'Green Monster' wouldn't be repaired until the December of '65, and couldn't be raced until January 1966 at the earliest. But few veteran Bonneville racing buffs thought there could be any racing on the flats in midwinter, when the water table on the speedway is at its highest and winter storms blast across the Great Basin with unpredictable, icy fury. From all indications it looks as though Craig Breedlove was now the undisputed Land Speed King of the World ... At least until the autumn of 1970, when the duel on the salt got under way once again. This time the contestant was the late Gary Gabelich in the beautiful rocket-powered 'The Blue Flame'.

Gary Gabelich ~ A Legacy of Speed

The X-I, a rocket-engined dragster which Reaction Dynamics Inc., built to demonstrate their ability to design and construct The Blue Flame *land speed record vehicle. The X-I delivered 2,500 lb thrust. The Blue Flame delivered 13,000 lb of thrust. Setting dragstrip records throughout the United States, the X-I proved to be a particularly successful project for the design team of Reaction Dynamics.*

On 23 October 1970, Gary Gabelich became the fastest man on wheels when he drove the 35,000 horsepower, rocket-powered *The Blue Flame* to a new World Land Speed Record of 622.407 mph (1001.664 kph) at the now famed Bonneville Salt Flats.

Gabelich was born on 29 August, 1940 in San Pedro, California, and when selected to drive *The Blue Flame*, he was far from a novice to speed. In his long career on the drag strips and dry lakes of Southern California, Gabelich drove almost every exotic piece of racing equipment on the market, ranging from gas and top fuel Funny Cars to the powerful jet dragsters.

He drove the mighty jet car *Untouchable I*, owned by drag racing veteran Romeo Palamides, and later handled another jet-powered racing machine owned by Mickey Thompson and Art Malone. In the summer of 1963, Gabelich achieved the ultimate dream of all top drag racing drivers, outduelling the national champion 'Big Daddy' Don Garlits in the first United States Drag Racing Association meeting.

The tiny 25 lb thrust prototype rocket motor from which was born the design concept for the final 22,000 lb maximum thrust LNG-fuelled rocket motor of The Blue Flame.

Gary Gabelich had worked for a spell with the giant North American Rockwell Corporation, undergoing long environment tests in space capsules under simulated zero gravity conditions in parabolic streaks across the sky, and making protracted parachute falls over the Pacific Ocean during which he photographed the simulated re-entry of space capsules for the early NASA Mercury project. Only when it became apparent he had no chance of being selected for astronaut training himself, did Gabelich quit his job and become a full-time drag racer. All of this richly qualified him to drive the prestigious rocket car *The Blue Flame*.

The dream of engineering a liquid-fuel rocket-powered car capable of beating Breedlove's 1965 record of 600.601 mph (966.528 kph) started with Ray Dausman, a slightly rotund and jovial young research technician with the Chicago, Illinois-based Institute of Gas Technology (IGT).

Dausman was far from impressed by the speeds attained by conventional nitro-burning dragsters and Funny Cars. At the very most they were clocking speeds in the low 200 mph regime. Dausman was thinking in faster terms, and discussed his highly ambitious plans with Dick Keller, a friend and colleague at the ICT.

The partners devised a three-phase initiative, that would commence with the development of a small-scale, 25 lb thrust prototype rocket motor to demonstrate their theory and their ability to construct such a powerplant. The unit was successfully ignited, and performed to specification with a six-second burn.

Having established the viability of their small-scale engine, the pair advanced to stage two, with the help of Pete Farnsworth, a professional dragster driver and automobile technician who had served briefly on the Don Garlits crew.

The trio formed a partnership in the form of Reaction Dynamics Inc., of Milwaukee, Wisconsin, and, with their own funds began building a rocket-powered dragster – the now legendary *RD X-1* or *Rislone Rocket*.

The dragster's engine was a slight variation of the 25 lb thrust prototype, producing 2,500 lb thrust, equivalent to approximately 2,800 bhp at full throttle.

Indeed, compared with a solid-fuel rocket engine, which is simply ignited and burns under full power until it has spent its energy, the liquid-fuel rocket can be controlled by step-throttling, not unlike an internal combustion engine.

A series of extensive trials proved not only the state-of-the-art engineering capabilities of the team, but the overall success of the *RD X-1* on drag strips throughout the United States, enabled them to secure the vital corporate sponsorship from both the Institute of Gas Technology and the Goodyear Tire & Rubber Company, for stage three of their project, the development of a rocket-powered Land Speed Record vehicle, which would run on liquified natural gas (LNG), in combination with hydrogen peroxide – *The Blue Flame*.

The *RD X-1* was retired soon after construction of *The Blue Flame* began. It was eventually sold to Snow Pony, a division of the Studebaker-Worthington Corporation, manufacturers of snowmobiles. On 14 February 1970, with Ky Michaelson at the wheel, the *RD X-1*, appropriately re-named *Sonic Challenger*, set a world snowmobile drag racing record of 114.57 mph (184.38 kph).

While Gary Gabelich was carving out a drag racing reputation on the West Coast, the Reaction Dynamics team, now under the learned direction of

project manager Dean Dietrich, had reached the point of negotiations with James McCormick of the Engineering Design Services Co, of Buffalo, New York, who agreed to join them in the development of the powerful rocket engine for *The Blue Flame*.

Such was the prestige of the project, Bill Fredrick the former butcher turned rocket propulsion experimentalist from Woodland Hills, California, joined the Reaction Dynamics team as telemetry consultant, and some two years later débuted the first of his own rocket cars, a three-wheeled lance called *Courage of Australia*.

By now, some 30 specialists from the Illinois Institute of Technology joined the project alongside the Reaction Dynamics crew, and over 70 students of the Institute were able to participate in the design of the vehicle, including Shashi Kurani, Dr Carl Uzgiris and Monoj Adhikari.

The engine, designated the RD HP-LNG-22,000-V, followed the basic engineering principle of the smaller 25 lb thrust prototype units, but the LNG, liquified by cooling to minus 258°F, passed from a helium-pressurised Alcoa aluminium chamber into the rocket motor: 75 per cent filtered through a central intake, with the remaining 25 per cent passing through a peripheral intake duct into a 'feathered' heat exchanger, while the hydrogen peroxide passed from a compressed air-pressurized stainless steel tank, through the outer jacket of the 22,000 lb thrust motor, to initiate the decomposition of the catalyst pack.

The subsequent superheated steam and oxygen flowed over the heat exchanger, converting the 25 per cent of LNG, into gas which ignited as it joined the heated oxygen flow. The resultant reaction raised the temperature to the point where the remaining 75 per cent of LNG, injected as a liquid,

Ray Dausman of the Chicago-based Illinois Institute of Gas Technology, with the 22,000 lb maximum thrust LNG-fuelled rocket motor used in The Blue Flame. *Design considerations favoured a rocket engine being less heavy than comparable-thrust turbines and thus improving that vital power to weight ratio. The Blue Flame engine weighed only 770 lb.*

As The Blue Flame *chassis nears completion, the slim, needle-like shape becomes apparent. Access to the propulsion system components is provided by removing the nose cone, the upper half of the central body span, or the rear tubular structures which envelope the engine and propellent control valves. In addition, small access panels are located on the vehicle for replenishing the propellents and high-pressure nitrogen and helium gases between runs at Bonneville.*

The central monocoque of The Blue Flame is 20 feet in length. Extruded aluminium H-beams and welded rings form a sub-structure to which the .040 inch thick fully-stressed aluminium skin is riveted. Hatch covers over the propellent tank and front wheel compartments are also stressed when bolted into position. The entire structure was held in alignment on a steel I-beam while being fabricated. The tubular structure at the rear of the chassis houses the propellent control valves, the 22,000 lb thrust LNG-fuelled rocket engine and parachute braking system.

ignited upon contact with the remaining oxygen.

The resultant thrust produced from the 17 inch diameter annulus (throat), delivered a maximum of 22,000 lb, equivalent to a staggering 58,000 bhp in a 20 second burn.

For the record attempt, Dausman and Keller decided the thrust ratio was sufficient to keep the engine throttled back to produce only 13,000 lb thrust, or an equivalent 35,000 bhp.

Design considerations for the vehicle led to an ogive-shaped fuselage which was adopted as the least resistant nose configuration, and a cross-section of the car's body was a rounded triangular shape. The front wheels (racing specifications dictated a four-wheeled vehicle) were housed in the underside near the front of the vehicle, forward of the driver-controlled canard (stabilizing) fins. For high-speed stability, the rear wheels extended beyond the rear of the vehicle, and had a wide track for roll stability.

The driver's cockpit was located aft of the propellant tanks and forward of the rocket engine, a driver preference. The semi-monocoque fuselage included ring-and-stringer construction in the central section of the car, and the rear of the vehicle had a welded nickel-steel tubular frame for additional strength because of the additional stresses of the powerful engine, wheel struts, tail-fin and parachute braking system housing. Steering was through the front wheels with a 91:1 ratio.

Many of the top names in high-speed driving were considered for *The Blue Flame*, including Craig Breedlove, Art Arfons and Mickey Thompson. But the dashing hot-rodder from San Pedro was selected.

Neither Gabelich nor his sponsors, the Institute of Gas Technology and the Goodyear Tire & Rubber Co. planned to attack the record head-on. Speeds would be steadily increased until all was ready for full-throttle runs.

The Blue Flame

Chassis and Body

Length:	38 feet 2.6 inches
Width:	26 inches
Height	8 feet 1.5 inches (from ground to top of tail fin)
Wheel Base:	25.5 feet
Track:	(front) 9 inches (rear) 84 inches
Weight:	6,608 pounds (Loaded)
Ground clearance:	9.5 inches
Frame:	20 foot, semi-monocoque aluminium centre span with welded tubular steel nose and rear sections
Body material:	Harvey aluminium sheeting 0.064 in thick (over 4,000 cs rivets hold the outer skin to the chassis)
Tyres:	8 x 25 in Goodyear (hand-made) bias-belted; special low-profile, high-speed treadless design. Inflation: 350 lb psi. Design speed: 1,000 mph
Braking systems:	Kelsey-Hayes 15 in diameter discs on the rear with pinion gear coupler flanges for use at 100 mph and below. Deist 'ribbon' drogue parachutes for high speeds: primary chute, 7.3 foot diameter for deployment below 650 mph; secondary chute; 16 foot diameter for below 250 mph; Automatic reserve systems with manual override
Steering ratio:	91:1 through the front wheels; ball-joint linkage with coaxial coil spring-cum-damper units
Steering lock:	3/4-turn of the wheel
Turning circle:	1/4-mile

Propulsion Specifications

Engine type:	Reaction Dynamics HP-LNG-22,000-V pressure fed bio-propellant rocket system
Thrust:	Step-Throttling from 13,000 to 22,000 lb (for the LSR run the engine was throttled to produce only 13,000 lb thrust from a 17 in diameter annulus 'throat')
Horsepower:	35,000
Fuel:	AGA – 75/25% mixture of Liquified natural gas and Hydrogen peroxide
Oxidizer:	Hydrogen peroxide
Pressurant:	Helium
Burn Time:	20 seconds at 13,000 lb thrust
Speed Capability:	750 mph
Cost:	$500,000

With the assembly of the streamline body panels near completion, The Blue Flame *stands in the Milwaukee workshop of Reaction Dynamics Inc.*

On 17 September, Gary Gabelich clocked a leisurely 185.086 mph (297.866 kph) on his inaugural run. But during this run, an engine backfire caused a minor explosion, melting the exhaust nozzle.

'We injected the fuel into the combustion chamber at too low a temperature,' explained project manager Dean Dietrich of the IGT. 'That caused the explosion, which doesn't appear to have seriously damaged any vital components.'

Three days later, 20 September, Gabelich was timed at 411.230 mph (661.80 kph) through the measured mile. 'It was a perfect run. This is the fastest I've ever travelled on land. It felt real good. It was out of sight.'

While *The Blue Flame* was recording speeds in the 400 mph (650 kph) range, for some reason the engine was producing only 11,000 of its 22,000 pounds of thrust capability. 'We're simply not getting the full thrust potential out of the car,' groaned Gabelich shortly after a 450 mph (725 kph) sortie. It was later discovered to be a malfunction in the fuel catalyst, damaged during the explosion on 17 September.

The team returned to base on 25 September to await the arrival of a new catalyst pack from Buffalo, New York.

Two weeks later, they were back on the salt. With the replacement catalyst in position, *The Blue Flame* made two runs through the mile attaining 462.321 mph (744.031 kph) and 478.770 mph (770.503 kph) burning only hydrogen peroxide. 'We were practically out of liquid nitrogen and we wanted to take no chances with the new catalyst pack,' said Dietrich. The runs, however, were not without incident.

Halfway through the first solo run on the course, Gabelich fired his braking chutes prematurely. It turned out to be a necessary manoeuvre, for he became separated from his oxygen mask and was forced to hold the oxygen line to the face mask with one hand and steer the speeding vehicle with the other, and a hurtling 35,000 horsepower rocket car, loaded with high-octane propellants is not easy to control.

Two days later another mishap occurred. This time the braking chutes failed to deploy and Gabelich finally halted the rampaging car four miles past the designated finishing marker at the end of the Bonneville speedway. Gary estimated the car was approaching 550 mph (885 kph) when he released the safety chutes on *The Blue Flame*, but nothing happened. 'Apparently enough radiant heat was coming off the exhaust system to melt the nylon shield on the chutes' casing,' said co-builder Dick Keller, 'The drogue guns fired, but with the nylon shields destroyed it was like firing a blank shell.' The problem was overcome by the fitting of aluminium shields to protect from the intense heat of *The Blue Flame's* roaring exhaust', the nylon ropes that held the chutes.

Seconds before the cockpit canopy was sealed on Friday, October 23, Gary Gabelich knelt by the silver-blue, needle nose of *The Blue Flame*. He caressed the shining nose of his car and talked to it in a whisper. 'Let's do it together, baby. Give me a good ride. Let's go, baby. You can do it. We can do it together, baby.'

At 11.40 am Gabelich, the former NASA would-be astronaut adjusted his love beads and cradled his St. Christopher medal in his hands.

Gabelich, now alone in the confinement of his cockpit, began the countdown sequence, 'Ten, nine, eight, seven, six, five, four, three, two, one ... Ignition!'

Gabelich pushed down the accelerator pedal and could feel the rush of fuel around him as it was forced toward the catalyst pack. He was forced back in the seat so hard he couldn't move his head to see the vital instrument panel and telemetry dials. In a split ear-shattering second, the rocket car disappeared in a stream of white smoke as it streaked toward the deep-blue horizon and the target, almost two miles down range.

At almost the same time all the vibration and noise vanished, as *The Blue Flame* roared over the top of the hard-packed salt. Gabelich now experiencing the full effects of the high g-force, aimed the car and continued to accelerate in an eerie silence caused by the increasing pressure as the car generated its own shock waves, now approaching speeds in the high subsonic region.

This time there were no problems on the salt as *The Blue Flame* blasted through the measured mile in 5.89 seconds. Speed: 617.602 mph (993.931 kph). The car was refuelled, the Deist braking chutes repacked. Again the 31-year-old driver knelt by the car's nose, rubbing it fondly, his lips moving, 'That was far out, baby, but we're not through yet. We've got to do it one more time and do it better. We can do it. Just you and me. We can do it. Now, let's go and do our thing together, you and me, baby, you and me.'

With 12 minutes remaining in the countdown, *The Blue Flame* flashed across the salt flats, accelerating through the mile in 5.739 seconds. The even faster, 627.287 mph (1009.518 kph) run cemented a new World Land Speed Record of 622.407 mph (1001.473 kph).

The remarkable *The Blue Flame* was the last in a golden era of record-breakers at the Bonneville Salt Flats, which saw John Cobb's record of 394 mph, set in 1947, rise to within sight of the sound barrier in a period of only seven years, from July 1963 to October 1970. Names such as Gabelich, Arfons, Thompson, Breedlove and the Summers brothers are well known to all involved with hot-rodding.

Shortly after Gabelich set his record in October 1970, Dausman and Keller began working on a design concept for a new vehicle with Mach 1 capabilities.

Basically a slender version of *The Blue Flame*, their new vehicle, officially dubbed *The American Way*, would utilize a similar power system, packing some 21,000 lb thrust, and once again Gabelich would drive.

The Institute of Gas Technology sponsored, The Blue Flame *with driver, Gary Gabelich.*

But Officer ... I thought you were Breedlove, otherwise I would have stopped.

Sadly, however, Reaction Dynamics were unable to secure the backing for another high speed foray financed by corporate America, and the project was shelved.

A sad footnote to the remarkable success of Gary Gabelich and the outstanding contribution he made to the world of land speed record-breaking, is that in January 1984 he was killed in a motorcycling accident close to his home in Long Beach, California. He was travelling at high speed when a truck pulled out in front of him and, in an attempt to avoid collision, Gary laid the bike down trying to slide under it, but didn't make it. Gary wasn't wearing a crash helmet, and died instantly.

He survived terminal speeds in excess of 600 mph, only to lose his life on a Freeway. Gary Gabelich was one of the most likeable guys in the record breaking business and will be missed by so many who return to the salt arena year after year in the wake of the true master of the art ... We'll all miss you Gary!

Chapter 5
Winners in Different Races

A delicate needle trailing a swirling vortex of fire and dust in testament to the violence of its passage, the Budweiser Rocket blasts through the Sound Barrier at a staggering 739.666 mph (1190.377 kph) or Mach 1.0106.

Richard Noble ~ A Briton Finally Does It!

P restige is more than just a word to an Englishman. It's a way of life. It was the driving force behind the motivation of men like John Cobb, Sir Malcolm and Donald Campbell, and more recently Richard Noble, who risked their lives for the sake of a new land or water speed record.

Richard Noble's abortive attempts to regain the World Land Speed Record for the United Kingdom never really got off the ground at Bonneville: the weather was against the Project Thrust team there in 1981 and again in 1982.

No sooner had the team arrived at the Bonneville course in 1982, than the Salt Flats disappeared under four feet of water. There was a sketchy fall-back plan, and the Project Thrust entourage set off for Gerlach on the edge of the Black Rock Desert, Nevada. They had heard through the bush telegraph that a potentially suitable site was to be found in the region, a vast alkali playa some 120 miles north of Reno.

Before *Thrust 2* could run on the prehistoric mud lake, Noble had to acquire a permit from the BLM (Bureau of Land Management), who are responsible for maintaining the environment and natural habitat of the region. Initial objections were thwarted when the citizen's of Gerlach and Empire lobbied the BLM; Noble and the enthusiastic townsfolk were given the 'green light'. It was go ...

In wintry conditions, with the thermometer reading around 43 °F and with more rain threatening, Richard Noble made another attempt at the World Land Speed Record on Thursday, 3 November at 11.59 am. Unfortunately, the surface conditions did not allow *Thrust 2* to be taken far enough back for a proper run-in to the measured mile. Nevertheless, the two-way average speed was 595 mph (960 kph).

The 4 November 1982 was to be the big day at Black Rock, the day Richard Noble would end an eight year struggle to realize his dream of exceeding the existing record of 622.407 mph (1001.664 kph) set by Gary Gabelich on 23 October, 1970 in the unique, rocket-powered *The Blue Flame*.

Before Noble could commence his assault on the record, the USAC timekeepers moved the timing traps one mile further north due to adverse weather conditions.

After spending almost an hour inspecting the car and talking with the designer John Ackroyd, Noble, looking more like a middle-weight wrestler in his black racing suit and face mask, climbs into the now familiar cockpit of *Thrust 2*. After running through a carefully typed check-list, and actuating a sequence of switches and assocated valves, Noble gives the thumbs up and the cockpit canopy is sealed.

Operations Manager, Eddie Elsom announces five minutes to the start of the first run. The red 'Palouste' turbine starting unit is connected to its socket adjacent to the offside front wheel, and soon the 'Palouste' whines into life, flames darting from its exhaust as it begins to spin *Thrust 2's* Avon turbine. A muffled thunder and a stream of heat haze from *Thrust 2's* exhaust, signals that the ex-Lightning fighter engine has ignited and as Noble builds up the power against the brakes the palouste is hurriedly disconnected and the panel covering its socket replaced. The turbine is now reaching a crescendo that sends vibrations through one's chest. Suddenly

Thrust 2 lurches forward with a crackling roar. Blasting white clouds, she slams away from the line with a stench of jet fuel, the earth trembles as the four ton leviathan gathers momentum, trailing the distinctive rooster tail of flying dust. Within 10 seconds she is lost to the eye as the reflective morning haze casts a watery sheen on the dry, sun-baked desert course. A voice crackles over the radio from control. 'It's a beautiful run ... 596.421 mph through the mile, 596.412 mph through the kilo.' Thrust pulls up at the 8½ mile mark, the course is declared clear and the mad rush begins as the crew converge on the end of the course for the turnaround. Noble, jubilant at the result, gets out of the cockpit and declares, 'I'm still alive'. If Noble can make a return run in excess of 650 mph he will have achieved the project objective, but there were problems. On the first run the car registered an incredible 20 degree yaw angle on occasions.

Tension is high, but controlled, and two minutes later Noble kits up again and climbs back into the cockpit to begin what he alone must know could be his very last attempt to regain the World Land Speed Record for the United Kingdom. The bowser pulls away having replenished the fuel tanks with Jet-A spirit, a short countdown commences and Thrust 2 is once more blasting its way toward the measured mile and Noble's dream.

The performance was poor and all hopes were soon dashed as the car sped on its course. Even before the run was over everyone knew the attempt to beat Gary Gabelich's record had failed.

The voice of the USAC timekeeper crackled once again over the radio from control, 'return run; 584.795 mph through the mile, 587.121 through the kilo.'

Emerging from the cockpit of Thrust 2, Richard Noble hugged his wife Sally, both obviously reflecting in silence ... So near, and yet so far.

Conditions at Black Rock on 4 November could barely have been more favourable, despite the pressures from the local environmentalists to have his earlier attempts temporarily banned. The vehicle, however, simply couldn't produce the required thrust to exceed the existing record.

Initial design considerations for the vehicle did not lead to an aerodynamic configuration that fell in the range from high subsonic to low

Thrust 2 photographed on the immense Black Rock Desert.

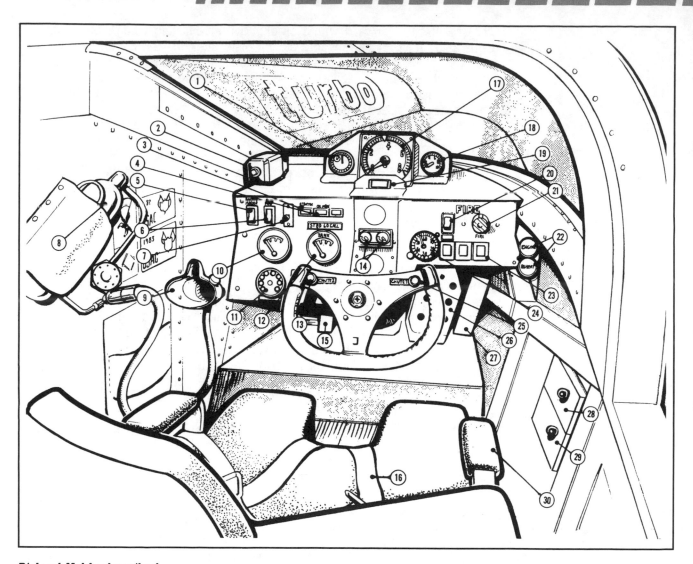

Richard Noble described driving Thrust 2 *as 'just like an automatic car — steering wheel and two pedals'. As the drawing shows, it is a right-hand drive automatic vehicle with a yoke type steering wheel. There was a great deal in the tiny cockpit demanding Noble's attention without in addition his having to follow the marker cones while travelling at 600 mph plus. As well as the two foot pedals —accelerator and brake — there is a foot rest, interestingly it is located next to the accelerator, for the crucial*

supersonic. The lower surface of the vehicle was flat, which, at high subsonic speeds would not dissipate the swell of pressure and boundary-layer build up approaching low supersonic speeds. The centre of pressure was located forward of the centre of gravity of the vehicle, alleviating the necessary counteraction against yaw tendencies, through the emplacement of two, short vertical stabilizing fins at the rear instead of a more appropriate single sharply raked stabilizing fin which would have significantly reduced the 20 degree yaw angle registered on occasions.

It must have been painfully obvious to John Ackroyd, who, having overcome earlier mechanical and aerodynamic setbacks in the United Kingdom and, indeed, the Bonneville Salt Flats, was now faced with a design concept which fell well below the required standard to capture the World Land Speed Record for the United Kingdom.

That evening in 'Bruno's Country Club' in downtown Gerlach, the Board of Thrust Cars Limited decided unanimously to abandon their assault on the record and project objective.

Looking strained under the subsequent pressure from his sponsors, Richard Noble pledged he would return to the United Kingdom to raise the necessary funds to return to the Black Rock Desert in 1983.

period of the run when Noble was decelerating. As with many modern day automobiles, the speedometer is rather optimistic; it reads up to 800 mph.
Key: 1 Engine rpm, 2 Fuel transfer timer, 3 Over-speed warning light, 4 Oil pressure warning light, 5 Battery master switch, 6 Fuel pump switch, 7 Engine starter button, 8 Filtered air breathing bottle, 9 Air mask, 10 Port side fuel tank, 11 Brake pressure indicator lights, 12 Starboard fuel tank, 13 Second parachute release button (for 375 mph and below), 14 Reheat nozzle position indicator, 15 Wheel brake pedal, 16 Seat belt, 17 0-800 mph speedometer, 18 Jet pipe temperature, 19 Reheat failure indicator, 20 Extinguisher test switch, 21 Extinguisher button, 22 Low pressure fuel shut-off, 23 Black box records, 24 Stop watch, 25 First parachute release button (for release at 600 mph plus), 26 Accelerator pedal, 27 Foot rest, 28 Power pack extinguishers, 29 Power pack chutes, 30 Arm rests (necessary for support at up to 5.5g).

In 1983 the Thrust team returned to Gerlach again; this time vital modifications had been made to the underside of the car, and the team had a realistic organisation strategy ... they meant business!

Thrust 2 refused to start.... Richard Noble sat patiently and tried again. Nine years is a long time to wait. Nine years to spend just $5^1/2$ seconds covering one mile of hard sun-baked desert. Attempting the culmination of a lifelong ambition, one could be forgiven for being nervous. Richard Noble could not afford that. He tried again. *Thrust 2* refused to start.

Everything else was perfect. The car had been polished. The wind sock on the mast at the Project Thrust base camp hung limply. Black Rock Desert, Nevada, was almost wind free. Memories of the almost monsoon conditions at Bonneville 12 months before were forgotten. It was just before 2 o'clock on Tuesday, 4 October 1983, the hottest time of the day. The ambient temperature was 73°F; perfect land speed record-breaking weather and better than at the Bonneville Salt Flats in 1981, better than Black Rock last year. Morale was high. So was the temperature in the cockpit of *Thrust 2* as Noble, dreaming of a place in the New Year's honours list waited for the verdict. A fuse had blown!

An ambition of a lifetime held up by a blown igniter fuse. Changing it was simple, the problem was that the service van was 15 miles away at the other end of the projected run, ready to turn *Thrust 2* round within the permitted limit of one hour. The radio buzzed, Noble waited, the fuse arrived and was fitted, the service van sped back across the mud flats for the 15-mile return journey. The wind sock had not moved, the temperature had not dropped. Richard Noble took his chance.

Hands firmly on the yoke steering wheel, left foot ready on the brake pedal, the other on the accelerator, Noble began to depress the pedal under his right foot. The high-pressure cock was opened and fuel from the 124 gallon tank began to enter the Rolls-Royce Avon 302 engine. The noise and the spectacle were matters of which Noble was oblivious. After all, he had driven this car before. He continued progressively to push down the accelerator pedal to full throttle, to the most important 59 seconds of his life. That was when Noble applied *Thrust 2's* kick-down to instigate the afterburn. The trick, as he puts it, is to hold the throttle to the floor for as long as possible on full thrust – in this case, 34,000 horsepower for 59 seconds.

The instruments showed that *Thrust 2* was running perfectly, Noble had pulled his heavy machine away from the line and concentrated on the distant marker buoys. Up to 350 mph *Thrust 2* is steered, after that she will run straight unaided. The difficulty is making sure the vehicle is pointing in the correct direction; from then on it's basically a question of squirting. Noble had had problems in seeing the marker buoys during previous runs, but now they were more visible and he kept the nose of the car 11 feet away from them, running parellel.

Thrust 2 broke the timing beam just over five miles away from the starting point at 2.38 pm. The first flying mile took 5.767 seconds, at a peak speed of 632 mph, (1017 kph) and an average of 624.241 mph (1004.616 kph).

The team turned *Thrust 2* around, refuelled her and prepared for the second run. From south to north there was a slightly longer run-up over six miles, and the mud was harder baked which would mean that there would be less drag on the wheels, which on paper should mean a quicker run.

For the second time Noble was catapulted across the Nevada desert, the nose of *Thrust 2* breaking the timing light at 24 minutes 38.724 seconds past 3 o'clock. A mere 5.599 seconds later, Noble had covered one mile. With his right foot flat to the boards, the Rolls-Royce engine had consumed the Avtur fuel at a rate of just under one gallon per second, and the average speed for the mile was 642.971 mph (1034.758 kph), with a peak reading of 650 mph (1046 kph).

Noble hit the right-hand button on the steering yoke and the 7ft 6in Irvin transonic parachute opened and began to slow the 8,500 lb vehicle and its passenger. The 24,000 lb of drag brought the speed down to around 375 mph before Noble hit the second button and a cluster of three more 'chutes opened and *Thrust 2* coasted to a leisurely 125 mph. Noble applied his left foot braking technique and the Girling disc brakes brought the machine to a halt.

Long before, it seemed, the timing computer had confirmed that history had been made; the official average speed was 633.468 mph (1019.465 kph). The chief steward of the United States Auto Club would sign the certificate. Project Thrust began nine years before, and now Britain held the new World Land Speed Record.

Richard Noble had, therefore, finally elevated himself to join a rare and unique group of men. But for how long will his record stand? There is certainly more than enough American money and technical know-how waiting and eager to snatch it back almost immediately.

Richard Noble's interest in speed was first sparked in 1952 when he was taken for a drive along the banks of Loch Ness by his father. There, tied alongside a jetty was John Cobb's boat *Crusader* being prepared for an attempt on the World Water Speed Record. Noble still recalls the impression this sight made upon his life. 'It was an absolutely beautiful looking thing: I thought, someday I would really like to do something like that.'

He collected all the information he could on the boat and developed an interest in jet-engines. It was the speed element of the *Crusader* that provided the real inspiration, and throughout childhood and adolescence a large part of Richard's reading was devoted to anything he could garner on speed records and the brave men who attempted them. Mixed with the reading were outline plans for a jet-powered car and eventually a contender for the World Land Speed Record.

It was not until 1974 that he was able to turn his ideas into tangible form and begin work on *Thrust 1*; the first pure thrust powered car ever to be built in the United Kingdom. By selling his family car Richard was able to raise £1,000 and bought a surplus Rolls-Royce Derwent jet engine that had been used in a Meteor fighter and began construction. 'I had never designed a car before in my life', he recalls, 'so it was a fundamental exercise and when completed it looked like a cathedral on wheels!'

Thrust 1 was built in private garages in Thames Ditton and Chiswick by Richard in his spare time. While the end result may have looked like a 'cathedral on wheels', in demonstrations it established Richard as a determined young man with a larger than life ego-trip ahead of him. Whether or not he was yet to be taken seriously as a potential land speed record contender was to be discovered. A salesman from Twickenham with a forced public school accent was, it was generally thought, hardly land speed material!

The car appeared on BBC's *Tomorrow's World* gaining valuable publicity. In March 1977, however, during a run at RAF Fairford, a wheel bearing seized and *Thrust 1* did a triple airborne roll at 140 mph (225.307

kph). Richard was able to climb out unscathed but *Thrust 1* was a total write-off.

The wrecked car was sold to a scrap merchant for £175 and this became the total working capital for the planned *Thrust 2*. It never occurred to Richard to abandon his ego, cut his losses and retire gracefully from the land speed record scene.

'I'd learned a lot from *Thrust 1*,' he claims, 'I knew that the next car would have to be professionally designed and I realised that the funding would have to come from sponsorship, for to do the job properly would cost very large sums of money.'

That the ill-fated *Thrust 1* had given Richard and his ambitions a high degree of credibility was soon made evident. Invited to give a lecture to a gathering of junior ranking RAF officers, Richard was asked exactly what he would need to give his next car a chance of bringing back the World Land Speed Record, he replied, 'An Avon engine from a Lightning fighter!' After the young officers consulted their superiors, he got the engine; a Rolls-Royce Avon 210 from an obsolete F2A Lightning that had been withdrawn from service. The price to Richard was 'nominal'.

More, however, was needed now than just an engine and some credibility. Richard needed a very competent engineer who could translate his dreams into reality. Unable to afford to advertise, Richard drafted a press release simply headed: 'Situation vacant – designer for 650 mph car! 'This novel and attention-seeking approach gained a lot of media exposure and attracted an enormous number of equally eccentric applicants.

On the learned recommendation of Ken Norris, who designed Donald Campbell's *Bluebird*, John Ackroyd was selected. John was at that time working as a contract designer with Porsche and had behind him a career that spanned aircraft and hovercraft, as well as automotive design. These were ideal qualifications but at that time there were insufficient funds in the sponsorship kitty to employ him full time.

Such was John's enthusiasm for the project that he put in long hours of his spare time at the drawing board getting the initial design concept together in addition to his demanding full-time employment with Porsche.

On Monday 12 March 1984 at the Royal Automobile Club, London, Richard Noble (left) was presented with the Castrol Segrave Trophy by Lord Montagu of Beaulieu. The designer of Noble's car, John Ackroyd, was awarded the Segrave Medal. The Segrave Trophy is Britain's premier award for achievement on land, water or in the air.

In 1977, a piece of very good luck came Richard's way with the offer by the *Daily Express* of a 1,000 square foot stand space free of charge at the Motorfair it was organizing at London's Earls Court. Though the stand space itself was free, Richard still had to pay contractors' fees for its construction so he sold advertising space on the stand in order to pay for it. 'It was a tremendous gamble; if we didn't succeed in getting the stand together our credibility would have been back at zero and the project dead,' he says. It was a close thing but public response at the exhibition was incredible.

Of the many thousands of visitors who visited the stand, one set were to prove very important indeed. A group of executives from TI Reynolds, one of the firms that had taken out advertising space on the stand, paid a visit. Richard says, 'The team and I pooled what little money we had left – it mounted to some £65 – and blew the lot on taking them to lunch'. It proved to be money well spent for the company responded with an offer to build, free of charge, the giant space frame chassis of *Thrust 2*, the biggest such chassis ever built in Britain at that time.

By May 1978, John Ackroyd had become a full-time member of the project team, Initial Services and Loctite UK having by this time responded to Richard's approaches and provided cash sponsorship for what they saw as a very exciting enterprise. By now in schools across the country the talk among class-rooms was of a new *Boy's Own* type hero who had emerged with a dream that was turning to reality.

Within a year, the spaceframe had been completed and the Rolls-Royce Avon installed, at which point the entire building programme was transferred to Project Thrust's new Isle-of-Wight base, a location chosen because it offered relatively cheap workshop facilities and contained a wealth of aircraft engineering expertise and skilled labour.

There were now five full-time members on the Project Thrust team. In addition to Richard and John Ackroyd these were, operations manager Eddie Elsom and development engineers Ron Benton and Gordon Flux. A further team of eight part-timers including an RAF Lightning engine specialist, and an electronics engineer. Others handled the accounts, publicity and transport and Sally, Richard's petite wife, the Thrust Supporters Club, membership of which was now growing to thousands in number.

The original Project Thrust concept had been that it would be a three-phase operation with *Thrust 2* being built and run in demonstrations purely as a fund raiser for the planned 'Thrust 3' which would be the actual land speed record vehicle. It soon became apparent, however, that the potential of *Thrust 2* was such that it would be able to exceed 650 mph and from that moment the illusive record came within sight.

By July 1980, *Thrust 2* in the form of a rolling chassis, was available for low speed tests under power and for a series of demonstration runs before the public at air displays and motor race meetings in the Home Counties. By doing this it gained enormous public interest as well as valuable and much needed publicity in the popular press and on television and radio.

Within a year, Noble had gone back to the RAF and negotiated the purchase of a more powerful Avon 302 series engine from a Lightning F6 fighter. This engine provided 20 per cent more power than the 210 series it replaced. It was this new engine, coupled with the determination and dedication of a select team of English 'gentlemen' that produced the required thrust to regain the World Land Speed Record for the United Kingdom.

The poster of Thrust 2 produced by Castrol after Richard Noble's record-breaking run, showing Castrol's historic involvement in land speed record breaking.

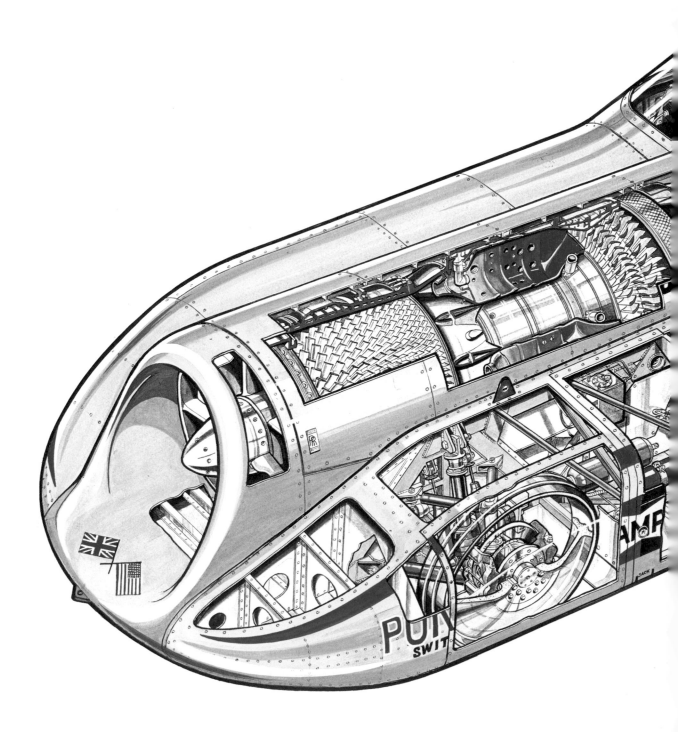

*Cut-away of Thrust 2
(Courtesy of Motor).*

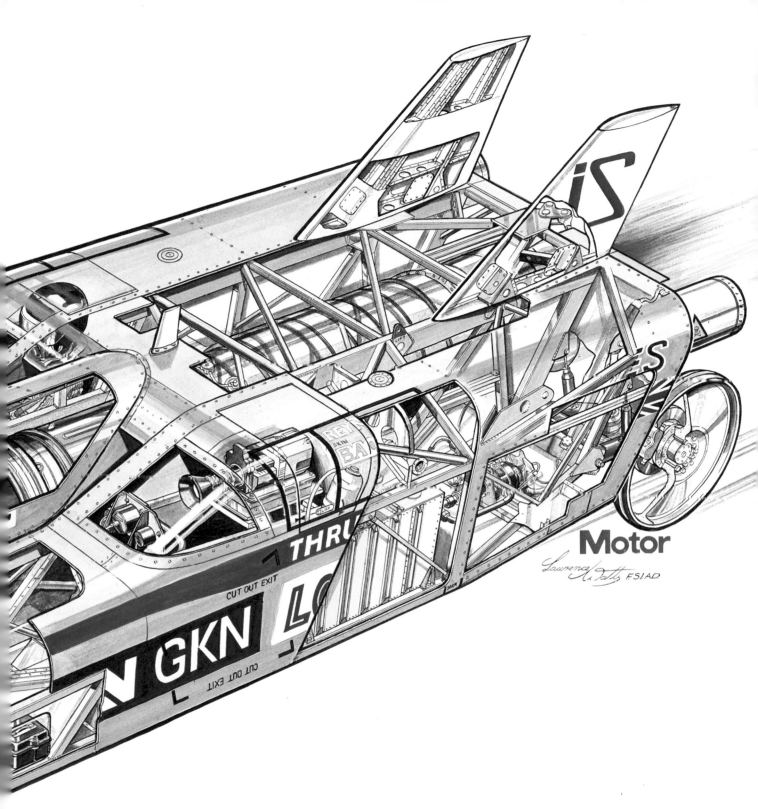

CUT OUT EXIT

GKN

THRU

iS

Motor

Lawrence Watts F.S.I.A.D.

Thrust 2 trailing a huge dust plume during its record breaking run.

Nine years after he dreamed the impossible dream, Britain's Richard Noble sped across the Nevada Desert at near supersonic speed to notch up a new World Land Speed Record, after 19 years of American dominance.

The tiny cockpit of the SMI Motivator, a combination of high technology and claustrophobia.

Bill Frederick and his team are the leader in the engineering and design of land speed record vehicles. The Success Motivation Institute-sponsored SMI Motivator was the testimony of Frederick's ability to create a car with supersonic capabilities. Both Hal Needham and Kitty O'Neal drove the car to speeds in excess of 600 mph in 1976. Seen here after completing a day of trials on the immense Alvord Dessert, Oregon.

A Project Speed of Sound team engineer making last minute checks of the power plant housing on the Budweiser Rocket prior to the assault on the sound barrier at the Edwards Air Force Base.

Gallons upon gallons of FMC hydrogen-peroxide rocket fuel awaits the summons of Bill Fredrick to power the mighty 48,000 horsepower, Romatec V4 rocket engine. The Budweiser Rocket used the equivalent of 650 gallons of fuel — 17 yards to the gallon.

A delicate needle trailing a swirling vortex of fire and dust in testament to the violence of its passage, the Budweiser Rocket blasts through the Sound Barrier at a staggering 739.666 mph (1190.377 kph) or Mach 1.0106.

The curious rear aspect of the Budweiser Rocket, showing the torsional flexing struts to the rear wheels and the exhaust outlet of the rocket motor. The only change in the vehicle between Bonneville and Edwards was the switch to a special hybrid bio-propellant system using hydrogen-peroxide as an oxidizer for polybutidiane, and a Sidewinder missile, producing a further 12,900 horsepower.

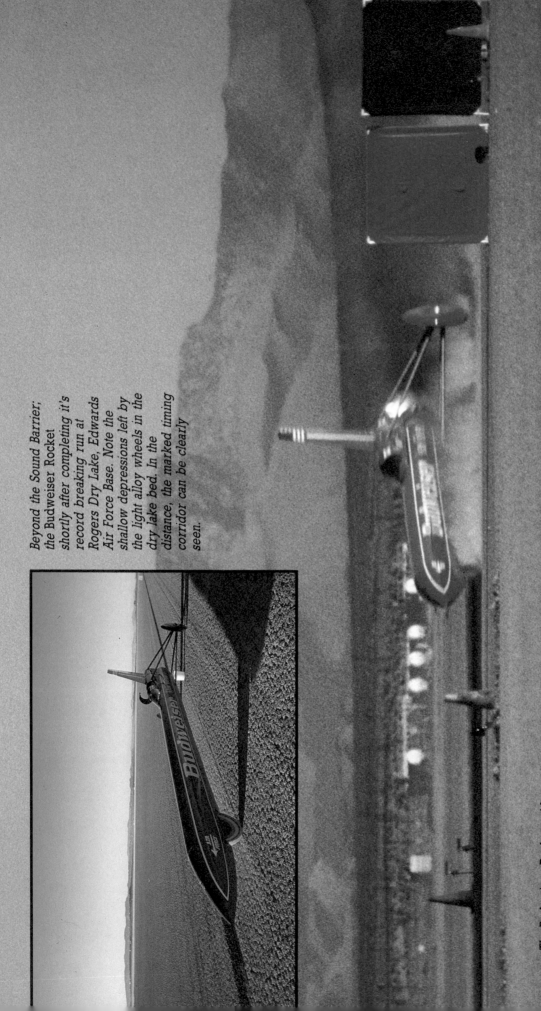

Beyond the Sound Barrier; the Budweiser Rocket shortly after completing it's record breaking run at Rogers Dry Lake, Edwards Air Force Base. Note the shallow depressions left by the light alloy wheels in the dry lake bed. In the distance, the marked timing corridor can be clearly seen.

The Budweiser Rocket with the rear wheels literally off the ground, roars through the timing corridor beyond the speed of sound. Observers heard only a small rumble like distant thunder, some said there was a supersonic boom.

Thrust 2

Length:	27ft 2in
Width:	8ft 4in
Height:	
Body	4ft 6in
Fin Top	7ft 2in
Ground Clearance:	5in
Wheelbase:	20ft 10in
Track:	
Front	LS Tyres 76 in
Rear	90in
LSR Wheels:	6ft 6¼in
	7ft 10¼in
Weights:	
Empty	8000 Lb
LSR Fuel & Driver	8500 Lb
Engine	2938 Lb

Power Unit: Rolls Royce Avon 302 with reheat
    Thrust at Max Reheat;   17,000 lb

Fuel: Avtur A-I,
    Capacity   124 gall
    Consumption at Max Reheat   50 gall/minute

Lubricants:
    Engine Oil   OX-38 12 Pints
    Turbo Pump Oil   OX-38 500CC
    Air Starter   OX-38 50CC
    Wheel Hubs   Kluber Isoflex Topaz NB52-12cc per bearing.

LSR Wheels:
    Material Hand forged L77 Alloy
    Size 30in O/D x 4in wide. Rolling Radius. 14.8in

Suspension: 4 Wheels independent
    Front – Nearly parallel Wishbones   1.5 in travel
    Rear – Trailing A Frames   1.5 in travel
    Springs Hollow Rubber compression and rebound
    Dampers 2 per wheel, gas/hydraulic
    Hubs Timken taper roller bearings

Steering: Rack and Pinion (Adwest) ratio 25:1

Braking:
    600 mph (24,000 Lb drag)   7ft 6 in dia Irvin transonic parachute
    375 mph (24,000 Lb drag)   Cluster of three Irvin 7ft 6in dia parachutes.
    125 mph   Lucas Girling wheel disc brakes

Structure:
    Frame: Tubular Steel – Reynolds 531
    Firewalls: 28SWG stainless steel with 277 Rockwool sandwich
    Skin: Aluminium Panels flush rivetted.
    Intake Nose: GRP 8 layers of .011" Resin 199.

Controls:
    Accelerator – Right foot pedal via lost motion box
    Wheelbrakes – Left foot pedal
    Steering – elliptical wheel
    Drag Parachutes – fired electrically from steering wheel mounted button
    Fuel tank cocks – push/pull cables
Instrumentation:
    Speedo 3.5in dia 0-800 mph range
    Engine speed %
    Jet pipe temperature
    Nozzle position Indicator
    Voltmeter
    Brake pressure tester
    Fuel levels
    Warning lamps for

A) Reheat fail
B) Oil pressure
C) Starter Overspeed
D) Fire

Switches:

A) Battery On/off
B) Fuel Pump
C) Ignition
D) Fire Extinguisher
E) Parachute Release

Starter system: Air start using LP compressed air supplied by an external Rolls-Royce Palouste 10 + /102 gas turbine.

Stan Barrett ~ Master of the Sound Barrier

When Hollywood stuntman Stan Barrett stopped pretending to be someone else, he became the fastest man on Earth, and successfully pulled off the stunt of his life, when he hurtled his three-wheeled 48,000 horsepower rocket car, the *Budweiser Rocket* across Rogers Dry Lake at the US Air Force Flight Test Centre at the legendary Edwards Air Force Base, California, to make history in becoming the first man to exceed the speed of sound on land.

He reached a terminal speed of 739.666 mph (1190.377 kph) or Mach 1.0106, with the help of a US Navy Sidewinder missile, becoming the first man to exceed the speed of sound in a land-bound vehicle. At exactly 7.26 am on 17 December 1979, Stan Barrett turned a page in automotive history.

The $1.2 million (£400,000) three-wheeler blasted off in a cloud of dust and, like a bright red needle with a huge ball of flame flying from its tail, scorched a path across the coffee-coloured dry bed of Rogers Dry Lake, high in the Mojave Desert. Barrett was 12 seconds into the run when, at an already staggering 612 mph (984 kph), he hit a button on the small butterfly steering wheel to fire the missile. 'I felt a lot of buffeting, then a period of smoothing out, and then it was like hitting a wall when the motors quit.'

Some claim that there was a supersonic boom. Other observers heard only a small rumble like distant thunder. Barrett covered the $5^3/4$ mile timed section of the course in seconds before a series of Deist braking parachutes were deployed, bringing the arrow-like projectile to a controlled halt at the end of the immense Rogers Dry Lake.

Engineered and designed by Bill Fredrick of Chatsworth, California, the *Budweiser Rocket* began its assault on the sound barrier in September 1979 on the vast Bonneville Salt Flats, the home of high-speed racing. After achieving a terminal speed of more than 638 mph on 9 September, however, further attempts at Bonneville had to be abandoned because the salt surface was so rough the vehicle was rocking back and forth on its two rear wheels. On one occasion at Bonneville, five working crew members were sprayed with rocket fuel when a press helicopter, carrying a CBS television crew, swooped over the car at the end of the run while they were emptying hydrogen peroxide from its fuel reserve chambers. They were rushed to the nearby Wendover clinic where they received treatment for burns.

Air Force permission to use the Edwards site came two months later, and the *Budweiser Rocket* resumed its sound barrier attempts on the same site where Chuck Yeager became the first man to attain the speed of sound in 1947. Then he flew the experimental Bell X-1 rocket plane, *Glamorous Glennis,* at 670 mph.

Fredrick, who started working with rockets as a hobby more than 20 years ago while still a teenager, incorporated space-age computer equipment into the car. Sophisticated telemetry gear relayed every function of the car back to a computer command post.

Bill Fredrick (right) working on the construction of the Budweiser Rocket. *The protruding tension pins (clecos) enable frequent and easy removal of the body panels for access to the propellant tanks and inboard instrumentation during construction.*

The 48,000 horsepower, hybrid design, Romatec V4 mono-propellant rocket motor of the Budweiser Rocket nears completion in Bill Fredricks' Romatec Research Laboratory, Chatsworth, California.

While supersonic aerodynamic theories had to be used, Fredrick says the vehicle is based on a simple design concept. 'You design for the smallest amount of frontal area and the largest amount of power available. That's why we have three wheels instead of four; it means a smaller frontal area and it's more stable at high speeds.'

Fredrick said, 'The thing you begin with is the size of the human body.' As a result the Budweiser Rocket's fuselage section is only 20 inches wide and 24 inches high. and 39 inches high at the top of the cockpit canopy. The vehicle, 39ft 2in long and 8ft 10in tall at the tip of the vertical fin at the rear, rides on a revolutionary new concept in high-speed tyre design of solid forged aluminium. At speeds in excess of 700 mph, the wheels were spinning at 9,200rpm and conventional rubber tyres would have disintegrated. Fredrick's confidence in solid tyres was proven in the prototype to the *Budweiser Rocket*, the successful *SMI Motivator*, which Kitty O'Neil and Hal Needham (owner of the *Budweiser Rocket*) both drove to speeds of more than 600 mph in 1976, on the vast Alvord Desert in Oregon.

For the engine of the Budweiser Rocket, Fredrick came up with a hybrid design, a Romatec V4 system, combining both liquid and solid propellants and producing 24,000 pounds of thrust – 48,000 horsepower. As he explains, 'The hydrogen peroxide filters through a catalyst and decomposes, giving you superheated steam and oxygen at temperatures of 1,370 degrees. That erodes the solid fuel which automatically ignites as soon as it's gaseous.'

In addition, to go supersonic Fredrick added 12,900 horsepower from a Sidewinder missile. Normally the Sidewinder is used as an air-to-air heat seeking missile by the US Navy and Air Force, and is not unlike the series used by the Royal Navy during the Falklands crisis.

No-one had ever driven at more than 700 mph. Stan Barrett's supersonic run was the culmination of three and a half months and 18 attempts, which began when he broke the previous timed speed on land – 622.407 mph – set by Gary Gabelich in the Institute of Gas Technology sponsored *The Blue Flame*, on 23 October, 1970.

The *Budweiser Rocket* used the equivalent of 650 gallons of fuel – 17 yards to the gallon.

It is not a long drive by conventional car from the sprawling ranch home of Stan Barrett in Bishop, California, to the Edwards Air Force Base where the assault on the sound barrier was made. Barrett's wife, Penny, a former member of the US ski team, and their children – David, eight, Stanton, seven, and five-year-old Melissa – went along.

Walking relaxed, in the comfort of his ranch home, Barrett told me, 'All the family knew the risks involved, that I might not come out of it. Penny and I talked to the children about it.'

After spending almost 30 minutes inspecting the car and talking with its owner, film director Hal Needham, Barrett climbed into the tiny cockpit of the *Budweiser Rocket*. Crew chief Kirk Swanson buckled him in and Bill Fredrick asked Stan to pray for God's blessing, gave the 'thumbs up' to the working crew and engineering support team, and the canopy was closed.

There was an ominous silence and after a wave from Kirk Swanson, arming the rocket commenced. After actuating the proper sequence of switches transmitted to the vehicle by Bill Fredrick on radio, who was kneeling on the course close by, Barrett increased the pressure, blasting clouds of hydrogen peroxide vapour from the exhaust outlet, 'She's ready to go, Stan,' called Fredrick who then started the countdown ... 3-2-1. Barrett depressed the accelerator with his right foot, igniting the engine. The rocket car blasted away from the line with a menacing roar and disappeared in a stream of white smoke, scorching a path across the dusty dry lake toward the unknown.

The rocket engine burnt for about 16-20 seconds (the thrust and length of burn are worked out by computer to achieve the desired speeds) with about another 50 seconds required to bring the car to a halt.

Inside the car, Stan Barrett had accelerated faster than any human being ever had in a land-bound vehicle. During the run he was subjected to an estimated 4 gs of force, or four times his body weight. He pulled over a further g at over 600 mph when he fired the Sidewinder missile. The car skipped at times on the first part of the run – as a result of tremendous acceleration which leaves wheel rotation catching up with the vehicle's speed. ''You could hardly see as the vibrations were so great along with the tremendous acceleration and speed. The 1/2 mile markers looked like telephone poles and I was afraid that I would not be able to distinguish where to fire the Sidewinder from all the jostling around. I saw the marker and fired the Sidewinder and felt some real hard thrust, the acceleration at that speed was tremendous with the boost that it provided. Nearly 5 seconds later, I felt some hard buffeting and then it smoothed out for an instant and then it was like I hit a wall, all the mass of air pressure we had pushed through with the multi-thousand horsepowered rocket caught us now as the engines quit. For a moment I didn't know where I was. I was afraid that the main chute had prematurely fired. I managed to purge the engine and release the main chute and felt another big jolt as the chute took hold. I slowed more, then released the second chute and finally slowed enough to apply the brakes''. Chuck Yeager was among the first to reach him. The 36-year old father of three pulled himself out of the car with the help of his friend, Hal Needham, amidst a crowd of onlookers, family friends and working crew, and hugged Hal. He then embraced his wife and children. An Air Force Northrop T-38 flew over at one hundred feet as a salute from one mach-buster to another. Although Barrett had become the first man to break the Sound Barrier on land, the historical event was not accepted by the FIA, as a new Land Speed Record. In order to be official, a record has to be set by averaging the speed of two runs through a one-mile timed course. Barrett had to wait nearly ten hours for the Air Force to confirm the speed.

In a telegram to Hal Needham, Colonel Pete Knight of the US Air Force broke the news. The car had exceeded Mach 1. It was official. Stan Barrett had indeed become the first man to break the sound barrier on land.

Barrett, a devout Christian, offered thanks to God – and celebrated with a large bowl of strawberry ice cream.

Watching the run was Chuck Yeager, who 32 years earlier broke the sound barrier in a rocket plane to earn his place in history. Yeager, now Air Force Brigadier (retired), who interviewed Barrett during the warm-up runs, pointed out, "It's far more dangerous than what I did. At that time, nobody knew what would happen should a plane go faster than sound. I had 42,000 feet of space between me and the ground to play with. ... Something goes wrong here, and Barrett's gone."

The successful sound barrier run of the *Budweiser Rocket* was monitored by extrapolation from a special United States Air Force (dish) tracking radar trace in addition to the rocket's own sophisticated computer telemetry equipment under the direct management of Earl Williams, a leading US computer consultant, and Joe Sargent, an ex-Northrop Corporation man who programmed NASA's computers for the Apollo II EVA lunar landing mission, seconded to Bill Fredrick's Project Speed of Sound team.

In a telegram to *Budweiser Rocket* owner Hal Needham, the United States Air Force said that along with engineering personnel from the rocket

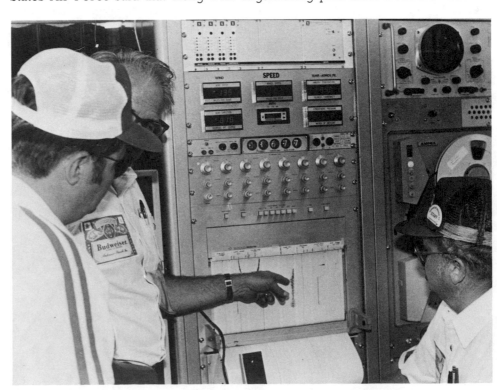

Sophisticated telemetry equipment relayed every function of the Budweiser Rocket *back to a mobile computer command post, manned by a team of specialists under the direct management of Earl Williams, the leading US Computer Consultant seconded to the 'Project Speed of Sound'. Joe Sargent (left) and Ray Van Aiken evaluate the telemetry readout after a successful 'low speed' trial run of the car at Bonneville.*

crew it had 'performed a review of the limited accelerometer, photographic, air speed and radar data taken during the speed of sound land speed attempt at Rogers Dry Lake at Edwards Air Force Base in November – December 1979. Within the accuracy of the speed measuring devices used, it is our judgement that the overall objective of obtaining Mach 1 (the speed of sound) with a land vehicle was achieved at 7.26 am on December 17, 1979.' The telegram was signed 'very sincerely Yours, Col. Pete Knight, Vice Commander, Air Force Flight Test Centre'.

Needham said 'We can't thank the Air Force enough. They have been so supportive and helpful, we couldn't have done it without them.'

The sound barrier has been broken, the enigmatic Stan Barrett has now travelled faster than a rifle bullet, literally out-running the very roar of his mighty 48,000 horsepower, hybrid rocket engine.

The Anheuser-Busch-sponsored Budweiser Project Speed of Sound team insist 'this was a high-technology scientific and engineering achievement'. Bill Fredrick and his remarkable crew of dedicated engineers, mechanics, telemetry and computer specialists are the foremost exponents of Land Speed Record breakers.

Some people thought breaking the sound barrier was a useless stunt 30 years ago, but today anybody can do it in supersonic Concorde. Who knows where the achievements of this project will lead?

Stan Barrett in the tiny cockpit of the Budweiser Rocket after becoming the first man to exceed the speed of sound on land at Rogers Dry Lake, Edwards Air Force Base. Interviewing Barrett is Chuck Yeager, the first man to break the sound barrier 'upstairs' in the legendary Bell X-1 rocket plane in 1947.

Beyond the Sound Barrier: the Budweiser Rocket shortly after completing it's record breaking run at Rogers Dry Lake, Edwards Air Force Base. Note the shallow depressions left by the light alloy wheels in the dry lake bed. In the distance, the marked timing corridor can be clearly seen.

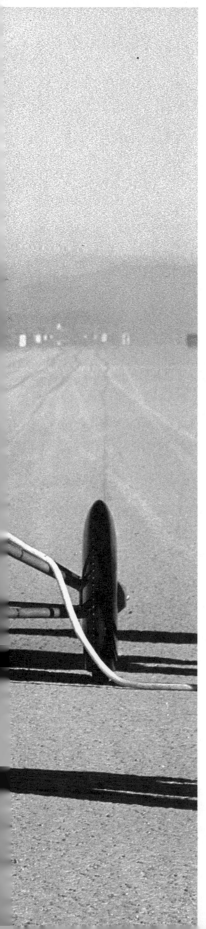

The Sound Barrier Team

The Driver

Stan Barrett – A protégé of Hal Needham who is one of Hollywood's top stuntmen, he performed virtually all the major stunts in *Hooper*, the film in which actor, Burt Reynolds played the role of a stuntman. Barrett has doubled for Reynolds and Paul Newman in numerous films including *Smokey and the Bandit* and *When Time Ran Out*. Stan Barrett's career in motion pictures began in 1964 after four years in the United States Air Force. Barrett entered the USAF after attending Roosevelt High School and Missouri Military Academy at Mexico, MO. He was seventeen when he reported for basic training at Lackland Air Force Base, near San Antonio, Texas, and was later sent across town to the School of Aerospace Medicine at Brooks Air Force Base for additional schooling in the altitude chamber with partial and full pressure suits, and ejection seat training.

In December 1960, Barrett reported to Chanute Air Force Base, near Rantoul, Illinois, for duty as a physiological training specialist. 'I was in the business of teaching airmen and officers the techniques of survival at high altitudes,' he recalled.

When he left the Air Force, Barrett wanted to continue his career in the medical profession. 'I went to the University of Oregon as a pre-med student. My work in the Air Force really gave me the interest for medicine as a career.

'But while in Oregon, I learned that a movie was being filmed nearby. I auditioned and got a small part in the Jimmy Stewart movie, *Shenandoah*, which led to my meeting Hal Needham and a career as a stuntman.' Barrett is a private pilot and has raced motorcycles. Former Golden Gloves (undefeated) lightweight champion in his hometown of St. Louis in 1959, he is a Black Belt in karate. Barrett was 36 when he drove the *Budweiser Rocket*, and lives on a ranch near Bishop, California with his wife and three children.

The Builder

Bill Fredrick – Started working with exotic propulsion systems as a teenager when he owned a 200-mile-an-hour plus jet dragster. Fredrick is now an aerospace industry consultant on rocket propulsion and as head of Fredrick's Inc., is a technical advisor to the motion picture industry on the use of rockets and studio equipment for special effects. Fredrick is also patenting a special combustion process that uses waste material to generate power. He designed, engineered and built the *Budweiser Rocket*, including its 48,000 horsepower motor, developed at the Romatec Research Laboratories, another company within the Fredrick stable. This is Fredrick's third rocket car. The first was the 27-foot, 12,000 horsepower rocket dragster *Courage of Australia I*, the Wynn's sponsored car in which Vic Wilson attained 311.41 mph in 5.107 seconds at the Orange County International Raceway in Irvine, California. This successful car was followed by the *SMI Motivator* in 1976, the prototype of the *Budweiser Rocket*, in which Kitty O'Neil and Hal Needham both drove to terminal speeds of more than 600 mph on the Alvord Desert in Oregon. Fredrick is currently working on the design concept of a rocket-powered boat, with which he plans to attack the World Water Speed Record in 1987.

The Mailgram sent by Colonel Pete Knight to Hal Needham confirming that the Budweiser Rocket had successfully exceeded the speed of sound.

```
MAILGRAM SERVICE CENTER
MIDDLETOWN, VA. 22645

4-0100485005002 01/05/80 ICS IPMRNCZ CSP LSAB
1 8054982206 MGM TDRN THOUSAND OAKS CA 01-05 1150A EST


AIR FORCE OFC OF PUBLIC AFFAIRS, WEST COAST
11000 WILSHIRE BLVD RM 10114
LOS ANGELES CA 90024


THIS MAILGRAM IS A CONFIRMATION COPY OF THE FOLLOWING MESSAGE:

 8054982206 TDRN THOUSAND OAKS CA 118 01-05 1150A EST
PMS HAL NEEDHAM, PRESIDENT, SPEED OF SOUND INC, CARE CBS SPORTS, ASAP, D
LR
REMOTE CONTROL BROADCAST BOOTH, STANFORD UNIVERSITY STADIUM.
PALO ALTO CA
DEAR MR NEEDHAM
IN COOPERATION WITH SPEED OF SOUND ENGINEERING PERSONNEL, THE AIR
FORCE HAS PERFORMED A REVIEW OF THE LIMITED ACCELEROMETER,
PHOTOGRAPHIC, AIR SPEED, AND RADAR DATA TAKEN DURING THE SPEED OF
SOUND LAND SPEED ATTEMPTS ON ROGERS DRY LAKE AT EDWARDS AIR FORCE
BASE IN NOVEMBER-DECEMBER 1979.
WITHIN THE ACCURACY OF THE SPEED MEASURING DEVICES USED, IT IS OUR
JUDGMENT THAT THE OVER ALL OBJECTIVE OF ATTAINING MACH ONE (THE SPEED
OF SOUND) WITH A LAND VEHICLE WAS ACHIEVED AT 7:26 A.M. ON DECEMBER
17, 1979.
THIS TELEGRAM CONCLUDES AIR FORCE PARTICIPATION AND COOPERATION WITH
YOUR SPEED OF SOUND ORGANIZATION. A DETAILED STATEMENT OF CHARGES
WILL BE PROVIDED AS SOON AS POSSIBLE. VERY SINCERELY YOURS
  COLONEL PETE KNIGHT
  VICE COMMANDER
  AIR FORCE FLIGHT TEST CENTER

11:53 EST

MGMCOMP MGM
```

The Owner

Hal Needham – King of the Hollywood stuntmen, Needham, 54, has certainly branched out. He wrote and directed the successful movies *Smokey and the Bandit I and II*, and directed *Hooper*, all of which starred Burt Reynolds, and directed *The Villain* with Kirk Douglas and Ann Margret. He started in films when he 'just walked in and knocked on the door' and got a bit part in the picture *Spirit of St. Louis* as a wingwalker. That was, says Needham, '25 years and 45 broken bones ago'.

Hal Needham got to know *Budweiser Rocket* designer/builder Bill Fredrick when he called on Fredrick to use some rocket propulsion systems for special effects in motion picture stunts. Needham drove the earlier Fredrick rocket car *SMI Motivator* to 619.99 miles an hour on the desolate Alvord Desert, Oregon in 1976.

The Car

Body width:	20 inches
Height of main body:	24 inches
Length:	39 feet 2 inches
Weight, dry:	3200 pounds
Weight, with fuel and driver:	5300 pounds

Suspension, F: Hydroelastic-pneumatic
Suspension, R: Torsional flexing of struts
Suspension travel: F: 2.0 in; R, 1.5 in
Front wheel: 3 x 30 inches, all-metal
Rear wheels: 3 x 32 inches, all-metal
Steering lock: $^3/_4$ – turn of the wheel
Turning circle: $^1/_2$ – mile

As for fuel, the *Budweiser Rocket* car burned a hydrogen-peroxide monopropellant at Bonneville, which produced less than half the engine's potential power. For the sound barrier run, the hydrogen-peroxide was used as an oxidizer for polybutidiane, and a Sidewinder missile, approved for Barret's run by the Pentagon, gave a final jolt toward the sound barrier. Total horsepower approaches 50,000. A body-width increase of only two inches would require approximately 2,000 more horsepower.

From a standing start, the *Budweiser Rocket* can accelerate from 0 to 140 mph (225 kph) in one second, and travels 400 feet in the first second. The vehicle attains a speed of 400 mph (644 kph) in 3 seconds. The driver experiences an estimated 4 g during acceleration.

Record Runs
(Speed timed on the principle of a one-way pass at terminal velocity)

9 September 1979	Bonneville Salt Flats	638.637 mph (1027.784 kph)
3 December 1979	Edwards Air Force Base	643.086 mph (1034.944 kph)
4 December 1979	Edwards Air Force Base	677.328 mph (1090.051 kph)
15 December 1979	Edwards Air Force Base	692.774 mph (1114.908 kph)
17 December 1979	Edwards Air Force Base	739.666 mph (1190.377 kph) or Mach 1.0106

Spirit of America III - Sonic II *The striking rear aspect of Craig Breedlove's 60,000 horsepower, pressure fed, bio-propellant liquid-fuel rocket car. With a 144 inch rear wheel track, the futuristic vehicle, when completed, should prove to be the ultimate in high speed stability.*

Chapter 6
The Future

The golden era of Land Speed Record-breaking came to a halt in 1970, but the pool of general technical knowledge became greater and greater, and it was this that gave birth to the jet and rocket dragsters of the early seventies. It is now three years since the World Land Speed Record was last broken and almost two decades since the Americans held the coveted timing slip, and American interest in the record has lain largely dormant. Now the pendulum is beginning to swing back with scheduled International competition on a scale that is without precedent in the history of land speed record-breaking, a situation highlighted by the successful breaking of the sound barrier in 1979 by Stan Barrett in the *Budweiser Rocket,* and more recently when Richard Noble broke the 13-year-old record in 1983 with *Thrust 2,* raising the record to 633.468 mph (1019.465 kph).

As many as seven different contenders flying the proud colours of four countries could be involved in the Great Race. For the first time since land speed record racing came into being in 1898, the Soviet Union has decided to enter the arena. Four cars with supersonic potential could represent the United States, while Australian industry is negotiating sponsorship for two exotic racers engineered around the design concept of Bill Fredrick's successful 1971 Wynn's-sponsored 6,100 lb thrust monopropellant hypergolic rocket dragster, *Courage of Australia 1.*

Prior to his tragic death in 1983, former land speed record holder Gary Gabelich of Long Beach, California, and five-time record holder Craig Breedlove, talked of a supersonic drag race at the Bonneville Salt Flats, but Gabelich's untimely death halted further plans for the duel. Craig Breedlove, however, has remained in the arena and plans his assault on the World Land Speed Record with his new 60,000 horsepower liquid-fuel rocket car *Spirit of America III – Sonic II,* with which he intends not only to return the record to the USA but also to break the sound barrier.

In Britain, the Author's 'Project Lionheart' team plan their assault on the record on the vast Wadi Rum desert in Jordan, with a ferocious 48,000 horsepower bio-propellant rocket car *Lionheart,* engineered and designed by Bill Frederick.

Art Arfons, who battled Craig Breedlove through two stormy years (1964-1965) and established three land speed records during that time, is now talking about the possibility of attacking the Sound Barrier in a new 5,000lb thrust, rocket-powered car dubbed *Firestone Mach 1.*

Auto racing veteran Mickey Thompson is currently rebuilding his 1968/1969 Ford *Autolite Special,* for an assault on Bob Summers' 20-year-old wheel-driven record. The car, renamed *Conquest 1* will use a significantly more potent fuel mix of 40 per cent nitromethane and 60 per cent hydrogen peroxide, and will be driven by Thompson's crew chief son, Danny.

Don Vesco, holder of the World Motor Cycle Land Speed Record, with a speed of 318.598 mph (512.733 kph), established at Bonneville in 1978 in the twin Kawasaki KZ 1000 cc-engined streamliner *Lightning Bolt,* is planning an attempt on the Summers record in a 21ft long, turbo-charged 3500 cc Offenhauser-powered six-wheeler, that is good for about 1100 bhp.

In the United States, a 35,000 lb thrust rocket-powered land speed record car was engineered and designed by Minnesota industrialist Tony Fox, of *Pollution Packer* fame, which he estimated could exceed the speed of sound and possibly 1,000 mph. No sooner had he completed the construction of a full size engineering mock-up of the vehicle. In 1977, Fox decided to freeze the project, directing his initiative to the development of the new Foxjet ST/600 aeroplane.

'Courageous' John Paxson co-driver of the Wynn's sponsored Courage of Australia *prototype.*

The 12,000 horsepower Wynn's-sponsored Courage of Australia was the first in a series of outstandingly successful thoroughbred rocket cars to be engineered and designed by Bill Fredrick. Powered by a 6,100 lbs thrust Fredrickinetics monopropellant hypergolic rocket system, the 27 foot dragster broke the timing beam at 311.41 mph in 5.107 seconds on 11 November 1971 at the Orange County International Raceway, Irvine, California, setting a new World Land Speed Record for the quarter mile.

Driven by Vic Wilson and John Paxson, the Courage of Australia was designed as the prototype for a land speed record car that was to be backed by an Australian consortium for an attempt on the record at Lake Eyre in 1972; due to the worldwide economic recession however, the project never evolved.

The *Proud American* and its 45 foot long spectacular 'Bonneville Boss' transporter are now owned by Jay Ohrberg of Corona Del Mar, California, and continue to draw crowds at Motor Shows and exhibition centres throughout the world.

Art Arfons' older brother Walt, who introduced the rocket age to land speed racing with a little help from Alex Tremulis, envisiges another rocket car or a steam-powered vehicle. A prototype steam-powered Grand Prix car has already demonstrated tremendous speed potential but is not recognized by the FIA, the world governing body for motor sport and record-breaking. Sadly, when I last spoke with Walt at his home in Bradenton, Florida, he was in very poor health and naturally had no immediate plans to evolve the project, although Walt's son Craig, may well pick up the gauntlet.

Bill Gaynor of Atwood, Colorado, plans an attempt on the World Land Speed Record with a four-wheel hydrogen-peroxide rocket car dubbed *The City of Sterling;* a remarkable vehicle, powered by seven, 6,500 lb thrust units, producing a combined maximum horsepower of 121, 278.

Thomas Palm and Paul Vickroy, will soon realise a life-long ambition of attacking the Summers Brothers' long-standing wheel-driven Land Speed

Record of 409.277 mph (658.636 kph), with their General Electric T-58 jet-turbine powered car named 'The Minnesota Land Speed Record Project'. Thomas Palm, of Brooklyn Center, Minnesota, is not a newcomer to the land speed record industry, for in 1981-1983 he was an active member of the British *Thrust 2* team. The experience he gained from Richard and indeed the entire 'Project Thrust' team will prove an invaluable asset in his own quest for a place in the land speed record books.

The illusive Ermie Immerso plans yet another attempt on the wheel-driven record, with yet another variation of the *Thunderbird* streamliner. For his latest attempt, the 62-year-old Southern Californian millionaire has designed his new car, *Thunderbird II* around two 860 bhp Avco Lycoming T53-L gas turbines, that were originally installed in an earlier Immerso streamliner, the *Thunderbird Turbine*.

Ermie Immerso plans his attack on the 20-year-old record at Bonneville in 1986, while at about the same time a strange looking vehicle could also join him in the salt arena in pursuit of the Summers Brothers' record, the 2,900 horsepower *Indy Challenger*.

Engineered and designed by Mike Spitzer of Indianapolis, Indiana, the *Indy Challenger* has been wind tunnel tested to 600 mph and should prove

Engineered and designed by Minnesota businessman Tony Fox of Pollution Packer fame, the 45 ft long, 35,000 lb thrust hydrogen peroxide rocket car Proud American, *seen here on its 'Bonneville Boss' transporter, was shelved in 1977 due to lack of interest in sponsorship from corporate America.*

to be quite a ride for driver, Ken Goodman.

The Soviet Institute for Automobiles and Roads in Kharkov recently announced their intention to attempt an assault on the World Land Speed Record with a Tumanskij R-11 gas turbine-powered car, the *Khadi-9*. Vladimir K. Nikitin, 'Master of Sport' and head of the Institute who developed the Soviet car recently told me through the services of a translator at the Novosti Press Agency in London: ''I have no doubt that the *Khadi-9* will be the fastest car in the world. We propose to overcome the sound barrier with it''.

Back in the United States, 41-year-old super-cool and publicity-conscious drag racing veteran, Slam'n Sammy Miller of Wayne, New Jersey, is poised to attack Richard Noble's 3-year-old record with the latest in a long-line of thoroughbred rocket cars bearing the generic name of *Vanishing Point*. The 37ft long projectile Miller has recently purchased is a big technological step beyond the last *Vanishing Point*. Powered by a GG Industries 14,000 lb thrust, hydrogen-peroxide rocket system, with a radial chemical rocket booster developing an additional 5,000 lb thrust, pent-up power is the message. Sammy estimates the car has Mach 1 capabilities, with a performance limit in excess of 800 mph (1290 kph).

The WSRA International Freedom Cup. Three 'dormant' liquid-fuel rocket motors mounted on a global plinth suggest a combination of romance and technology in the quest for the World Land Speed Record.

'Spirit of America III ~ Sonic II'~ Improving the Breed

Who would have ever thought then that a $^1/_{25}$ scale Revell model kit of a 1932 Ford coupe and roadster, offering authentic hot rod parts and pieces, from dropped axles to hot engines to chrome wheels, would have caused so much excitement for the young Craig Breedlove, growing up in the tranquil coastal community of Mar Vista, California.

At that time drag racing had barely evolved into an organised activity. A trip to the dry lakes was considered an adventure, when the only pit stop between Los Angeles and Mojave was a small winery in Adelanto, where the local 'Zinfandel' white wine became synonymous with El Mirage and Harper lake meets, and it took a lot to wash the dust from your throat after a weekend meeting.

Inspired by his successful assembly of the model Ford coupe, the inquisitive young Breedlove embarked on a career as a practising exponent of the 'strip and modify' society. At the age of thirteen he told his father he wanted to build the real thing. Within two years the young Californian had built his first classic street rod, a chopped and channelled, five-window '34 Ford coupe with a blown flathead V-8 and four Stromberg carburettors, that was typical of engines running on the lakes in the early days.

It took a couple of days to unwind after a thrilling day at the dry lakes. Then it was back to building and planning for the next outing. Most of the bench racing sessions were held at the famed Scully's Café.

It wasn't the dry lakes, however, that echoed to the roar of Breedlove's souped up Ford coupe. It was the public streets and highways. Street racing was the 'in' thing in Southern California. On any given night in the dazzling post-war era, hundreds of 'hot rods' could be found at the drive-ins around Los Angeles.

Picadilly's drive-in was one of the first and most popular of the Los Angeles area at the end of the war. It nestled in the corner of Washington Place and Sepulveda Boulevard, and at the witching hour, it resembled the present day pits of a major drag race meeting.

When Breedlove was sixteen he took his hot rod to the Bonneville race course and achieved a mean 154 mph (248 kph) on alcohol, taking his neighbourhood car club, the 'Igniters', into eighth place with 112 mph (180 kph) in the quarter mile.

In the years that followed, the Craig Breedlove story reads like a chapter from the book of the American Dream. In a span of less than 29 months, he established and held the World Land Speed Record for the United States on five separate occasions. Improving the breed with every run, Breedlove became the first man to exceed the 400,500 and 600 mph barriers, in what was to be a phenomenal, albeit very short-lived, blaze of success. The tides of time and destiny began to turn on the dashing, patriotic champion of the American people.

Breedlove's personal life fell to pieces, he lost a lucrative contract with the American Motors Corporation, and if that wasn't enough for the young Craig Breedlove, a torrential storm and ensuing flood destroyed his entire workshop in Torrance, the birthplace of the 'Spirits', destroying just about everything he owned and cherished, including two prized jet-turbines. Breedlove lost almost everything, but not his gusto and fighting determination. He gathered what remained of his tattered life and embarked on a new career in property. Over a period of time he rebuilt his workshop, made a number of successful investments in Baja, and began working on a rocket dragster.

Breedlove knew that another crack at the record would require rocket propulsion to deliver the required thrust. To test his theory he called on Jerry Elverum and Ron Gardner whose experience of rocket propulsion and telemetry would prove invaluable in the engineering and design of a prototype liquid – fuel rocket system for the dragster. Within a year, Craig Breedlove realised his dream of driving his own rocket dragster, the *English Leather Special* on the famed Bonneville speedway. The year was 1973.

It was a successful venture for Breedlove and his team, for not only did it mark his return to the salt after an absence of 8 years, it served admirably as a marketing tool for his life-long ambition to engineer and drive the first car to exceed the speed of sound. Only three years before he drove the *English Leather Special* he had lost the opportunity to drive the Institute of Gas Technology sponsored *The Blue Flame,* when, amongst a short list of no less than five selected candidates, including Art Arfons and Mickey Thompson, Breedlove was pipped to the post to drive the first rocket-powered car to set an official World Land Speed Record, by his life-long friend, the late Gary Gabelich.

From 1973 on, Breedlove and his company, Spirit of America Enterprises grew from strength to strength. The rocket dragster was modified and renamed, the *Screaming Yellow Zonker,* and soon Craig was joined by his grown son, Norm, to work on the final chapter of the Craig Breedlove story – the *Spirit of America III – Sonic II* – with which they were going for the ultimate record – the speed of sound on land.

In 1979 however, Stan Barrett became the first man to exceed the speed of sound on land at the wheel of the *Budweiser Rocket,* with a staggering 739.666 mph (1190.377 kph) or Mach 1.0106.

Breedlove ignored the success of the *Budweiser Rocket,* claiming that the 'Project Speed of Sound' did not attempt to meet the requirements for FIA recognition of a land speed record attempt, and that the speed attained was monitored by 'an extremely tenuous calibration' by a United States Air Force NORAD early warning radar system.

There is a whole stack of data and telemetry computations to support the success of the *Budweiser Rocket,* including the extrapolation from the radar trace and readings from sophisticated timing equipment.

Indeed, if the USAF NORAD early warning radar system is extremely tenuous, then the defence programme of the United States of America has one hell of a problem. Whatever is said and indeed written on the subject, one must not forget the objective of the 'Project Speed of Sound' was to exceed the speed of sound, and that objective was achieved on the 17 December 1979, and at no time have they ever claimed to have broken the World Land Speed Record, thus, they were not required to conform to FIA requirements.

Four years later Britain's Richard Noble drove the Rolls-Royce Avon 302 jet-powered *Thrust 2* to an official FIA World Land Speed Record of 633.468 mph (1019.465 kph), bettering Gary Gabelich's long standing record by 11.061 mph. Moreover, and perhaps even more impressive, *Thrust 2* had eclipsed Craig Breedlove's existing jet car record by 32.867 mph.

Now, at the age of 47 Craig Breedlove, the courageous man who grasped the World Land Speed Record for the United States in the 1960s,

Craig Breedlove.

The Ultimate Speed Trap ... Craig Breedlove's pursuit of a supersonic dream. A pause for thought at El Mirage!

Norm Breedlove.

after 30 years of British dominance, is set to regain the record yet again, in a ferocious 60,000 horsepower rocket car.

The new *Spirit of America III – Sonic II* vehicle is an all-composite structure powered by a pressure-fed, liquid-fuel, bio-propellant rocket system, developing a thrust of 30,000 lb. Engineered and designed by Jerry Elverum, Vice President and Head of Energy Systems Division TRW Inc., the liquid-fuel rocket system of the new 'Spirit' is a hybrid design combining a 50/50 mixture of Super 'Citgo' unleaded fuel, and monomethyl hydrazene, using nitrogen tetroxide as an oxidizer, with a pressurant of nitrogen gas. For the fuel chambers, Breedlove called on the state of the art expertise of James Leslie, PhD, President of Advanced Composite Products and Technology Inc., who developed a unique manufacturing process for Teflon-lined, Kevlar filament-wound high pressure 'explosion resistant' fuel tanks which will provide an 80 per cent saving in the overall power-to-weight ratio of the vehicle.

Breedlove, who last broke a Land Speed Record of 600.601 mph (966.528 kph) in November 1965, has spent almost 20 years gathering funds and engineering expertise for his 'farewell' assault on the record and it is believed that the vehicle, when fully developed, will have the capability of attaining speeds in excess of 1,000 mph.

The *Sonic II's* futuristic technology aspects include a highly specialized aerodynamic composite engineering concept for optimum lift and drag coefficiency, designed by the legendary Brandt Goldsworthy, President of Goldsworthy Engineering Inc, and one of the world's foremost pioneers in the field of reinforced plastics and composite construction methods.

Craig Breedlove has assembled a team of technical manpower, comprising some of the top people from every field of the aerospace and composite engineering industry, and he intends to promote the vehicle as America's entry and team vehicle of the World Speed Record Association, in a planned series of international land speed competitions.

The World Speed Record Association (WSRA) was formed in 1984 as a promotional body for land, air and water speed record attempts. The primary concern of the WSRA is to help promote its international team members speed record attempts which will be held under FIA or FIM rules. Along with creating exposure for its members, overseeing their speed record programmes and aiding with obtaining sponsorship, the WSRA plans to create and operate a permanent World Speed Record Museum featuring special cameo displays of the cars, boats and planes of past records. Also on display will be associated memorabilia, and future plans include the production of educational films and publications on the men and history of speed records plus the creation of a trophy – the International Freedom Cup – which will be given in recognition of new world speed records and outstanding contributions to the record-breaking industry, not unlike the prestigious 'Castrol Segrave Trophy' presented to Richard Noble in 1984.

In Breedlove's fluent land speed language, "By organizing the United States World Speed Record Team, the American people can individually participate in supporting their vehicle via a membership fee which will entitle them to receive a newsletter, T-shirt, decal, photograph and membership card admitting them to view the historical runs of *Sonic-II.* In addition, membership names will be placed in our 'on-board' computer to further enhance their participation in the record-breaking event. The car is designed with an 'on-board' video camera which will enable the television audience to ride visually in the cockpit with me".

Spirit of America III – Sonic II

Length:	44 feet 10 inches
Width:	23 inches
Height:	3 feet 9 inches
Width at Rear Wheel:	12 feet
Fairings:	
Fuselage Maximum Diameter:	37 inches
Estimated Weight Loaded:	7,800 pounds
Wheel Base:	305 inches
Wheels: solid forged	
aluminium diameter:	(front) 33 inches
	(rear) 31 inches

Propulsion Specifications

Engine Type:	Pressure Fed Bio-propellant Liquid Rocket
Thrust:	Step-throttling From 13,000 to 30,000 lb
Fuel:	Citgo – 50/50 mixture of Super Unleaded Gasoline and Monomethyl Hydrazene
Oxidiser:	Nitrogen Tetroxide
Fuel tanks:	Teflon lined, Kevlar Filament wound high-pressure fuel chambers
Pressurant:	Nitrogen Gas
Burn Time:	24 seconds at 30,000 lb thrust
Estimated Speed Capability:	1,000 mph
Approximate Horsepower:	60,000

By the time Craig Breedlove and his crew chief son, Norm are ready to try for Mach 1 in the Spring of 1987, their vehicle will represent more than 100,000 man hours in design and construction at a cost in excess of $1.1 million in labour and materials. Spirit of America Enterprises is proposing to operate the venture on a non-profit making basis until the vehicle has established a new World Land Speed Record for the United States, upon which, under the auspices of the WSRA, a significant purse will be negotiated with sponsors based on the successful achievement of their objectives.

To break the existing record, Breedlove's third *Spirit of America* must attain speeds in excess of the 633.468 mph set by Richard Noble in 1983. To exceed Mach 1, Breedlove must add more than 108 mph to Noble's top speed, which would add 140 plus mph to his last record set in 1965.

The computer gives the car a speed potential of 1,000 mph, Breedlove claims. "We're going to be trying for 750 mph to take care of the latest 'official' land speed record and break the sound barrier, which at sea level is 740 mph. The *Sonic-II* will deliver sufficient sustained thrust for 24 seconds, which will be enough to maintain Mach I through the measured mile."

At present, the development of the vehicle has advanced to the construction of a full-scale fibreglass engineering mock-up, which recently made it's debut on the El Mirage dry lake, where, at the age of thirteen, Craig Breedlove first became obsessed with the idea of breaking a World Land Speed Record, but the proposed venue for the attempt will be one of a number of sites already considered, including Bonneville, the Edwards Air Force Base, Mud Lake, Tonopah Nevada, and the Roach Dry Lake. The WSRA and Spirit of America Enterprises are currently negotiating a number of delicate sponsorship agreements, and there is whisper on the land speed 'grapevine' that the Chrysler Corporation could possibly become a major sponsor of the project, using the *Sonic II* as a unique automobile and truck marketing tool, but as yet, no firm commitment has been reached. Breedlove, however, is confident that a corporate sponsor will once again participate in the quest to regain the World Land Speed Record for the United States of America.

There is an ironic post-script to this comeback run. In 1986, Breedlove will be 48, the age of the late John Cobb, when he drove the 'Railton-Mobil-Special' to a new World Land Speed Record of 394.20 mph (634.267 kph) on 16 September 1947; a record that would stand until 1963, when the dashing 26-year-old Craig Breedlove drove the General Electric J47 jet-powered *Spirit of America* to a new record of 407.45 mph (655.696 kph).

It took two decades and some hard, lean years to get back to his dream, and still Breedlove remains philosophical: "It is great to achieve a goal, but I think sometimes it's better to keep reaching for one. What people fail to see is that most of the fun of catching a dream is in getting there. Once you have your dream, you are back to square one".

'Lionheart'- Crusader of the First Order

The proudest of all nations in the competition for the World Land Speed Record has been Great Britain, which has often knighted its heroes and treated them like royalty. From 11 March 1929 to 12 November 1965, a British subject held the record for the ultimate in automotive speed. Englishmen have held the record for more than forty-eight years since it was first established in 1898.

The men, and the women, who have reached into the unknown thresholds of speed are clearly not ordinary mortals. For John Cobb, the motivation was an obsession with excellence, for the indefatigable Sir Malcolm Campbell, it was undoubtedly a way of life, and for Richard Noble, it was possibly a quest for a knighthood that never came. But in common with most single minded Englishmen, dedication led them all to eventual success.

Somewhat earlier than 1965, Americans Craig Breedlove, Art Arfons and Tom Green set world speed records, but they did so in unworldly exotic projectiles powered by jet engines. The British 'purists' were among those who refused to accept something on wheels driven by jet thrust as an automobile. Twenty years later, Britain finally conceded to the Americans' use of unlimited power, and once again, holds the World Land Speed Record ... with a jet.

It sometimes takes a British success to awaken the Americans, and when

Richard Noble scorched a path back into the land speed record books in 1983 he woke a sleeping giant.

America is poised to return with a vengeance, with a team led by Craig Breedlove, himself, a living legend whose success and high-speed forays have been financed by corporate America.

Shortly after 10.00 p.m. on Friday, 23 October 1970 I received a long-distance call from Dean Dietrich of the Institute of Gas Technology, excitedly hailing the news that Gary Gabelich had exceeded Craig Breedloves' 1965 record with a pass of 622.407 mph (1001.473 kph) at the wheel of *The Blue Flame*. I naturally shared his excitement, but at the same time could not help thinking, "where on earth would this leave Britain, ... what possible chance would we have competing, yet alone regaining the World Land Speed Record from the Americans, now they were incorporating the principles of rocket-propulsion in land-bound vehicles".

Several years earlier I had read a signed article in the May, 1966 issue of *Popular Mechanics*, by Alex Tremulis (the brilliant designer and aerodynamicist, who rigged the extra rockets on Walt Arfons *Wingfoot Express II)*, extolling the virtues of rocket power in future land speed record attempts.

There are benefits in favour of both jet and rocket power for land speed record vehicles, but the final selection is often determined by what the contender can acquire. The rocket does not need an air intake, so wheels, fuel chambers, driver and engine can be placed in line, achieving a slim, pencil body spoilt only by having to place the rear wheels on a wide track for stability. The low drag coefficient, combined with a high power-to-weight ratio offers rapid acceleration, enabling a short run to be used. However, some critics of rocket propulsion have a tendency to claim that a large proportion of the vehicle's weight is composed of fuel, thus, when consumed the vehicle becomes 'light and lively'. For the rocket car to maintain peak speed for an 'official mile' against the colossal drag encountered near Mach 1, the car would need to carry a drastically increased fuel payload, but by combining a bio-propellant of both solid and liquid fuels, the payload is significantly reduced. On the other hand, a jet-powered car needs to suck in vast quantities of air and the immense intake for this pushes the other main components and instrumentation aside, making for a greater frontal area and considerably more drag than a rocket lance. The result is a far heavier, bulkier machine with lower acceleration. However, the fuel weight is not quite so critical and the vehicle could give a stable ride, allowing the performance to be fully exploited and held for the statutory mile. The battle between these two schools of thought was closely fought, that was until 1979, when Stan Barrett exceeded the speed of sound with a 48,000 horsepower rocket car, eclipsing all previous timed speeds by more than 117 mph (188 kph). The rocket era had come of age.

As a land speed record vehicle is not intended for production, it would be particularly expensive to develop a purpose-built jet engine, so usually an existing, surplus turbine unit is selected. They are powerful, light and reliable. Richard Noble and John Ackroyd had been fortunate in being able to obtain a Rolls-Royce Avon 302 engine complete with reheat unit from a surplus RAF Lightning fighter. This 25 ft long unit weighed 3,700 lb and was able to produce 17,000 lb of thrust at full reheat. Ackroyd then applied his engineering expertise to arrange all salient components around the power unit, in the best possible configuration to suit any conflicting interests such as frontal area, visibility, safety, weight distribution, stability, accessibility and of course, cost. With what little deviation he could allow from the basic rules of aerodynamics, Ackroyd engineered one of the most 'Slippery' jet-powered vehicles of all time. But with speed being the primary and, indeed, overall objective, of any land speed record vehicle, *Thrust 2* will almost certainly be the last in a golden era of jet-powered vehicles to pursue the World Land Speed Record.

The road to building a land speed record car is not an easy one, it takes nature, however, considerably longer to produce a diamond!

In September 1978, I prepared a feasibility study into the possibility of building a rocket-powered land speed record vehicle with Mach 1 capabilities. My findings were simple ...

The usual situation is that the men with the initiative and required technology to build the car often lack the required funds. And the companies who could provide the financial resources and furnish components are not easy to convince. It isn't that they don't want to participate, for many companies recognize the enormous marketing potential of helping to set a new World Land Speed Record. The strength of motor sports as a marketing tool is attested to by the growing number of companies, automotive and otherwise, that 'want in'.

Campaign reported: "After a pit stop that lasted several years, motor-sport is roaring back as a fast track to sales victory for auto marketers ... The 1960's adage, 'Win on Sunday; sell on Monday' has new life".

Many companies, particularly in the United Kingdom, are simply cautious; a caution born of a steady stream of paper tiger projects appealing for help. A situation highlighted in 1977 by David Gossling's tragic 'Project Blue Star'.

It is, to say the least, difficult for busy executives to evaluate and separate the legitimate from the oddball. Consequently, it has become extremely difficult for a car designer/builder to get a favourable reply to any large scale proposal.

On paper a project will often look feasible, but without major financial assistance and logistic support it is often totally impractical.

Unlike conventional motor sport, sponsorship of a land speed record car is indeed a unique opportunity for a company, for every record set is in itself a unique achievement, resulting in a marketing platform of international prestige. This factor alone is attested to by the number of companies that have committed their corporate identity to sponsorship of land speed record projects; The Goodyear Tyre & Rubber Company, Firestone, The British Petroleum Company Limited, Anheuser-Busch Inc, Champion, the GKN group of companies, The Southland Corporation, Faberge Inc, to name but a few, all of whom have gained enormous product enhancement as a result of sponsorship.

For 'Project Lionheart' I wanted to combine romance with state of the art technology and efficiency. What was required was a vehicle, of unbelievable power, that would not only be capable of attaining speeds in excess of Mach 1, but had the visual attraction of meaning business. The answer was rocket power, and the solution to that was Bill Fredrick.

When I first approached Bill about the possibility of building the car, back in 1980, it was a comforting thought, whilst listening to him extolling the virtues of rocket-propulsion in ground effect vehicles, that Fredrick and his team had a wealth of experience gained from successful projects such as *The Blue Flame, Courage of Australia 1, SMI Motivator* and, indeed, the remarkable *Budweiser Rocket,* all of which harnessed the power of rocket propulsion as a means of delivery.

While Fredrick began working on the design of the vehicle I began the arduous search for sponsorship. In the many months that followed I touched base with no less than 380 potential sources of corporate sponsorship, in both the United Kingdom, Europe, the Middle East and Australasia, while at the same time searched the globe for a potential venue for the attempt.

It is no good engineering a sophisticated car without somewhere to run it. This must be flat, hard and smooth with sufficient room to allow for acceleration and deceleration, and last, but certainly not least, it must be accessible and available – if at all possible, within a region that a potential sponsor could apply a cost-effective marketing programme. One of the most suitable sites explored was the vast Wadi Rum desert in Jordan; access was no problem, and the surface was as smooth as glass. Sadly, however, very few companies have a marketing outlet in Jordan, although Saudi Arabia and the Gulf States have a long and traditional link with the Hashemite Kingdom. The ideal venue would be a site within a 100 mile radius of a major city, a catchment area with unlimited access, Craig Breedlove and Bob Kachler of the World Speed Record Association are currently negotiating with a major US Corporation based in Las Vegas, the possibility of staging a permanent land speed record venue on Roach Dry Lake, midway between Las Vegas and Reno, Nevada. If they are successful in their quest, the event, greatly enhanced by the sponsorship of The Southland Corporation (7 Eleven) and The Du Pont Company is planned for the Spring of 1987, and it is envisaged that the venue will see regular international competition with Australian, English, and American (and possibly Russian) teams all trying to exceed Mach 1 and, indeed, the great automotive goal – 1,000 mph on land.

To fulfil the objective of 'Project Lionheart', it is our intention to raise the World Land Speed Record to a two-way average speed in excess of Mach 1, conforming to the rules determined by the FIA.

The present rules state that the speed registered is the average achieved over a common measured mile in both directions, the second run taking place within one hour of the first. Thus, the 'measured' mile must lie in the middle of the prepared course, determining equal run-up and braking distance at either end.

It is the objective of 'Project Lionheart' to break Richard Noble's official record, set in 1983, and attain a two-way average speed exceeding Mach 1 with a 48,000 horsepower bio-propellant rocket-powered, four-wheeled projectile appropriately dubbed *Lionheart.*

Engineered and designed by Bill Fredrick *Lionheart* will be *the* state-of-the-art in land speed aerodynamic engineering. While supersonic aerodynamic theories had to be used, the vehicle is based on a simple design concept, adopted from the *Budweiser Rocket:* design for the smallest amount of frontal area and the largest amount of power available.

The primary consideration is the size of the human body; and it is for this reason, the vehicle fuselage is a mere 20 inches wide and 24 inches high, increasing to 39 inches above the cockpit canopy.

The vehicle, 41 feet in length and 8 feet 10 inches high at the top of the vertical tail fin at the rear, rides on solid forged aluminium wheels with a vee-shaped tread and keel for lateral bite. Considerably lighter than conventional pneumatic tyres, they reduce overall and unsprung weight as well as gyroscopic forces. At speeds in excess of 800 mph, the four alloy wheels will be rotating at 10,100 rpm, at which speeds conventional rubber tyres would disintegrate. The rear wheels are 3 x 32 inches, and the front closely paired wheels are 3 x 30 inches. The steering is 28 degrees lock-to-lock with a turning radius of $\frac{1}{2}$ mile. *Lionheart* will be extremely easy to control under power and is capable of being driven from lane to lane under full power without losing stability, although it is unlikely this will happen during the land speed record attempt.

Design considerations for the vehicle led to an aerodynamic configuration for pure supersonic ground effects. The lower surface of *Lionheart* tapers to a 'V' to dissipate the enormous swell of pressure and boundary layer build-up approaching supersonic speeds. The centre of pressure is located aft of the centre of gravity of the vehicle to counteract the tendency to yaw and to eliminate flight characteristics, through the emplacement of a sharply-raked stabilizing fin at the rear.

An ogive shape was adopted as the least resistant nose configuration, and a cross-section of the vehicle's fuselage would show a rounded, tear drop shape. The closely paired front wheels are housed in the underside of the vehicle, forward of the in-board controlled canard fins. For high-speed stability, the rear wheels extend beyond the rear of the vehicle, and have a 12 foot wide track for roll stability.

The driver's cockpit is located aft of the propellant tanks and forward of the multiple rocket engines. The semi-monocoque fuselage includes ring-and-stringer construction in the central section of the car, and the rear of the vehicle has a welded nickel-steel frame, utilizing square and round chrome-moly tubing for additional strength to compensate for the stress of the engines, torsional flexing wheel struts, tail fin, gyro-controlled ejection capsule and Deist braking parachute system. The safety system includes one 12 foot diameter drag chute for below 1,000 mph (1609 kph), and the secondary drogue for speeds below 600 mph is 16 feet in diameter. All pyrotechnically activated.

In addition, safety will be complete by the incorporation of a gyro-controlled ejection capsule, a revolutionary new concept in high-speed safety. The driver is protected from impact and fire by being isolated within the strong capsule, surrounded by two-inch thick mineral wool firewalls with stainless steel backing. The driver is firmly harnessed into a form-fitting seat of energy absorbing foam and all controls and instrumentation are easy to reach from the supine position.

For the engine, Fredrick arrived at a hybrid design combining both liquid and solid fuel propellants, producing 24,000 pounds of thrust, 48,000 horsepower. In addition, to attain Mach 1 we have incorporated a radial chemical rocket booster engine from a Raytheon AIM-7F solid-state air-to-air Sparrow missile, producing a further 15,000 horsepower.

For the primary engine, hydrogen peroxide is used as an oxidizer for polybutidiane, which filters through a catalyst and decomposes, producing steam and oxygen at temperatures in excess of 1,370 °F. This element erodes the solid fuel which ignites as soon as it becomes gaseous. The engine, a Romatec V4, is the same system that was used on Fredrick's last rocket car, the successful *Budweiser Rocket*. The combined power of the Romatec V4 and the Raytheon AIM-7F booster, will yield the required thrust to attain a terminal velocity of 1,000 mph. The propulsion configuration is such that the centre-line of thrust will be balanced along the centre-line of the vehicle. The system has been designed to enable the engine ignition sequence to be made in stages or combined.

Don Vesco ~ Assault with a Deadly Weapon

On 28 August 1978 Don Vesco set the World Land Speed Record for motorcycles with a speed of 318.598 mph (512.733 kph) in the twin Kawasaki KZ 1000 cc-engined streamliner *Lightning Bolt*.

Now, almost a decade later, Vesco is set to wrestle with Bob Summers' 20-year-old wheel-driven record in a 21ft long, Offenhauser powered six-wheeler.

Vesco's latest streamliner, *Sky-Tracker I*, took shape within its double-wall monocoque tub of 0.080-inch thick 2024-T6 aluminium sheet. Suspension, supporting three-quarter-inch thick aluminium bulkheads mounted to each end. Shoe-horned between the wheels is one turbo-charged $3^{1}/2$-litre Drake Offenhauser engine (used by many of the successful Indy 500 cars), that is capable of producing anything up to 1100 bhp. The streamlined fuselage encasing this power measures a mere 25 inches wide and 35 inches high.

As far back as 1980 Vesco sent preliminary drawings of the vehicle to frame builder Rob North in San Diego, California, who has worked with Vesco on just about all of his record-breaking motorcycles since 1972, and would build the tub for the six-wheeler.

Vesco despatched another set of drawings to Bonneville and drag racing chassis builder Steve Rhodes in El Cajon, California, to fabricate the chrome-moly swinging arms, engine mounts and engine-compartment support struts. These components went for final assembly to Vesco's shop in Temecula, California.

While Rob began fitting some 2000 stainless steel rivets into the tub, Vesco organized delivery of the 14mm Uniroyal drive-belts, pulleys, pneumatic switches, electric tachometers, and turbo and injection pieces. Then Don turned his attention to building the bulkheads, belt-drive jackshafts and belt tensioners. Belt drive isn't new to Vesco; both of his earlier streamliners, the twin 1500 cc Yamaha TX750 four-cylinder engined *Silver Bird* and the *Lightning Bolt* linked the powerplants' crankshafts together with toothed belts. The small 22-tooth sprockets allowed by available space were half the size demanded by usual engineering requirements. Vesco discovered that frequent replacement short-circuited belt shearing, but the situation was marginal. The hot confines of an engine cowling is no place for chains; lubricants tend to spit onto the hot engines and exhaust pipes causing choking fumes that can fill the cockpit and blind the driver; a snapped chain can destroy valuable components – parts that are particularly costly and time consuming to replace. Belts are bulkier and require larger sprockets, but they are strong, light and demand no lubrication. Vesco designed the new 'liner around the requirement dictated by using belt-drive.

Since only one engine is used there is no need for crankshafts to be linked together by belts, as was the case in earlier Vesco streamliners, and extensive crankshaft and crankcase modifications weren't required. Only the right-hand crankcase covers were modified; the forward one for clearance in the skid's retracted position, and the rear to drive the fuel pump. The standard clutch assemblies received 100-per cent-stronger stainless steel springs.

Two atmospheres of combustion heat and pressure would blow the stock head gaskets. Even solid copper gaskets would move around without a method of crimping the sealing material in place. A simple drag racing technique solved the problem. O-ring grooves were machined into the cylinder sealing surface and another – just slightly larger – in the cylinder head. Metal wire O-rings that stand proud in these grooves crimp the copper gasket when the cylinder-head retaining bolts are tightened, locking the gasket in place.

The Dunlavy camshafts lift the valves 0.10 inch more than standard lift, while offering about five degrees less valve duration. These cams act on standard KZ650 followers, and S & W springs control the valves.

Touching a button in the cramped cockpit signals twin Murdoch air shifters to move pneumatically the dual gearchange levers, while microswitches simultaneously signal the ignitions off; Vesco would gearchange his way to speeds in excess of 400 mph with the touch of a button. An identical button triggers downchanges. This system is not untested technology for drag bikes have used it successfully for some years. Shifting two linked transmissions simultaneously, however, is a new departure. Should one engine find a false neutral or even fail to select, the twin tachometers would register contradictory readings. To allow Vesco to grab the correct gear and re-synchronize the shifters, a small button on the top of each tach' upshifts that transmission only, bypassing the other.

The normally taken-for-granted task of clutch operation required a thorough rethink for Vesco and his team: A cramped, narrow cockpit wouldn't allow the luxury of a standard lever with its comfortable leverage; 100 per cent stronger clutch springs aggravated the problem; and cable friction, amplified by its long-distance cockpit-to-engine-compartment passage, forced Vesco to use pneumatic clutch actuation. A stock Kawasaki starter lock-out switch in the clutch lever signals an air cylinder to disengage the clutch.

One of the two 23 inch diameter alloy front wheels that were fitted to Sky-Tracker I. *To enhance traction, Vesco machined grooves into the wheels' contact surfaces.*

Previous control-linkage problems at critical moments of record attempts compelled Vesco to opt for non-cable controls; salt-soaked cables rusted, frayed and eventually broke – always at the worst time. The only cable in the new streamliner swings the small turbo inlet butterfly valve; all other controls are 12 volt-operated or pneumatic systems. Fuel shut-off and tow-release are solenoid-only actuated; turbo-wastegate, skids, parachute releases, clutch and gearchanging are electrically-triggered pneumatic air-cylinder operations. Two 280-cubic-inch tanks at 200 psi charge this system, and two standard KZ1300 batteries supply electric current – one for ignition power, the other for solenoid power. All systems are "total loss" – spent nitrogen is replenished prior to each run and batteries are replaced when necessary.

The machine's only brake, on the rear wheels, mimics Indianapolis racing car technology having a Hurst Airheart internally-vented rotor and four-piston caliper. Two Deist parachutes serve as emergency backup. The high-speed parachute, triggered by a standard Kawasaki front brake light lever switch, is a 5.5 foot ribbon-type drogue. The low-speed chute, activated at speeds under 300 mph, is an eight-foot quad-panel. If the streamliner capsizes onto its slick, cylinder body, the parachutes pull the rear end behind the front, preventing roll-over like a pencil on a table top – provided Vesco actuates them in time! Once the streamliner swaps ends, the parachutes are free to wrap themselves uselessly around the fuselage.

The tubes that house these fabric brakes are integrated with the aluminium 8.5 gallon fuel tank – a space-saving tactic. A 1.75 gpm fuel demand required this large tank despite the short, five-mile runs.

Conventional pneumatic tyres, ideal for motorcross racing and the family saloon, present a hazard to a record machine; they are prone to pitching tread, vulnerable to punctures, quick to wear out and costly to replace. When inflated to 100 psi, the pressure required to resist heat build up, the tyres' smooth, treadless carcasses make you feel as if you're riding on steel – the rubber is about as thick as thin-wall tubing. Pneumatic tyres just aren't available anywhere. Goodyear and Firestone haven't built suitable high-speed-rated tyres since 1972, and these companies are simply not interested in developing costly 400 mph plus motorcycle tyres. After all, how many 400 mph motorcycles are there?

Originally, Vesco intended to use the nine-year-old Firestone automotive tyres, but he was concerned about deterioration – not only of the rubber but of the nylon in the cord. Moreover, another potential hazard lay in tyre growth. The 600 x 18 Firestones would grow about 1.5 inches at 375 mph – too much for the swinging arm, and for comfort. Don Vesco is not interested in testing a tyre's ability to hold air pressure at speeds in excess of 400 mph.

There's another danger in using pneumatic tyres at Bonneville, and a matter that is a weighty problem for Gregg Morgan and his team at the Salt Lake District Office of the BLM. When an engine blows up, it seeds the course with shrapnel, sometimes for miles. Bits of shattered engine casing, jagged rod pieces and severed, rusting bolts wait in hiding to sabotage 100 psi tyres. And when a 100 psi balloon tyre pops, you get one hell of a speed wobble   possibly your last.

What do you do when you can't get tyres? If you're Vesco, you ride on the rims ...

Pioneered by Bill Fredrick of *SMI Motivator* and *Budweiser Rocket* fame, solid forged aluminium wheels are now adopted by just about all land speed record contenders, all of whom claim to be the first to use this revolutionary new concept in high-speed tyre design.

Machined from forged 7075 aluminium-alloy rings, x-ray inspected, sonic tested and heat treated, Vesco's rubberless hoops bolt to quarter-inch-thick

The scattered remains of Sky-Tracker I after a high-speed tumble at Bonneville in 1985. The vehicle is currently being rebuilt for an all-out assualt on the wheel-driven record.

aluminium discs. Their contours were shaped on a giant electronic tracer lathe from the cross-section of a road racing slick.

The strongest argument against all-metal wheels centres are their lack of self-aligning torque. The corded tyre casing of a pneumatic tyre produces this wonderful phenomenon. When the front tyre of a motorcycle loses contact with the running surface momentarily and then contacts the surface with the wheel pointed off the direction of travel, the contact patch instantly squirms into alignment with the true path of the speeding motorcycle. The tyre casing distorts and produces a torque that pulls the wheel into alignment with the direction of travel. At speeds over 30 mph, self-aligning torque lends much stability to a motorcycle, to say nothing of speeds over 300 mph. Vesco argues that a speed wobble at 300 mph is nearly impossible to correct anyway, so ...

Thirteen hundred pounds and Don's survival will be riding on these 'tyres'. What works is simply what Vesco makes work. If he rode on hoops made from man-hole covers, he'd probably figure a way to make them go at 400 mph.

Vesco conceived several concepts for traction such as an epoxy and abrasive paint mix; steel studs such as ice racers use; and machined grooves similar to standard tyre tread. Machining grooves into the contact surfaces proved to be the most logical and certainly the safest answer for the front tyres. Forces at speeds in excess of 400 mph could split the studs like bullets, which might then make them puncture the fuel tank or radiators or foul the braking-parachutes, not to mention the rear pneumatic tyres. The paint stands ready should the groove tread slip.

Ribbed with 0.040 inch deep grooves, the two, closely paired 23-inch diameter front wheels steer, but not in the conventional way. The centre-steering hub, borrowed from the 300 mph streamliner, has a central kingpin; the centreline of the steering stem exactly intersects the centreline of the axle. This gives about eight inches of trail depending on what angle the kingpin is set at. Vesco will run with his tried-and-proven hub, but a new hub, with the kingpin offset behind the axle providing trail closer to motorcycle standards, waits to be tested. Although this trail dimension is important, Vesco feels that adjustments to kingpin rake more drastically affect high-speed handling.

Technically a six-wheeler, the Offenhauser powered vehicle looks little different from Vesco's motorcycle streamliners ... the only major difference is that there are two, 25 inch diameter rear wheels bolted together at the back ... in addition to the closely paired alloy front wheels, there are two,

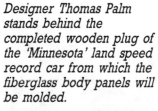

Designer Thomas Palm stands behind the completed wooden plug of the 'Minnesota' land speed record car from which the fiberglass body panels will be molded.

*Craig Breedlove and the car with which he aims to regain the World Land Speed Record for the United States.
The* Spirit of America III - Sonic II. *A ferocious 60,000 horsepower, pressure fed, bio-propellant rocket car.*

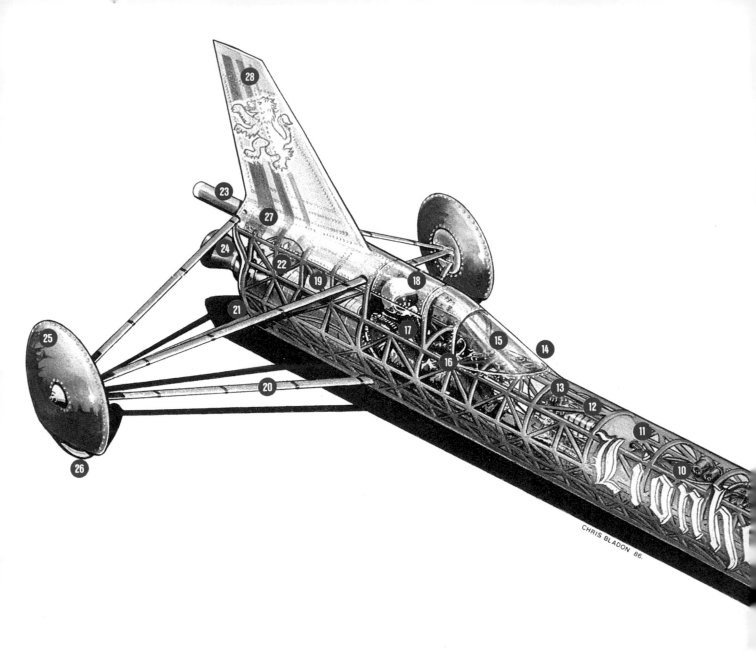

CHRIS BLADON 86.

Lionheart: *Britain's attempt to exceed the speed of sound.*

1. Air cylinder
2. On board fire fighting system
3. Propellant regulator valve
4. Front wheels. 3 x 30 in
5. Driver-controlled horizontal canard fins
6. Hydrogen peroxide propellant tank
7. Liquid hydrogen tank
8. Liquid oxygen oxidiser tank
9. Liquid oxygen fill/drain disconnect
10. Axial instrumentation funnel
11. Propellant tank pressurization line
12. Increased-power hydraulic servo controls
13. Discrete-component circuitry
14. Instrumentation and propulsion system display
15. Sierracin windscreen
16. 'Butterfly' steering wheel
17. Fire resistant suit with umbilical attachment facility
18. GEC Lexan full-pressure helmet with life support
19. Combustion chamber
20. Torsional flexing struts
21. Vernier
22. Romatec V4 hydrogen peroxide rocket engine
23. Raytheon AIM-7F solid-state 'Sparrow' missile booster engine
24. Expansion nozzle
25. Aerodynamic wheel fairing
26. Rear wheels. 3 x 32 in
27. Deist drag chute housing
28. Fixed vertical stabilizer

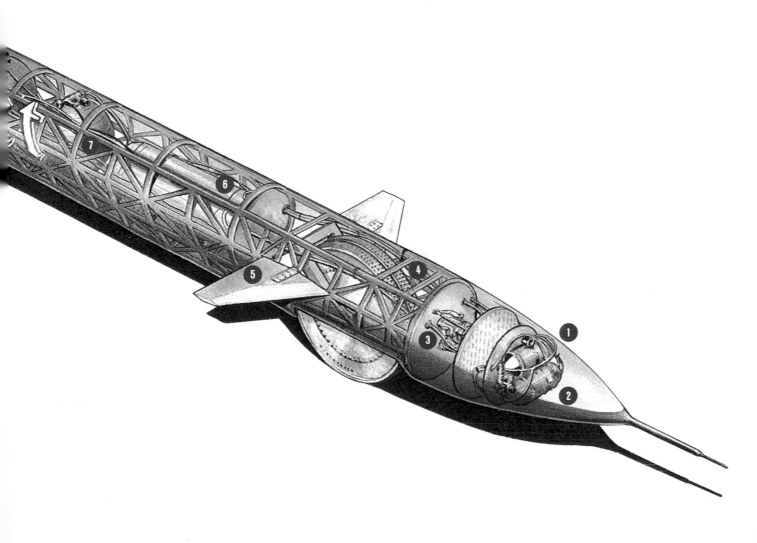

A study in attention ... Don Vesco and Sky Tracker I.

The turbocharged 3500cc Offenhauser engine of Sky-Tracker I.

On 28 August 1978, Don Vesco of Temecula, California, became the world's fastest man on two wheels, averaging 318.598 mph (512.732 kph) in the twin Kawasaki KZ, 1000 cc-engined streamliner Lightning Bolt.

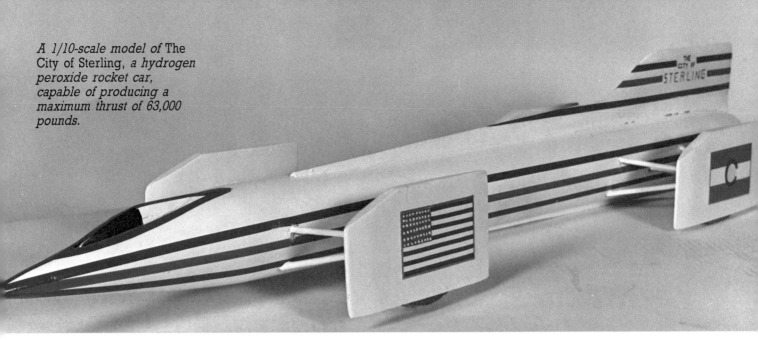

A 1/10-scale model of The City of Sterling, *a hydrogen peroxide rocket car, capable of producing a maximum thrust of 63,000 pounds.*

One of seven 6,500 lb thrust, hydrogen peroxide rocket units that will power The City of Sterling.

The stainless steel hydrogen peroxide tank already in central situ above three of the carbon steel nitrogen oxidization tanks carefully mounted within the spherical air frame of The City of Sterling *rocket car.*

The construction of the wooden plug of the Minnesota land speed record car.

Thomas Palm with the completed full scale engineering mockup of the General Electric T-58 turbine engine that will power the 'Minnesota'.

Powered by two 860 bhp Avco Lycoming T53-L gas turbines. Ermie and Marvin Immerso's Thunderbird II *is but a variation on their previous cars entered for the race for the wheel-driven record.*

Ernie and Marvin Immerso's Thunderbird Turbine *at Bonneville in 1977. A four-wheel drive streamliner, fitted with two 860bhp Avco Lycoming T53-L gas turbines.*

Driver, Ken Goodman and the Indy Challenger.

18 inch diameter, static stabilizing wheels protruding from the streamliner, slightly aft of the driver cockpit,

"There's nothing bizarre about a streamliner's handling," says Vesco, "other than in the proportions". Strapped in his claustrophobic cockpit by seat belts, shoulder harness and wrist restraints, Vesco can't apply subtle body lean to help maintain balance. Have you ever tried to ride a bike this way?

A 3 foot tall motorcycle might seem tiny, but one that's over 20 feet long is like a billboard to a wispy crosswind. The slightest breeze blowing against a streamliner's fuselage, tries to pivot the body around the tyre's contact patch – much the same as it would to a normal bike. Counter-steering input corrects this problem, but with no body lean (and no self-aligning torque) a gust can cause high-speed weaving (or skid) that human reflexes can't correct. Vesco doesn't like to run in breezes over five or eight mph, and neither does Britain's Alex Macfadzean, who miraculously survived a 170 mph crash in pursuit of the British 500 cc Motorcycle Land Speed Record.

Macfadzean, 40, was testing the 500 cc Suzuki-powered streamliner *Penetrator* at Bruntingthorpe Proving grounds, a former U.S. Air Force Base near Leicester, in preparation for an assault on the record when a crosswind caught the machine and it veered out of control and onto a grass verge where it overturned several times before coming to a halt. Luckily for Alex he survived to tell the tale with only minor neck and facial injuries.

Don't expect to see any tall dorsal fins on *Sky-Tracker I*. It was once considered essential to fit a tail fin to aid directional stability; but over the years Vesco has had experience with several sizes and shapes of fins – all bad. He believes a high-speed motorcycle needs the aerodynamics of a bullet.

Shortly after noon, on 22 August 1985, almost seven years to the day he established the World Land Speed Record in the streamliner's motorcycle predecessor, Vesco launched the six-wheeler down the Bonneville speedway, approaching the timing traps at a staggering 299 mph. The port stabilizer wheel hit a salt buckle and rolled the streamliner, sending the vehicle and its intrepid driver tumbling down the course for almost a quarter of a mile. The steamliner was almost a write-off, but Don emerged from the wreckage unscathed.

Vesco and brother, Rick are currently rebuilding the machine for yet another assault on the Summers Brothers' record in 1986 in a project appropriately named 'Project 425 mph'.

Now he waits for his 400 mph future, with a machine that's simply one-third science, one-third faith, and three-thirds pure Vesco.

'Project 1000 ~ The City of Sterling' ~ Motive for a Mission

One man's concern for the needs of young, handicapped and retarded children living under difficult circumstances in north eastern Colorado, has inspired the biggest single sponsorship appeal ever undertaken in the quest for the World Land Speed Record.

Project 1000 was conceived in 1979 by 45-year-old Bill Gaynor of

Atwood, Colorado, as a method of establishing a new land speed record with a rocket-powered vehicle, *The City of Sterling*.

Inaugurated as a three goal initiative, the primary objective of Project 1000 is to use the success of *The City of Sterling* as a fund raising vehicle to establish a foundation which will continually administer to the needs of handicapped and retarded children under the age of 21. It is envisaged that through the promotional medium of the project, sufficient funds will be raised to build a permanent facility in Sterling, Colorado, which will provide free the very finest technological, medical and therapeutic care available for the needs of these unfortunate children. With proper support and growth, the boundaries will be ever increasing and could eventually encompass a nationwide programme throughout the United States. Indeed, 50 per cent of the gross income received in the event of the success of *The City of Sterling* establishing a new World Land Speed Record will be used for these purposes.

The second goal of Project 1000, has been to establish a foundation which will administer financial and practical support to families in Bill Gaynor's local community of Logan County, Colorado, who have been the unfortunate victims of a catastrophy; such as a terminally ill child or close relative, a major fire or similar mishap. Twenty per cent of the gross income from the project will be allocated to goal two, with any annual surplus from this fund being credited to the primary goal.

The third and final goal of the project is based on the foundation of a trust fund, providing essential educational assistance to local and County students at the discretion of the Project 1000 Board of Directors. Fifteen per cent of the gross income will be allocated to goal three, and again, any surplus will be added to the funds of goal one. The remaining 15 per cent of income will be distributed at the discretion of Bill Gaynor and his Board of Directors.

The aerodynamic design applied to *The City of Sterling* is without precedent in the field of land speed engineering, though visual comparison with any earlier land speed record vehicle might perhaps suggest a loose resemblance to the jet-powered *Flying Caduceus*.

The vehicle, 42 feet 8 inches in length and 7 feet 6 inches high at the top of the vertical tail-fin, has been designed to an aerodynamic specification that falls in the range from high subsonic to low supersonic. A spherical fuselage has been adapted as the area rule for transonic flow and dissipation of pressure and boundary-layer build-up approaching supersonic speeds.

Design considerations for the vehicle have led to the centre of pressure being located aft of the centre of gravity, with the nose dropped 6 inches from the centre line. As speed increases, the fuel load moves towards the rear of the vehicle, the resultant downforce on the nose is increased due to the inclined plane effect, maintaining the relative centre of gravity at the point of actual centre of gravity.

Tyres for the speeds Bill Gaynor and his team are contemplating are unobtainable, so the vehicle will ride on four solid forged aluminium wheels with a 'vee' shaped tread and keel to stop side-slipping.

Over each front and rear suspension, between the fuselage and wheel fairings, is a supersonic aerofoil, adjustable to either a positive or negative angle of attack to eliminate flight characteristics and to compensate wheel loading dictated by telemetry readings fed to a computer via strain gauges on the suspension.

The business end. A complement of seven 6,500 lb thrust units are mounted in the tail of the vehicle.

The driver-controlled pneumatic air-brakes on the remarkable The City of Sterling.

The driver's cockpit is located forward of the propellant tanks and multiple rocket engines, with steering aerodynamically-operated through hydraulic spoilers on the nose of the vehicle.

For the engine, Gaynor has come up with a hybrid system comprising a complement of 7 – 6,500 lb thrust hydrogen peroxide units, producing a combined maximum horsepower of 121,278. All performance items are based on 70 per cent concentrated hydrogen peroxide. The concentration can be upgraded to 90 per cent, yielding increased thrust. Upgrading can be accomplished without any modifications to the vehicle or changes in pressure settings. This will increase the total thrust from 45,000 lb to 63,000 lb.

At the wheel of *The City of Sterling,* Bill Gaynor will be able to fire any number of engines from 1 to 7, and no matter how many are ignited, the propulsion configuration is such that the centre line of thrust will be balanced along the centre line of the vehicle. The control system has been engineered to enable the engine ignition sequence to be fired in stages, from one to three, the operation of which can be controlled by the driver or a computer.

The computer is of Hewlett-Packard design, and is programmed to monitor telemetry and essentially control the vehicle, although the driver has manual over-ride on all inboard control functions, if desired.

The two-phase braking system conceived for the vehicle is based on the incorporation of two, 4 foot square air-brake panels hinged flush, one on each side of the vertical tail fin, operated by torque-limited servo 'linear drive', with a maximum deflection when fully opened of 60 degrees, which can be driver-controlled or computer-operated.

In addition, Gaynor has incorporated a revolutionary concept in the design of the parachute braking system. While the basic principle is conventional tube-loaded, the drogue is pyrotechnically activated, and can be fired manually or by computer. The spent chute is released by crewmen, the empty tube removed and a new pre-loaded tube is installed and hooked up, enabling easy handling and allowing a quick turn-round for the return run.

Bill Gaynor was born on 2 June 1940, in Sterling, Colorado, and was raised on a farm in Atwood, Colorado. He graduated from Sterling High School in 1958, and served in the United States Marine Corps until 1962. Following this Bill had a variety of jobs in Colorado as a heavy equipment operator and truck driver, and returning to Sterling in 1963, he worked as a teller at Security State Bank, and was a part-time student at North Eastern Junior College. He received his AAS degree in 1967, and then entered Embry-Riddle Aeronautical Institute, Daytona Beach, Florida. After earning his degree in aeronautical engineering, Bill taught algebra, calculas, differential equations, subsonic aerodynamics, wind tunnel disciplines and aircraft design at the Institute.

For three years, Bill was with Midrex Division of Midland Ross Corporation as Manager of Engineering Operation, and was in charge of construction and 'start-up' operations on many projects in the United States, Germany, Sweden and Africa. It was at this time that he began to develop a talent for innovative solutions to all types of problems, ranging from mechanical to electrical to process flow and control. Primarily, these were highly complex iron ore reduction plants, and while in Germany he began to design a car which could break the sound barrier.

From 1973 to 1976, Bill had returned to Sterling, Colorado, and was appointed Executive Vice President of the Ceres Ecology Corporation, a company devoted to the design, research, development and construction of manure processing plants. In this capacity, Bill's talent as a practical and innovative engineer really came to the surface. Much of the processing equipment had to be invented and Bill is now the holder of mechanical and process patents. Bill worked on projects in America, Mexico, France, South Africa and Brazil. In less than two years he became a Corporate Vice President, and continued with Ceres until 1979.

During the next year, Bill was to become Vice President and Engineer for Valley Dehydrating Co., Inc., Atwood, Colorado, and was involved in the construction and operation of an experimental proxan plant. During the one year contract Bill had with Valley Dehydrating, he was involved with U.S. Department of Energy engineers in the development of new process and equipment specifications for the proxan process. However, his interest in developing a potential supersonic car compelled him to leave the company, and he spent the next six months completing the design of *The City of Sterling* rocket powered vehicle.

From December 1980 to November 1981, Bill served as Vice President of Business Development at Security State Bank in Sterling, Colorado.

Because of Bill's broad knowledge of light to heavy industry and his ability to present projections and facts in a professional manner, he was assigned the task of bringing new industry to Sterling, Colorado. He rose to the challenge and acquired Evans Railcar which employs 70 people and Nichols Tillage Tools, employers of 65 people. In 1981, he moved to Nichols Tillage Tools and now acts as Vice President of Engineering. Bill's chief role with Nichols is in plant automation. To this day he is building robots to handle one of the more difficult material handling problems.

Bill and Denise Gaynor have three children and have made their home in Atwood, Colorado, at the site where *The City of Sterling* is currently being built. Denise is a very active member of the Project 1000 Team, acting as Corporate Secretary.

Presently, there are 21 members on the Project 1000 Team. Each person has specific responsibilities with regard to construction, engineering evaluation and the planned record attempt. The team is under Bill Gaynor's supervision, and in addition to designing and engineering the car, he will drive it.

The team is divided into an Operational Team, led by Crew Chief Tom Luckey of Sterling, Colorado. Tom was one of Gaynor's first choices for the Project 1000 Team because of his experience and ability to construct equipment to fine tolerances, coupled with a diverse background in metals and metal fabrication. The Organizational Team is headed by Richard Kloberdanz. It was Rich's ability to adopt sound management techniques in a time of economic instability and his ability to handle complex mechanical problems in practical ways that impressed Gaynor.

In tandem with the three goal initiative of the project, Bill Gaynor and his team plan to launch Project 1000 in three phases. Phase 1, to establish a new World Land Speed Record by breaking the existing record of 633.468 mph (1019.465 kph), set by Richard Noble in *Thrust 2* on 4 October 1983; Phase 2, to establish a new World Land Speed Record above the speed of sound; and finally, Phase 3, to establish a new World Land Speed Record at a speed in excess of 1,000 mph.

Bill Gaynor plans his attempt on Noble's record in the Autumn of 1987 at the Roach Dry Lake, although he is currently exploring the possibility of running *The City of Sterling* on the Alvord Desert, Oregon, a venue suggested to Gaynor by the author.

Basic satisfaction of a method to attain the goals of Project 1000 is through the medium of sponsorship of the car and associated costs necessary in the assault on the World Land Speed Record. Income from the

The nose section of the vehicle takes on a sleek and purposeful form.

sale of television rights, product endorsements, product development rights and other miscellaneous income associated with Project 1000 will provide the necessary funds to enable the accomplishment of their major goals.

In the United States, Project 1000 is becoming a household name, with a growing national audience interested in the attempt by a man to travel on land at a speed in excess of 1,000 mph. Moreover, the direct relationship of Project 1000 with goals of assisting young handicapped and retarded children has increased the popularity of the marketing efforts of Bill Gaynor and his team.

Many businesses, both local and national, have already joined the growing list of contributors by supplying services, materials, components, and other items of logistic support to Project 1000. There is naturally a great pride in participating in a project with such a worthy cause.

The construction of *The City of Sterling* is progressing at a rapid pace, because of a dedicated team of human beings who have a common desire to help the young of America, and who have faith in the objectives of their project. This is a team who willingly offer their talent, knowledge, experience and ability to make it successful. At times, progress must have seemed slow, and solutions to problems not always easy or immediately at hand, but the team found the answers together. They have shared every moment helping each other build the car to Bill's exacting design.

For Bill Gaynor and his team, Project 1000 is a living dream. A dream that began in November 1979 and one that will continue throughout their lifetime and beyond.

The Minnesota Land Speed Record Project

As a youngster growing up in the North Star State of Minnesota, Thomas Palm dreamed of driving cars faster than anyone else.

"I have always had a great interest in jet and rocket cars. All through High School I was working on cars, changing engines, tuning them up, doing a little street racing and just generally having a good time," he recalls. But how many get the chance to foster their dreams and ambitions into a workable project?

For 26-year-old Thomas Palm and his life-long friend and associate, Paul Vickroy, their childhood dreams have emerged from a chrysalis of passion to a 20th century adventure in the form of The Minnesota Land Speed Record Project.

The story began in the summer of '77. Tom and Paul were fresh out of High School and enjoying a holiday before taking up their chosen careers. It was during this time that they began discussing building the 'ultimate' car – a twin jet-engined land speed record car.

Tom produced some rough drawings of the car and even built a small rocket-propelled model of the thing, but the experiment was short-lived. During one 'fire-up', the model became airborne and came down with a nose-crunching thud. So much for rocket cars!

In September 1977, Tom joined the US Air Force, and served as a Titan II missile crew chief stationed in Texas and Kansas. During his four years in the Air Force, the design of their jet car progressed. "Hours and hours of research into jet engines, aerodynamics, other LSR cars and race car chassis design were well spent in my opinion, although some folk thought I might be a little crazy designing a jet car."

While Tom was in the Air Force, Paul had continued with his chosen job as an auto mechanic, now working full time with his father. But it wasn't until Tom left the Air Force that things really began to develop. During his last year in service, he heard about the annual Bonneville Speed Week races, and at about the same time, happened across a small article on Britain's LSR project, Thrust 2 in *Popular Mechanics* magazine which stimulated his interest even more. Without further ado he made plans to visit relatives on the West Coast and to stop at the famed salt flats to see what Speed Week was all about. "I remember parking across the street from the State Line Casino in Wendover about midnight, then waking up to the Utah sun glaring in my eyes. "The first thing I did, even before eating or going to the bathroom, was to head down to the salt flats ... Ah! the famous Salt Flats ... This was it. Mecca! The home to the fastest cars in the world. To say I was in heaven was an understatement ... I tasted it; yep, it's salt all right."

They were racing everything imaginable at Bonneville that season, but it was a poster of Thrust 2 adorning the side of a BLM (Bureau of Land Management) trailer that caught Tom's eye. There was the car he had read about in *Popular Mechanics,* on its way to Bonneville for an attack on the World Land Speed Record right after Speed Week. By this time, Tom had been joined by Paul and his new bride Debbie. "I looked at Paul and said 'we have to find out more about this situation,' so we knocked on the door of the trailer and introduced ourselves to Gregg Morgan, the BLM Outdoor Recreation Planner. At first we didn't mention anything about our own project to him so he probably thought we were just curious about Thrust 2."

"Then came a moment I will never forget," he recalls. "I took Paul to one side and said, 'should I tell him?' Paul shook his head 'yes' and I started telling Gregg about 'The Minnesota Land Speed Record Project'. Before this, we really didn't talk to too many people about the project because it was too far out or unbelievable for most people to believe in what we wanted to do – But not Gregg! I began by showing him some of the drawings I had done of the car. Needless to say he was impressed. He said he wanted to tell Eddie Elsom about our project, since he was the Operations Director for Thrust and he would be here later in the week. Just the thought of meeting the Thrust 2 team was overwhelming."

By the end of the week, Paul and Debbie had to leave Bonneville since they only had a week of their holiday left, and wanted to head north before making their way home to Brooklyn Center, Minnesota. If only they had stayed a day longer. The Thrust 2 entourage wheeled in the very next day. The entire caravan made their way through town and parked in one of the old abandoned hangars at Wendover Air Force Base, now just the local airport. "I hung around a little watching and listening to the team members and the spectators. I talked to a few people who wanted to know a little more about the car and by that time I practically knew all about Thrust 2 from listening to the team and reading the newsletters Gregg had copies of. One person even asked if I was on the team. Then Gregg introduced me to Eddie Elsom, Gordon Flux, Ron Benton, John Ackroyd and Brian Ball. I was helping a little, taking a few boxes of components out of the Ford van that had broken down, when Gordon Flux asked me if I could take apart a Ford rear axle. I said I had never done it before, but would give it my best shot." By this time the rest of the team were either too tired from the long haul through Nevada or were busy unpacking things to be able to work on the van. Thomas Palm had suddenly realised he was part of the Thrust 2 working crew. "I dove under that van and began to rip and tear into the axle. Before long I was covered in dirt and grease, but I didn't mind. Hell, I was working on a truck used for Project Thrust."

Toward evening, Eddie Elsom asked Tom if he would like to stay in the hangar during the night to watch over the car. By that time they knew they could trust him, since he had taken by far the greatest interest in the car and project out of just about all the people the Thrust team had met in Wendover. So by nightfall, the doors of the hangar were closed till they were only about ten feet open. Tom drove his car in front of the narrow opening and parked it there for the night.

"That night was truly a night to remember. Although no people showed up, that hangar seemed alive. The wind was blowing just enough to make the place creak and groan from every little beam and brace. I even got up three times to see if anyone or anything was making the noise from the back of the hangar. I guess I did such a bang-up job that Eddie Elsom asked me if I would spend the next night doing the same thing, since they wouldn't be able to get on to the salt till the next day. So I did."

Paul Vickroy and Thomas Palm in front of wooden plug full scale mock up of the Minnesota LSR car.

The following day the whole Thrust 2 convoy drove out to the salt flats and set up camp. Tom was asked if he would like to share the motorhome at night for security with Charles Noble, Richard's brother and Bob Pakes the photographer, his reply was obvious ... "I said sure; the rest of the night we spent reading articles about the project in *Hot Rod* magazine written by Peter Holthusen, and chronicled in the British motorsport newspaper *Motoring News* by David Tremayne.

After Thrust 2 broke the World Land Speed Record, Tom returned to Minnesota with a wealth of practical experience gained through his involvement with the project, but what he lacked was pure Bonneville racing experience before anyone would take their jet car project seriously. So he began researching vehicles and aerodynamics to evaluate a design concept that had been proven and that could be modified to suit their needs. That was when Tom came across an article on the Volkswagen ARVW diesel car. They had found what they were looking for. A forward driver position, rear engine, and impressively aerodynamic. They had the basic shape and then began designing a simple chassis that would accommodate petrol engines, either single or tandem. But they still felt that they wanted to build something different.

It was on their way to a car show in Eden Prairie, Minnesota that Tom and Paul hit upon their powerplant. "Both Paul and I had seen an article on Don Garlits' turbine-engined dragster and were quite impressed by the power of such a light engine. On the way down I began talking of how we needed something unique," Tom recalls, "something that had not been done in this state yet. Then it hit us. We must have both thought of it at the same time. We looked at each other and smiled ... A Turbine Car! How outrageous! How different! How do you make one? So by the weekend, I had drawn out a rough idea of what would later become the Minnesota wheel-driven LSR car."

That was three years ago, In the meantime, the design of their car has steadily progressed and they have continued to accumulate data on the development and design of high speed cars. The turning point for the project came when Thomas Palm found a copy of a paper written for the American Society of Automotive Engineers by the man who had helped Bob and Bill Summers design the remarkable *Goldenrod*. The paper was exactly what they needed.

"After reading the paper some three or four times I decided to compare our car with the *Goldenrod*. I used the formula and figures in the paper and came up with some surprising results," he recalls. "With a drag estimate of 0.18, which from the wind tunnel testing of a $1/10$ scale balsawood model of the car would later prove to be uncannily accurate, I found that with 1,400 horsepower available from our engine, our car had a good chance of breaking 450 mph. What we needed now was some accurate wind tunnel data on a model of the car and an accurate idea of the engine size to help us design the drive train and chassis."

The design of their car was further refined and was beginning to emerge as a serious challenger to the 20-year-old wheel-driven Land Speed Record of 409.277 mph (658.636 kph) set by Bob Summers at the wheel of the *Goldenrod* on 12 November, 1965.

Tom made hundreds of telephone calls around the United States to try to get as much information as possible on the T-58 turbine engine and related high technology components. That led him to Tim Arfons, son of veteran LSR driver Art Arfons, for the engine, and to Iowa State University and Dr

William James, head of the Aerospace Engineering Department, for the vital wind tunnel testing. It was during this time that Tom and Paul joined the World Speed Record Association in Studio City, California, and enrolled the 'Minnesota Land Speed Record Project' with Gary Baim who runs the WSRA from a suite of offices on Ventura Boulevard.

Over the next couple of months Tom spent a great deal of time talking over their project proposals with Tim Arfons and Dr James, and finally set a date for the wind tunnel testing of 12 January 1985.

Shortly after the completion of the tunnel tests Tom made his way to Akron, Ohio to visit Tim and Art Arfons. "I arrived at the Arfons' Pickle Road workshop at around 10.00 am. I met Tim first, then was shown around the shop. What I had come for was to get the dimensions of a T-58 engine, so a full scale engineering mock-up could be made to assist in designing the chassis and drive train. So I sat down and began to measure, making sketches as I went, then dimensioning each one. By two o'clock I was done. I then met Art Arfons for the first time. A super guy! Real down to earth and not at all like some of the other LSR car drivers one meets."

After his return from Akron, Tom began to develop the engine and build a full-scale mock-up of the T-58 turbine, then, with the help of Paul Vickroy, started the layout of the chassis and drive train.

The 'Minnesota Land Speed Record Project' reached three milestones over the next few months. The first was the design and construction of the wooden plug from which the fibreglass body moulds will be made. After many hours of drawing the sectional views of the car, Tom began cutting, glueing and nailing the plywood together. The second milestone was the completion of a full scale mock-up of the General Electric T-58 turbine engine, which "impressed the heck out of Tim Arfons when he saw it for the first time", Tom recalls. This engine, complete with engine front mounting points and rear power turbine coupler is being used for the design of the steel tube space frame, front suspension and drive train systems, until they have raised enough capital to buy the real thing.

The third, and certainly not the least important, of the milestones was the news that Bill Summers has agreed to supply them with some of the drive train components. "He is very interested in our project, and has no second thoughts on helping someone beat their long-standing record," Tom recently told me; and knowing the Summers Brothers as I do, this gesture is not at all surprising, in the competitive, yet true team spirit of the enterprising land speed record industry.

The 'Minnesota Land Speed Record Project' is the first in a series of record breaking cars being designed and built by V.P. Research Inc., with the aim of breaking the existing wheel-driven Land Speed Record. Due to be completed in 1986, the 23 foot long streamliner should be capable of attaining speeds in excess of 450 mph, and will actually be attempting to break two existing world records. The first being the wheel-driven record, and the second being the turbine-driven record of 403.10 mph (648.728 kph) set by Donald Campbell at Lake Eyre in 1964 with the *Bluebird-Proteus.* The primary objective of the Minnesota LSR Project however, is to utilize all available resources to build the World's fastest wheel-driven car, and to date no less than seven sponsors have come forward with support. As yet, it is not sure who will drive the car, but one thing that is sure, is that the dedication and professional approach of Thomas Palm and Paul Vickroy will lead them to eventual success in their quest for the World Land Speed Record for wheel-driven vehicles.

```
┌─────────────────────────────────────────────────────────────────┐
│                    'Minnesota LSR Project'                        │
│  Type:                    Mid Engine, Four-Wheel-Drive, Single    │
│                           Passenger, Wheel-driven LSR Car         │
│  Structure:               Steel Tubing Space Frame with           │
│                           Aluminium Inner Panels, Stainless Steel │
│                           Firewalls, and Kevlar Body Panels       │
│                                                                   │
│  Engine:                                                          │
│  Type:                    General Electric T58 Jet Turbine        │
│  Horsepower:              1,400 shp                               │
│  With Water/Alcohol Injection:   1,700 shp                       │
│  Length:                  59 in                                  │
│  Weight:                  320 lb                                 │
│  Dimensions:                                                     │
│  Length:                  23ft 3in                              │
│  Width:                   38in                                 │
│  Height:                  39in                                │
│  Wheelbase:               165in                               │
│  Track F/R                28in/31in                           │
│  Ground clearance F/R:    3in/4in                             │
│  Aerodynamic Drag Coefficient:   .110                         │
│  Estimated Weight:        3,000 lb                            │
│  Estimated Top Speed      500 mph                            │
└─────────────────────────────────────────────────────────────────┘
```

'Thunderbird II'- Variation on a Theme

On the lower slopes of speed, velocity is often thought of as a sensory delicacy. A thrill. A hedonistic treat, a euphoric rush, to be experienced at considerable expense and risk. For veteran dry lakes' tycoon Ermie Immerso, the risks have been there, but so has the wealth to support the expense.

Ermie Immerso is a Southern Californian millionaire who has spent the best part of 40 years building, and often driving, his exotic racing machines, and cementing new speed records in record-breaking passes at Bonneville and on the vast dry lakes of the Mojave Desert.

His prosperous business in the sub-tropical community of Rancho Dominguez, near Compton, California, develops and manufactures high-performance equipment for endurance, racing and record cars. His first successful vehicles to appear on the salt stage were the *Lakester's,* which were built around surplus Second World War plastic fuel 'belly' tanks from USAF fighter planes such as the Curtiss P-40 and the versatile North American P-51 Mustang, which were used as lightweight bodies for small capacity Class 'A' record breakers. The most celebrated of Immerso's 'A' jobs was the *Kraft Auto Special,* powered by two blown Chryslers, with a combined horsepower rating of 900. Unique was the word for the twin blower setup on this vehicle. With the all aluminium panelling removed, two flywheel chain-driven blowers on each side of the driver's compartment come into full view, along with the batteries, full tanks and other sundry automotive components that accompanies a *Lakester* driver down the long black 'oiled' line of the Bonneville Speedway.

Altogether, Immerso has established 15 US National speed records at Bonneville. One of the most memorable cars was the *Dean Van Lines Special* which was fitted with a potent Lincoln V8 engine with a displacement of 430 cu in. This vehicle was followed by what was to be the first in a series of potential record breakers adopting the *Thunderbird* livery. Powered by four Ford V8s, the latest Immerso racing machine went on to pull crowds of fascinated speed 'groupies' to the magnet of the 1962-64 Bonneville Nationals.

In September 1976, Ermie and Marvin Immerso turned up on the salt with what appeared to be the original *Thunderbird,* save for the incorporation of a power-plant consisting of two gas turbines. The streamliner, appropriately dubbed the *Thunderbird Turbine,* still retained the now familiar venerated emblem of the totemic *Thunderbird.* In the mythology of some North American Indians, thunder, lightning and rain are personified as a huge bird ... the Thunderbird. The latest project to emerge from the stable of Ermie Immerso Enterprises Inc. is *Thunderbird II.* Engineered and designed by Ermie, Marvin Immerso and Dean Moon, this current project started four years ago, and is basically a variation on a theme of the earlier *Thunderbird Turbine,* a four-wheel drive streamliner, fitted with two 860 bhp Avco Lycoming T53-L gas turbines, taken from surplus US Army Hughey helicopters, that were originally installed in the *Thunderbird Turbine,* which Marvin drove at Bonneville in 1977 to a two-way average speed of 264.90 mph (426.224 kph).

Unfortunately, on a later run through the mile, another driver, who shall remain nameless, completely wrecked the car; leaving only himself and the two turbine engines worthy of salvage.

Designed to attain 500 mph, *Thunderbird II* is set to chase the 20-year-old wheel-driven Land Speed Record.

The two turbines of *Thunderbird II* are mounted side-by-side, the left-hand Lycoming driving the front wheels and the right-hand one, the rear wheels, coupled by a synchronizing differential. A single tail fin acts as a stabilizer and to counteract the tendency to yaw, with the driver's cockpit blending into its lower, leading edge.

The streamlined vehicle, which weighs in at approximately 5,000 lb, is now shod with custom-built Mickey Thompson high-speed tyres. Because of the sophisticated Immerso/Moon designed synchronized differential and the complicated arrangement of the coupling, the car will be subjected to a lengthy series of static evaluation and low speed 'shake-down' trials before an attempt is made on the Summers' long-standing record. Indeed, it is this complicated arrangement that has led many sceptics of Immerso's latest venture to doubt the ability of the car attaining the required speeds, however willing its wealthy owner/driver.

Ermie Immerso plans to attack the record in 1986, by which time he will be 62 years old, and the famed Bonneville course will once again see a *Thunderbird* go for it!

Mike Spitzer's 'Indy Challenger' - Strange but True

Veteran drag racing chassis builder Mike Spitzer is planning an assault on Bob Summers' wheel-driven Land Speed Record from his renowned

Indianapolis based race car facility on East 30th Street.

At a press conference at this year's California Speed & Performance Show in Indianapolis, Spitzer announced his intention to pursue the land speed record with a conventional piston-powered car dubbed the Indy Challenger.

Engineered and designed by Mike and Dean Spitzer, at thirty-six feet long and just 19 inches wide at the rear, the vehicle is powered by four Chevrolet aluminium small block V8 engines mounted in line and coupled in pairs, the front pair are fuel injected and drive the front wheels, and the rear engines are blown, driving the rear wheels. The displacement of each engine is 400 cu in, with an estimated combined 2,900 bhp produced by all four engines at 8,200 rpm. The 5400-pound streamliner is also equipped with unique rear-end drive units and dual three-speed planetary type transmissions, custom-built by the Chicago-based, Strange Engineering

Mike Spitzer's 2,900 horsepower Indy Challenger *with which he plans to attack Bob Summers' long standing wheel-driven Land Speed Record of 409.277 mph (658.636 kph).*

concern, who were quick to remark; "Spitzer's *Indy Challenger* is Team Strange's strangest race car yet."

The front engines are not supercharged because the solid forged aluminium wheels at the front of the vehicle cannot handle the additional horsepower when the nose starts to lift at speeds in excess of 400 mph. All four engines feature timed injection and computerized monitoring and control, which will prove invaluable during the record runs.

Spitzer and his driver, Ken Goodman have explored several possible sites for their attempt on the 20-year-old wheel-driven record, including a 22-mile graded stretch of Lake Eyre, near Muloorina in Australia, made famous by Donald Campbell in his record-breaking pass in July 1964, at the wheel of the *Bluebird-Proteus*. The conditions at Bonneville over the past four years have been relatively poor for speed trials, although 1985 saw the return of the salt to its true and purposeful form. Indeed, Gregg Morgan, the US Bureau of Land Management Outdoor Recreation Planner for the Salt Lake area, recently completed a survey of a 44,000 acre salt plain in preparation for the 1985 Bonneville Nationals, and told me the salt was in "great condition; the best it's been for years".

Spitzer and Goodman plan a series of low speed 'shake-down' runs on either Winnemucca Dry Lake, north of Reno, Nevada or the immense Black Rock Desert, the chosen venue for Richard Nobles' successful 1983 mission to regain the World Land Speed Record, "For Britain and the Hell of It". Whilst the possibility of running the *Indy Challenger* in Australia has indeed been explored, the logistics of mounting such a venture outside of the United States would present the project with an unnecessary burden, when there is an abundance of potential land speed venues within a 1,000-mile radius of the team's Indianapolis headquarters. Moreover, if the conditions at Bonneville remain stable in 1986, the famed Salt Flats could see the *Indy Challenger* participate in a season of competition without precedent in the history of man's quest for the World Land Speed Record.

Ken Goodman of Fowler, Indiana, has been driving Top Fuel dragsters for 25 years, the last being a Spitzer chassis AA/Funny Car. Ken is no stranger to acceleration, and has been involved with the construction of the *Indy Challenger* from the conception of the project in 1983.

The vehicle has already been subjected to a series of intensive wind tunnel tests to 600 mph, and with a drag coefficient of .109 the aerodynamic performance of the car at record speeds is assured, generating sufficient downforce on the front wheels to keep them in contact with the ground at all times. A comforting thought for driver, Ken Goodman.

For Mike Spitzer the *Indy Challenger* could prove to be a 'double', for he recently debuted his new streamlined Top Fuel dragster in which he plans to go after all of Mickey Thompson's old acceleration records set in the sixties. In common with a number of his fellow American land speed contemporaries, Spitzer and his team are members of the recently formed WSRA.

Attracting sponsorshop of any land speed record attempt is not an easy task, particularly at a time when no less than four US projects have been launched with the same objective of eclipsing Bob Summers' 1965 wheel-driven Land Speed Record. Mike Spitzer has already secured the sponsorship pledges of ten corporations, including Windfield Tool Co., Inter-Tec, JFZ Brakes, Sutton-Garten Co., Vincent Metals, Hedman Hedders, Autosports Fibreglass, Pasco Auto Paint Specialists, and, of course, Strange Engineering.

Indy Challenger

Engines:	4 Chevrolet small block V-8 engines mounted in line and coupled in pairs, the front pair driving the front wheels, and the rear pair driving the rear wheels. The cubic inch displacement of each engine is 400 cu in. The estimated horsepower of all four engines is 2900 hp at 8200 rpm
Fuel Supply:	80 gallons of straight alcohol
Transmissions:	Two 3-speed planetary type transmissions. Ratios: 1st 2.6:1; 2nd 1.5:1; 3rd 1.19:1
Clutches:	Two triple disc clutches, hydraulically activated
Rear End Drive Units:	Units completely custom built by Strange Engineering in Chicago
Wheels:	Aluminium Forged. No tyre will be used. Witdh of tread contact area: 5 inches wide, 24 inches in diameter. Design speed: 600 mph
Braking System:	JFZ spot brakes mounted on the front and rear drive units for use at 100 mph and below. Parachutes for high speeds. Pilot chute for 500 mph speeds with 20 foot final chute for speeds under 250 mph
Overall Length:	36 feet
Wheelbase:	282 inches
Front Tread:	22 inches
Rear Tread:	19 inches
Total Car Weight:	5400 pounds
Car Height (at Front Wheels):	29 inches
Car Height (at Cockpit Canopy):	42 inches
Car Height (at Stabilizer Fin):	60 inches
Estimated Top Speed:	500 mph
Ground Clearance:	3 inches
Frame:	2″ X 2″ and 2″ X 3″ tubing – .100 wall thickness
Body:	6061 T-6 aluminium supplied by Vincent Metals – .050 thickness
Frontal Area:	8.3 square feet
Coefficient of Drag:	.109

The 'Khadi 9' Experiments - Russia Takes an Interest

In 1818 a Russian explosives expert, Nikolai Ivanovich Kilbalchich, was arrested and sentenced to death for his part in an assassination plot against

Tsar Alexander II. While awaiting execution in Orekhovo-Zuyevo he sketched a design for a man-carrying platform propelled by gunpowder cartridges fed continuously to a combustion chamber. The chamber, filled with heated air, would transmit a steady flow of hot gas producing energy for propulsion.

Kilbalchich's sketches were not discovered until after the Russian Revolution in 1917. In the meantime, a Russian genius of humble birth, Vladimir K. Nikitin, left his home on the bleak steppe of the West Siberian Plain to search for work in the Ukranian city of Kharkov.

During his early years as a student at the Kharkovskiy Avtomobilno Doroshnij Institut (Soviet Institute for Automobiles and Roads), Nikitin filled his notebooks with advanced ideas for racing cars and with the arithmetic of jet-propulsion. In 1941 he published his first treatise on jet-propulsion in land bound vehicles. He considered a whole range of propellants, but was convinced the only practical scheme was that of the conventional gas turbine. The engine he proposed comprised an air compressor delivering to a combustion chamber where fuel – usually of a kerosene type – was continuously burned at constant pressure to deliver a steady flow of hot gas to drive a turbine connected to the compressor. Except for that extracted by the turbine, all energy in the jet was used to propel the engine by direct reaction, the hot gas being accelerated through a suitably profiled nozzle. Inspired by the sketches of Kilbalchich, he developed a small prototype of what is now generally accepted as a turbojet.

In 1951 Vladimir K. Nikitin was appointed 'Master of Sport' and head of the Institute.

The first car to emerge from the Institute's design laboratory was the 'Kharkov L-250', a unique vehicle with enormous capabilities. Driven by Eduard Laurent, the streamliner established no less than 12 USSR records, three of which are claimed to have been higher than existing world records

From left to right; Vladimir K. Nikitin, Dimitri Filtshin, Nikolai Klubov, Grigori Gulayev and Kirill Pokryshkin, at work on the Tumanskij R-11 gas turbine engine of the Khadi-9 *in the engineering laboratory of the Kharkovskiy Avtomobilno Doroshnij Institut (Soviet Institute for Automobiles and Roads), in Kharkov.*

for the class. The L-250 had a wide front track and narrow rear track, and the chassis was a single hollow backbone through which the drive passed to all four independently sprung wheels. Most remarkable of all was the engine – although not the gas turbine favoured by Nikitin – a supercharged two-stroke of 10 litres, working on the swash plate principle; that is to say with a central 'wobble plate' instead of a crankshaft, actuated by the radially disposed pistons and connecting rods; the whole unit measured only 25 inches in diameter but produced an estimated 250 bhp at each of the four wheels.

Together with the Institute's automobile design students, Nikitin went on to develop a further eight streamliners, establishing a total of thirty-two USSR records, 9 of which were said to be higher than existing World Land Speed and endurance records.

On 2 October 1967, Vladimir K. Nikitin finally realised his dream of designing and driving a gas turbine-powered car, the 350 bhp *Khadi-7*, with which he established a terminal speed of 246.09 mph (395.469 kph) on the Institute's high speed test track facility at Lyubotin, west of Kharkov.

Not satisfied with the speed and power-to-weight ratio of the *Khadi-7* Nikitin assigned his most experienced automobile engineer and designer, 33-year-old Dimitri Filtshin, to join him in the development of a gas turbine-powered car with Mach 1 capabilities.

On 17 March 1970, Nikitin produced an engineering mock-up of the proposed vehicle and announced that he was to build a car with the objective of eclipsing Craig Breedlove's World Land Speed Record of 600.601 mph (966.528 kph), set with the *Spirit of America – Sonic 1* on 15 November 1965. Nikitin said; "I have no doubt that it will be the fastest car in the world. We propose to overcome the sound barrier with it". Within six months, the 30-foot long car, *Khadi-9* emerged from the Kharkov laboratory for what was to be the first in a series of high speed test trials on the Lyubotin test track. "Because of the risks involved, we plan to control the vehicle by using radio signals rather than a human being at the wheel," said the Soviet design team. "That is, until we are ready to try for the record!"

The inaugural runs of the un-manned *Khadi-9* proved to be a great disappointment for Nikitin and Filtshin. The highest terminal speed attained by the vehicle was a mere 369.74 mph (593.56 kph). Nikitin was convinced the problem was again, one of power-to-weight ratio. The *Khadi-9* weighed in at 3 tons, and the multiple gas turbine engines could not produce sufficient thrust to power the leviathan.

After much deliberation, the car was completely rebuilt. It was a long and daunting task for Nikitin and Filtshin, but, on 10 October 1978, the modified *Khadi-9* was rolled out to what was almost a State procession, for shortly after he had announced the Soviet challenge to Breedlove's record, Nikitin had learned that the United States of America had raised the record he had planned to beat, to a staggering 622.407 mph (1001.664 kph), in the rocket-powered *The Blue Flame*, driven by Gary Gabelich. Furthermore, he had learned that the United States were planning to surpass the speed of sound with a three-wheeled, rocket powered car on the Daryácheh ye Namak salt lake, near Quom in neighbouring Iran.

For the engine, Nikitin chose the outstandingly successful Tumanskij R-11 gas turbine developing 11,240 lb thrust. Designed by Sergei Tumanskij, the R-11 turbine is normally used in the Soviet Mikoyan MiG-21 (Fishbed) interceptor which entered production in 1956.

The shape of the *Khadi-9*, evolved after extensive wind-tunnel tests on a beautifully laminated scale redwood model, was broadly that of a missile, with the long, slender fuselage and enclosed cockpit, forward of the power plant. The two front wheels were closely paired, giving a 9 in track, whereas the rear wheels were wide-tracked, 7 ft apart, with a wheelbase of 23.5 ft. Remarkably, the tyres were of Firestone low-pressure, aircraft stock, although, as Nikitin explained, "For the sound barrier attempt we plan to use Soviet-made all-metal wheels".

The front wheels had a ball-joint linkage with co-axial coil spring-cum damper units, and steering was at the ratio of 91:1, only slight wheel movement being desirable with the delta arrangement. *Khadi-9* thus had a turning circle of 1/4-mile! The rear axle was solid and unsprung, and although provision was made for fairings over the wheels, it was found that the handling, if not the appearance, was better without them. Braking was by Grigori-Vasilii anti-skid type 15 in diameter discs on the rear wheels, not unlike the Dunlop Maxaret. In this system a small wheel spins at high speed, driven by its rubber rim in contact with the main wheel. If the latter locks, the small wheel stops rotating, and via special valves instantly eases pressure on the brakes, thus restoring rotation. In addition, two drag parachutes were fitted, one 7.3 ft in diameter for below 650 mph, and the other 16 ft in diameter for below 250 mph. The chassis comprised a 30 ft semi-monocoque centre span in aluminium with welded steel tubular nose and rear sections, neatly clad in riveted glass fibre sheeting.

On the morning of 6 November 1978, Vladimir K. Nikitin, Dimitri Filtshin and their team of automobile design students, made their way to the Institute's high speed test track facility at Lyubotin, for the first long-awaited manned test run of the *Khadi-9*. In temperatures well below zero, Nikitin climbed into the cockpit, directly above the front wheel housing. Filtshin, standing beside the car on the frozen test track, gave the OK for engine

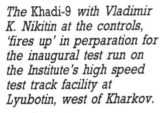

The Khadi-9 *with Vladimir K. Nikitin at the controls, 'fires up' in perparation for the inaugural test run on the Institute's high speed test track facility at Lyubotin, west of Kharkov.*

The Khadi-9 *comes to a halt at the end of the 50,000 ft high-speed test track with driver Vladimir K. Nikitin in the cockpit. Although poker faced he has just become the holder of the Soviet land speed record with a timed speed of 524.016 mph (843.322 kph). Next, the speed of sound!*

start. The design students in attendance resembled a team of scientists and doctors adorned in their sable fur hats to shield the biting wind, a far cry from the sun-burned, oil-smeared mechanics and drivers one would normally see on the blinding salt of Bonneville or El Mirage.

Nikitin depressed the ignition pedal with his right foot, and the Tumanskij R-11 gas turbine whined into action. At full thrust, the car was fighting to be released against the brakes, when Nikitin released the brake pedal from under his left foot, the car lunged forward, and with a mighty, tormented scream from the jet-pipe, the *Khadi-9* roared down the 50,000 ft, high-speed test track, trailing a rooster-tail of steam and ice thrown up from the frozen surface of the track. Surprisingly, during the 7 second run, the car never appeared to slide or even skid on the track. The timed speed for the first run was 524.016 mph (843.322 kph). Unfortunately, Vladimir K. Nikitin was unable to make a return run due to severe weather, and, though he established a new Soviet record for the mile, his ambition was far from fulfilled. He recalls, "the objective of *Khadi-9* is to exceed the speed of sound".

Sadly for Nikitin, on 17 December 1979, Stan Barrett became the first man to exceed the speed of sound in a land-bound vehicle, when he drove the 48,000 horsepower 'Budweiser Rocket' to that goal.

Recognising the enormous potential of racing on a dry lake or salt flat, Vladimir K. Nikitin plans his assault on the World Land Speed Record with the *Khadi-9* in either August or September 1987, on the immense Verkhniy Baskunchak salt lake in the lowlands of Prikaspiyskaya Nizmennost north of Astrakhan in the Kazakhstan. With a potentially untapped speed of 1,285 mph (2,070 kph), Nikitin and Filtshin are confident their vehicle will pass Mach 1, and for the first time since the inception of the World Land Speed Record in 1898, there is a serious Soviet challenge for the record. Indeed, already the Studio City, California-based World Speed Record Association have explored the possibility of inviting the Soviet land speed team to the United States of America for their attempt on the record. As yet, Vladimir K. Nikitin has not discussed the offer. Only time and fortune stand between them!

'Vanishing Point'- The Wayne Attraction

With more than 10 years experience of driving Top Fuel dragsters and Funny Cars behind him, Sammy Miller of Wayne, New Jersey is about to embark on the wildest ride of his career at the wheel of the latest in a long line of progressive rocket-powered cars, bearing the generic name of *Vanishing Point*.

Slam'n Sammy Miller, 43, gave up Fuel Driving in 1974 to join Tony Fox's famed *Pollution Packer* racing team, upon the retirement of Vern Anderson.

Pollution Packer was probably the most famous of all the early rocket cars, and was the first to run under NHRA (National Hot Rod Association) sanction. During a three-day period – 29 September to 1 October 1972 – drivers Vern and Dave Anderson, Ky Michaelson and Paula Murphy combined to set no less than 13 national and international acceleration records with the *Pollution Packer*, in the unlimited and category 'C' classes at Bonneville.

A record of 322.323 mph (518.617 kph) established by Dave Anderson in the quarter mile, required a terminal velocity of nearly 479 miles an hour, with an elapsed time of 4.99 seconds.

Sammy Miller's best run in *Pollution Packer* was 348 mph in 4.4 seconds against John Paxson in the *Armor All* rocket car.

It was about this time that Miller decided to build his own rocket car, in the shape of the *Spirit of 76*. Engineered by Race Car Engineering in Tarzana, California, the double-A Funny Car ran a best of 283 mph in 5.4 seconds, with a 3,500 lb thrust rocket engine.

Financially the car was far from successful, but in terms of experience the gain was enormous. For his next rocket car, the 2001/R Chevrolet Vega Funny Car *Vanishing Point*, Sammy used a 5,000 lb thrust motor, which is equivalent to about 10,000 horsepower. *Vanishing Point* was often seen on the drag strips in the United States, England and Sweden, blasting away from the line, breaking records for the standing quarter mile wherever and whenever he ran, before it was written off in an end of season slide at Santa Pod Raceway.

Sammy replaced the Vega with an even more impressive 2002/R Ford Mustang *Vanishing Point* Funny Car, powered by a GG Industries solid-state rocket engine developing 12,000 lb thrust/24,000 horsepower, which,

Slam'n Sammy Miller.

together with Sammy's radial rocket dragster *Oxygen*, demonstrated his ability to engineer and design a vehicle with Mach 1 capabilities.

Oxygen was undoubtedly the prototype for Sammy's new Land Speed Record car. It was a sleek, azure coloured dragster of straight line supremacy, sporting a vertical tail fin, slightly aft of the enclosed cockpit.

With Miller at the wheel of *Oxygen* and Al Eirdam in *Vanishing Point*, the dynamic duo gave Britain and Europe the quickest and fastest side-by-side races they'd ever witnessed.

Not content with acceleration on land, Miller – like Henry Ford in 1904 – turned to ice!

Sammy Miller replaced the wheels of *Oxygen* with skids, and, on 15 February 1981, took the vehicle to a new World Ice Speed Record on the frozen surface of Lake George in upstate New York, with a spectacular pass of 247.93 mph (399.00 kph).

Miller spoke with the author shortly after the run: "Way back in '68 veteran drag racer, Chuck Suba drove Tony Fox's 2,500 lb thrust, hydrogen peroxide rocket-powered snowmobile *Sonic Challenger* to a terminal speed of 153 mph ... but that was fun and games," he said. "This run alone sure demonstrates I am the World's fastest accelerating man ... and this is on ice. Man, wait and see what I can do on salt".

As far back as 1977, Sammy Miller had toyed with the idea of building a car to attack the World Land Speed Record, which then stood at 622.407 mph (1001.664 kph). Sammy made contact with Dick Keller, who, as Manager of Project Development with Reaction Dynamics, helped to develop the 22,000 lb thrust RD HP-LNG-22,000 V rocket engine for *The Blue Flame*.

For the Land Speed Record car, Keller explained to Sammy that he would need to develop a rocket motor with sufficient power to attain speeds in excess of 760 mph, and then all Sammy had to do in theory was aim the car at the measured mile and blast through the timing traps in less than five seconds. Easier written than accomplished. Keller estimated the cost of the attempt would be about $385,000 – small in comparison with *The Blue Flame* project which cost the Institute of Gas Technology some $800,000 (and which, taking inflation into account, would probably cost twice as much today).

The reason behind the decrease in required capital expenditure on the project is mainly due to significant advances in rocket technology and to the availability of well-documented computer telemetry on the propulsion elements of land-bound (ground effect) vehicles.

Sammy did not agree with Keller's theory that a rocket motor would need to be specially developed for the car, and felt sure he would find a surplus NASA unit lying dormant somewhere in the United States.

For the engine, Miller turned to George Garboden of GG Industries in California, who had developed the units for his earlier rocket cars, and had a number of motors based on the design concept of the Apollo lunar descent engines. Garboden came up with a hybrid design, 14,000 lb thrust unit, weighing a mere 97 lb and developing 28,000 horsepower. It was exactly what Sammy had in mind.

In addition, Sammy purchased an efficient radial rocket booster engine producing a further 5,000 lb thrust/10,000 horsepower to complement its already awesome power units for the final jolt toward the sound barrier.

Miller and his partner, Rory 'Chip' Calhoun, began working on the design of the LSR vehicle in March 1982, but without substantial backing from corporate America, they were about to shelve the project, when, in September, Miller received a call from Ky Michaelson, a rocket propulsion experimentalist, whom he knew from *Pollution Packer* days, back in 1974.

Ky had engineered and designed a rocket car from his Bloomington Minnesota-based Space Age Racing Inc, for Kitty O'Neil of *SMI Motivator* fame.

On 7 July 1977, Kitty drove Ky's lance, unimaginatively dubbed the *Michaelson Rocket Car*, to a two-way average speed of 207.739 mph (334.323 kph) at Bonneville.

The run proved to be a disappointment for Michaelson, and for O'Neil, who only the previous year had driven Bill Fredrick's *SMI Motivator* to 512.710 mph (825,126 kph) on the Alvord Desert, Oregon.

Michaelson was convinced that with the right power unit his rocket car was capable of exceeding the speed of sound.

In an agreement, veiled in secrecy, Miller is reputed to have offered $80,000 for the *Michaelson Rocket Car*, minus the SAR 13,000 lb thrust rocket engine. Michaelson accepted and without further ado, transported the 'spent' projectile to Miller's workshop in New Jersey.

Miller and 'Chip' worked around the clock, sand-blasting the vehicle of it's previous owner's red warpaint, and began the arduous task of mounting the GG Industries 14,000 lb thrust unit in situ.

The hydrogen peroxide fuel, weighing 11.61 lb per US gallon, is contained in a 125-gallon stainless steel chamber, pressurised by a pair of wire-wound, aluminium nitrogen tanks, wrapped in fibreglass.

Located forward of the driver cockpit, the hydrogen peroxide propellant will be pressure fed using nitrogen tetroxide as an oxidizer, much like Craig Breedlove's *Spirit of America III – Sonic II*.

Engineered from 4130 moly-chrome $1^3/4$ in tubing, the chassis of *Vanishing Point* is bronze-welded and finished in highly polished aluminium to ease the transonic air-flow and reduce the drag co-efficiency while approaching its anticipated supersonic speeds.

At 37 feet long, and rising to 8 feet at the top of the vertical tail-fin at the rear, *Vanishing Point* rides on four solid alloy wheels, the rear 32 inch diameter wheels have a 10 foot wide track for roll stability, while the front 30 inch diameter wheels are closely paired on a central hub enabling a low centre of gravity to be achieved.

Ky Michaelson's design was clearly based on Gary Gabelich's *The Blue Flame*, although the frontal aspect would suggest a remarkable resemblance to the *Budweiser Rocket*. There are no canard fins forward or aft; Sammy is relying totally on a 13.6 sq ft frontal area with a prominent 'stoop' to eliminate flight characteristics. Fully laden with driver and fuel, the *Vanishing Point* LSR car weighs in at 4,900 lb.

The 28,000 horsepower engine is currently on test and performance evaluation in Sammy's latest rocket-powered Funny Car, the 2003/R Pontiac Trans Am, which made it's first full pass at Santa Pod Raceway during the 1985 Anheuser-Busch sponsored 'Budweiser Cannonball Race', surpassing the 300 mph barrier with an elapsed time of 4.28 seconds for the quarter mile.

Sammy estimates the Trans Am is capable of becoming the World's first 400 mph Funny Car, using the 14,000 lb thrust unit from the LSR car. But he has bigger things in mind ... 800 mph to be exact!

Sammy Miller plans his attempt on the World Land Speed Record for

Powered by a GG Industries 14,000 lb thrust, 28,000 horsepower hydrogen peroxide rocket system in addition to a further 5,000 lb thrust from a radial rocket booster, the Vanishing Point LSR car will be a new dimension for Sammy Miller.

the Spring of 1987, in competition for the World Speed Record Association's 'International Freedom Cup'.

Miller estimates *Vanishing Point* will take around 18 seconds to attain 785 mph, with the 5,000 lb thrust booster firing at about 13.5 seconds into the run.

With an estimated positive g of no more than 3-4 during the acceleration phase, the LSR run should be just like a Sunday drive for Sammy. When he established his World quarter mile records with accelerations of 0-60 mph in 0.28 seconds and 0-100 mph in 0.36 seconds, he pulled over 12 g momentarily.

In the pioneering days of the World Land Speed Record attempts it was generally thought that terminal speeds in excess of 85 mph would cause the driver to 'black-out' due to the lack of oxygen supply to the brain at such high speeds, yet today conventional family saloon cars are built with sufficient power to exceed such speeds with no such effects on the driver occupant!

For many years it was generally felt that the sound barrier, even in the technological age we live today, was far from possible, yet alone safe. The military jet, and indeed Concorde, fly supersonic speeds on a daily basis, yet, as the layman might say, "in a jet you have plenty of room for manoeuvre", but a car travelling at such speeds would simply disintegrate within its own shock waves.

It took a well organized and highly professional team of engineers and telemetry technicians, and, above all, the supreme courage of one man, to prove the armchair critics and their theories wrong, and that man was Stan Barrett – a true pioneer and crusader of the first order.

Indeed, as Stan once told me; "Talking supersonic is one thing ... driving it is quite another".

But who will break the 1,000 mph barrier?. Has man in his quest for speed on land finally reached a barrier that is simply too formidable to penetrate? There is certainly no shortage of contestants prepared to try!

What will the future hold? The possible has been done, the impossible will be done!

Vanishing Point rides on four solid forged aluminium wheels. Picture shows one of the 32 inch diameter rear wheels.

Appendices

Appendix 1
Evolution of the Land Speed Record

Date	Place	Driver	Nationality	Car	Engine(s)	Flying kilometre			Flying mile		
						Time(s)	km/h	mph	Time(s)	km/h	mph
8.12.1898	Acheres	Gaston de Chasseloup-Laubat	F	Jeantaud Electric	1 x Fulmen 40 bhp electric	57.0	63.158	39.245			
17.1.1899	Acheres	Camille Jenatzy	B	CITA	1 x Fulmen 40 bhp electric	54.0	66.667	41.425			
27.1.1899	Acheres	Gaston de Chasseloup-Laubat	F	Jeantaud Electric	1 x Fulmen 40 bhp electric	51.2	70.312	43.690			
27.1.1899	Acheres	Camille Jenatzy	B	CITA	1 x Fulmen 40 bhp electric	44.8	80.357	49.932			
4.3.1899	Acheres	Gaston de Chasseloup-Laubat	F	Jeantaud Electric Profilée	1 x Fulmen 40 bhp electric	38.8	92.783	57.653			
29.4.1899	Acheres	Camille Jenatzy	B	CITA No 25 La Jamais Contente	2 x Fulmen-Jenatzy 60 bhp electric	34.0	105.882	65.792			
13.4.1902	Nice	Léon Serpollet	F	Gardner-Serpollet Oeuf de Pâques	1 x Serpollet 2.95 x 3.54 in. 4 cyl. electric 106 bhp (S)	29.8	120.805	75.065			
5.8.1902	Ablis	William K. Vanderbilt	USA	Mors Z Paris – Vienna	1 x Mors 4 cyl. 9.2 l. 60 bhp	29.4	122.449	76.086			
5.11.1902	Dourdan	Henri Fournier	F	Mors Z Paris – Vienna	1 x Mors 4 cyl. 9.2 l. 60 bhp	29.2	123.287	76.607			
17.11.1902	Dourdan	M. Augieres	F	Mors Z Paris – Vienna	1 x Mors 4 cyl. 9.2 l. 60 bhp	29.0	124.138	77.136			
7.3.1903	Clipstone	Charles S Rolls	GB	Mors Z Paris – Vienna	1 x Mors 4 cyl. 9.2 l. 60 bhp	27.0	133.333	82.849			
17.7.1903	Ostend	Arthur Duray	B	Gobron-Brillié Paris – Madrid	1 x Gobron-Brillié 4 cyl. 13.5 l. 110 bhp	26.8	134.328	83.468			
7.1903	Dublin	Baron de Forest	IRL	Mors 'Dauphine' (Paris-Madrid)	1 x Mors 70 bhp	26.6	135.338	84.095			
10.1903	Clipstone	Charles S Rolls	GB	Mors 'Dauphine' (Paris-Madrid)	1 x Mors 70 bhp	26.4	136.363	84.732			
5.11.1903	Dourdan	Arthur Duray	F	Gobron-Brillié (Paris-Madrid)	1 x Gobron-Brillié 4 cyl. 13.5 l. 110 bhp	26.4	136.363	84.732			
12.1.1904	Lake St Clair	Henry Ford	USA	Ford The Arrow (New 999)	1 x Ford 4 cyl. 16.7 l. 72 bhp				39.4	147.047	91.371
27.1.1904	Daytona	William K. Vanderbilt	USA	Mercedes-Simplex 90	1 x Mercedes 4 cyl. 11.9 l. 90 bhp				39.0	148.555	92.308
31.3.1904	Nice	Arthur Duray	F	Gobron-Brillié Paris-Madrid	1 x Gobron-Brillié 4 cyl. 13.5 l. 110 bhp	25.2	142.857	88.767			
31.3.1904	Nice	Louis Rigolly	F	Gobron-Brillié 'Gordon Bennett'	1 x Gobron-Brillié 4 cyl. 13.6 l. 130 bhp	24.0	150.000	93.206			
31.3.1904	Nice	Louis Rigolly	F	Gobron-Brillié 'Gordon Bennett'	1 x Gobron-Brillié 4 cyl. 13.6 l. 130 bhp	23.6	152.542	94.785			
25.5.1904	Ostend	Pierre de Caters	B	Mercedes Simplex 90	1 x Mercedes 4 cyl. 11.9 l. 90 bhp	23.0	156.522	97.258			
21.7.1904	Ostend	Paul Baras	B	Darracq 'Gordon Bennett'	1 x Darracq 4 cyl. 11.3 l. 100 bhp	22.0	163.636	101.679			
21.7.1904	Ostend	Louis Rigolly	F	Gobron-Brillié 'Gordon Bennett'	1 x Gobron-Brillié 4 cyl. 13.6 l. 130 bhp	21.6	166.666	103.561			
13.11.1904	Ostend	Paul Baras	F	Darracq 'Gordon Bennett'	1 x Darracq 4 cyl. 11.3 l. 100 bhp	21.4	168.224	104.530			
24.1.1905	Daytona	Arther E. Macdonald	USA	Napier L48	1 x Napier 6 cyl. 15 l. 90 bhp				34.4	168.419	104.651
25.1.1905	Daytona	Herbert L. Bowden	USA	A Mercedes Flying Dutchman II	2 x Mercedes 60 4 cyl. 9.2 l. 60 bhp				32.8	176.635	109.756
31.1.1905	Daytona	Herbert L. Bowden	USA	B Mercedes Flying Dutchman II	2 x Mercedes 60 4 cyl. 9.2 l. 60 bhp	20.6	174.757	108.589			
15.11.1905	Arles	Frédéric Dufaux	CH	Dufaux Brighton	1 x Dufaux 4 cyl. 26 l. 150 bhp	23.0	156.522	97.258			
30.12.1905	Arles	Victor Hémery	F	Darracq V8	1 x Darracq V8 ohv. 22.5 l. 200 bhp	20.6	174.757	108.589			
23.1.1906	Daytona	Victor Hémery	F	Darracq V8	1 x Darracq V8 ohv. 22.5 l. 200 bhp	19.4	185.567	115.306			
25.1.1906	Daytona	Louis Chevrolet	USA	Darracq V8	1 x Darracq V8 ohv. 22.5 l. 200 bhp				30.6	189.334	117.647
26.1.1906	Daytona	Fred H. Marriott	USA	Stanley Steamer Rocket	1 x Stanley 2 cyl. horizontal 900-1,000 lb p.s.i. 120 bhp (s)	18.4	195.652	121.573	28.2	205.448	127.659
8.11.1909	Brooklands	Victor Hémery	GB	Benz No. 1 Blitzen Benz	1 x Benz 4 cyl. ohv. 21.5 l. 200 bhp	17.761	202.691	125.946			
16.3.1910	Daytona	Barney Oldfield	USA	Benz No. 1 Blitzen Benz	1 x Benz 4 cyl. ohv. 21.5 l. 200 bhp	17.04	211.267	131.275			
23.3.1910	Daytona	Barney Oldfield	USA	Benz No. 1 Blitzen Benz	1 x Benz 4 cyl. ohv. 21.5 l. 200 bhp				27.33	211.988	131.723
23.4.1911	Daytona	Robert Burman	USA	Benz No. 1 Blitzen Benz	1 x Benz 4 cyl. ohv. 21.5 l. 200 bhp	15.88	226.700	140.865	25.40	228.096	141.732
24.6.1914	Brooklands	L.G. Hornsted	GB	Benz No. 3	1 x Benz 4 cyl. ohv. 21.5 l. 200 bhp				29.01	199.711	124.095
12.2.1919	Daytona	Ralph De Palma	USA	Packard '905' (Liberty Racer)	1 x Packard Liberty V12 ohc. 14.8 l. 240 bhp @ 2,400 rpm	14.86	242.261	150.534	24.02	241.200	149.875

Land Speed Records — the six speed columns are the flying kilometre (s, km/h, mph) followed by the flying mile (s, km/h, mph).

Date	Venue		Driver	Car	Engine(s)	s	km/h	mph	s	km/h	mph
27.4.1920	Daytona	USA	Tommy Milton	Twin Duesenberg Double Duesey	2 x Duesenberg straight-eight ohc 5 l, 92 bhp at 3,800 rpm	14.40	250.000	155.343	23.07	251.133	156.047
6.4.1922	Daytona	USA	Sigmund Haugdahl	Wisconsin Special	1 x Wisconsin 6 cyl, single ohc, 12.5 l, 250 bhp	13.80	260.869	162.097	19.97	290.117	180.270
17.5.1922	Brooklands	GB	Kenelm Lee Guinness	Sunbeam	1 x Sunbeam Manitou 60°, V12, single ohc, 18.3 l, 350 bhp @ 2,100 rpm	16.73	215.182	133.708	27.87	207.880	129.171
23.6.1923	Fano	DK	Malcolm Campbell	Sunbeam Blue Bird	1 x Sunbeam Manitou 60°, V12, single ohc, 18.3 l, 350 bhp @ 2,100 rpm	16.41	219.378	136.315	26.14	221.639	137.720
19.6.1924	Saltburn	GB	Malcolm Campbell	Sunbeam Blue Bird	1 x Sunbeam Manitou 60°, V12, single ohc, 18.3 l, 350 bhp @ 2,100 rpm	15.40	233.766	145.255	26.07	222.234	138.090
26.6.1924	Arpajon	F	J G Parry Thomas	Leyland-Thomas No 1	1 x Leyland Eight straight-eight, single ohc, 7.3 l, 115 bhp				27.75	208.780	129.730
6.7.1924	Arpajon	F	René Thomas	Delage DH La Torpille	1 x Delage 60° V12, ohv, 10.6 l, 280 bhp @ 3,200 rpm	15.62	230.473	143.210	25.12	230.638	143.312
12.7.1924	Arpajon	F	Ernest A D Eldridge	Fiat Special Mephistopheles II	1 x Fiat type A-12, 6 cyl, 24-valve, single ohc, 21.7 l, 300 bhp	15.32	234.987	146.014	24.675	234.798	145.896
25.9.1924	Pendine	GB	Malcolm Campbell	Sunbeam Blue Bird	1 x Sunbeam Manitou 60°, V12, ohc, 18.3 l, 350 bhp	15.305	235.217	146.157	24.63	235.226	146.163
21.7.1925	Pendine	GB	Malcolm Campbell	Sunbeam Blue Bird	1 x Sunbeam Manitou 60°, V12, ohc, 18.3 l, 350 bhp	14.83	242.751	150.038	23.878	242.635	150.766
16.3.1926	Southport	GB	Henry O'Neal de Hane Segrave	Sunbeam Ladybird	1 x Sunbeam-Coatalen 75°, V12, dohc, 12 cyl, 4 l, 306 bhp @ 5,300 rpm	14.687	245.115	152.307	24.108	240.320	149.328
27.4.1926	Pendine	GB	J G Parry Thomas	Higham-Thomas Special Babs	1 x Packard Liberty 45° V12, ohc, 26.9 l, 400 bhp	13.213	272.459	169.298	21.419	270.490	168.075
28.4.1926	Pendine	GB	J G Parry Thomas	Higham-Thomas Special Babs	1 x Packard Liberty 45° V12, ohc, 26.9 l, 400 bhp	13.08	275.229	171.019	21.099	274.593	170.624
4.2.1927	Pendine	GB	Malcolm Campbell	Napier-Campbell Blue Bird	1 x Napier Lion 12-cyl, ohc 'broad arrow', 22.3 l, 450 bhp	12.791	281.448	174.883	20.663	280.387	174.224
29.3.1927	Daytona	USA	Henry O'Neal de Hane Segrave	Sunbeam (Slug)	2 x Sunbeam Matabele, 2 cyl, V12, dohc 22.5 l, 435 bhp	11.02	326.679	202.989	17.665	327.973	203.793
19.2.1928	Daytona	USA	Malcolm Campbell	Napier-Campbell Blue Bird	1 x Napier Lion 12-cyl, ohc 'broad arrow', 22.3 l, 450 bhp				17.395	333.063	206.956
22.4.1928	Daytona	USA	Ray Keech	White Triplex (Spirit of Elkdom)	3 x Packard Liberty, V12, ohc, 12 cyl, 25.9 l, 400 bhp				17.345	334.024	207.553
11.3.1929	Daytona	USA	Henry O'Neal de Hane Segrave	Irving Napier Special Golden Arrow	1 x Napier Lion 12 cyl, ohc, 'broad arrow', 26.9 l, 925 bhp	9.66	372.671	231.567	15.56	372.341	231.362
5.2.1931	Daytona	GB	Malcolm Campbell	Napier-Campbell Blue Bird	1 x Napier Lion supercharged 12 cyl, ohc, 'broad arrow', 26.9 l, 1,450 bhp	9.09	396.040	246.088	14.65	395.470	245.733
24.2.1932	Daytona	USA	Sir Malcolm Campbell	Napier-Campbell Blue Bird	1 x Napier Lion supercharged 12 cyl, ohc, 'broad arrow', 26.9 l, 1,450 bhp	8.90	404.494	251.341	14.175	408.722	253.968
22.2.1933	Daytona	USA	Sir Malcolm Campbell	Campbell-Rolls-Royce Blue Bird	1 x Rolls-Royce 'R' Supercharged V12, ohc, 36.5 l, 2,300 bhp	8.21	438.489	272.465	13.23	437.916	272.109
7.3.1935	Daytona	USA	Sir Malcolm Campbell	Campbell-Rolls-Royce Blue Bird	1 x Rolls-Royce 'R' Supercharged V12, ohc, 36.5 l, 2,300 bhp	8.10	444.444	276.165	13.01	445.322	276.710
3.9.1935	Bonneville	USA	Sir Malcolm Campbell	Campbell-Rolls-Royce Blue Bird	1 x Rolls-Royce 'R' supercharged V12, ohc, 36.5 l, 2,300 bhp				11.955	484.620	301.129
19.11.1937	Bonneville	USA	George E T Eyston	Thunderbolt	2 x Rolls-Royce 'R' supercharged V12, ohc, 36.5 l, 2,350 bhp	7.165	502.444	312.203	11.56	501.179	311.418
27.8.1938	Bonneville	USA	George E T Eyston	Thunderbolt	2 x Rolls-Royce 'R' supercharged V12, ohc, 36.5 l, 2,350 bhp	6.48	555.555	345.206	10.42	556.011	345.489
15.9.1938	Bonneville	USA	John Rhodes Cobb	Railton	2 x Napier Lion supercharged 12 cyl, ohc 'broad arrow', 26.9 l, 1,250 bhp	6.39	563.380	350.068	10.28	563.583	350.194
16.9.1938	Bonneville	USA	George E T Eyston	Thunderbolt	2 x Rolls-Royce 'R' supercharged V12, ohc, 36.5 l, 2,350 bhp	6.26	575.080	357.338	10.07	575.336	357.497
23.8.1939	Bonneville	USA	John Rhodes Cobb	Railton	2 x Napier Lion supercharged 12 cyl, ohc 'broad arrow', 26.9 l, 1,250 bhp	6.05	595.041	369.741	9.785	592.094	367.910
16.9.1947	Bonneville	USA	John Rhodes Cobb	Railton Mobil Special	2 x Napier Lion supercharged 12 cyl, ohc 'broad arrow', 26.9 l, 1,250 bhp	5.68	633.803	393.827	9.132	634.398	394.196
9.9.1960	Bonneville	USA	Mickey Thompson	Challenger	4 x Pontiac V8 pushrod, ohv, 6.7 l, 700 bhp				8.854	654.359	406.60
17.7.1964	Lake Eyre	AUS	Donald Campbell	Campbell-Norris Bluebird-Proteus CN7	1 x Bristol-Siddeley Proteus 4,100 hp gas turbine	5.67	634.920	394.521	8.93	648.783	403.135
12.11.1965	Bonneville	USA	Robert S Summers	Goldenrod	4 x Chrysler Hemi 426, V8, ohv, 6.9 l, 603 bhp	5.46	659.341	409.695	8.796	658.667	409.277

Unlimited Records

Date	Venue		Driver	Car	Engine(s)	s	km/h	mph	s	km/h	mph
5.8.1963	Bonneville	USA	Norman Craig Breedlove	Spirit of America	1 x General Electric J47-GE-15 5,200 lb thrust jet	5.4785	657.114	408.312	8.8355	655.722	407.447
2.10.1964	Bonneville	USA	Tom Green	Wingfoot Express	1 x Westinghouse J46-WE-8 6,200 lb triple jet	5.389	668.027	415.093	8.7125	664.980	413.199
5.10.1964	Bonneville	USA	Arthur Eugene Arfons	Green Monster	1 x General Electric J47-GE-17 5,200 lb thrust jet	5.15	699.029	434.356	8.2945	698.491	434.022
13.10.1964	Bonneville	USA	Norman Craig Breedlove	Spirit of America	1 x General Electric J47-GE-17 5,200 lb thrust jet				7.6805	754.331	468.719
15.10.1964	Bonneville	USA	Norman Craig Breedlove	Spirit of America	1 x General Electric J79-GE-3A 15,000 lb thrust jet				6.8405	846.961	526.277
27.10.1964	Bonneville	USA	Arthur Eugene Arfons	Green Monster	1 x General Electric J79-GE-3A 15,000 lb thrust jet	4.111	875.699	544.134	6.7075	863.755	536.712
2.11.1965	Bonneville	USA	Norman Craig Breedlove	Spirit of America - Sonic 1	1 x General Electric J79-GE-3A 15,000 lb thrust jet	4.027	893.966	555.485	6.485	893.391	555.127
7.11.1965	Bonneville	USA	Arthur Eugene Arfons	Green Monster	1 x General Electric J79-GE-3A 15,000 lb thrust jet	3.907	921.423	572.546	6.244	927.873	576.553
15.11.1965	Bonneville	USA	Norman Craig Breedlove	Spirit of America - Sonic 1	1 x General Electric J79-GE-3A 15,000 lb thrust jet	3.723	966.962	600.842	5.994	966.573	600.601
23.10.1970	Bonneville	USA	Gary Gabelich	Blue Flame	1 x RD HP LNG 22,000-V liquid fuel rocket 13,000 lb thrust (?)	3.5485	1014.513	630.389	5.784	1001.666	622.407
4.10.1983	Black Rock D	GB	Richard Noble	Thrust 2	1 x Rolls-Royce RG 146 Avon MK 302C, 17,000 lb thrust jet	3.528	1020.408	634.052	5.683	1019.468	633.468

The Highest Speed Ever Attained by Any Wheeled Land Vehicle

Date	Venue		Driver	Car	Engine(s)	km/h	mph
17.12.1979	Edwards AFB	USA	Stan Barrett	Budweiser Rocket	1 x Romatec V4 bio-propellant rocket, 24,000 lb thrust & Sidewinder missile 4-6,200 lb thrust, 48,000 bhp (R)	1190.377	739.666

(equals Mach 1.0106)

Note: *Unless otherwise stated all engines are of the internal combustion type*

(S) = Steam.
(R) = Rocket.

Appendix 2
Record~breaking Cars on Public Display

A considerable number of land speed record cars still survive today; the list below shows where they may be seen on public display.

Camille Jenatzy's 1899 *La Jamais Contente:* Musée National de la Voiture et du Tourisme, Château de Compiègne, Oise, France.

Henry Ford's 1904 Ford *999* (sister car to the *Arrow*): Henry Ford Museum, Dearborn, Michigan, USA.

Fred Marriott's 1906 Stanley *Rocket:* remains of the car are in the Museum of Speed, South Daytona, Florida, USA; engine remains in the National Museum of American History, Smithsonian Institution, Washington DC, USA.

Barney Oldfield's 1910 *Blitzen Benz;* Daimler-Benz AG Museum, Mercedesstrasse, Stuttgart (Untertürkheim), West Germany.

Kenelm Lee Guinness's 1922, 350 hp Sunbeam: National Motor Museum, Beaulieu, Hampshire, England.

Ernest Eldridge's 1924, 300 hp Fiat Special *Mephistopheles:* Fiat Centro Storico, Via Chiabrera, Turin, Italy.

The Spirit of America on permanent display in the Museum of Science and Industry, 57th Street and Lake Shore Drive, Chicago, Illinois, USA.

Craig Breedlove's remarkable 1965, Spirit of America — Sonic 1 *stands sentinel on display in the Indianapolis Motor Speedway Corporations, Hall of Fame, Indianapolis, Indiana, USA.*

Henry Segrave's 1926, 4-litre V12 Sunbeam, rebuilt in 1932 by Sir Malcolm Campbell: currently owned and raced in British Vintage events by Neil Corner. A second car, fitted with a Napier Lion engine, is currently raced as the Sunbeam-Napier.

J.G. Parry Thomas's 1927 *Babs:* dug out of the Pendine Sands in 1969 by Bangor University lecturer, Owen Wyn Owen, and currently nearing completion of restoration.

Henry Segrave's 1927, 1,000 hp Sunbeam: National Motor Museum, Beaulieu, Hampshire, England.

Fritz von Opel's 1928 *Rak 2:* Deutsches Museum, Museumsinsel 1, Munich, West Germany.

Henry Segrave's 1929, *Golden Arrow:* National Motor Museum, Beaulieu, Hampshire, England.

Malcolm Campbell's 1935 *Bluebird:* Alabama Motor Speedway Hall of Fame, Talladega, Alabama, USA.

George Eyston's 1938 *Thunderbolt:* at the outbreak of World War II the car was on an exhibition tour in New Zealand, where it was later destroyed by a fire in Auckland; engine remains can be seen in the Museum of Transport and Technology, Western Springs, Auckland 2, New Zealand.

John Cobb's 1938-47 Railton-Mobil Special: Museum of Science and Industry, City Museum, Birmingham, England.

Donald Campbell's 1960-64 *Bluebird-Proteus:* owned by Campbell's widow, Tonia and on loan to the National Motor Museum, Beaulieu, Hampshire, England. Negotiations broke down in 1980 for the conversion of the car for the projected

The interior of The National Motor Museum, Beaulieu, Hampshire, England, with the impressive display of four historical land speed record cars; From the front, Kenelm Lee Guinness's 1922, 350 hp Sunbeam; Henry Segrave's 1929 Golden Arrow, and 1927 1,000 hp Sunbeam, and finally the familiar lines of Donald Campbell's 1964, Bristol-Siddeley Bluebird-Proteus.

assault by Craig Breedlove on Bob Summers' wheel-driven World Land Speed Record.

Dr Nathan Ostich's 1960 *Flying Caduceus:* William F. Harrah Automobile Museum, P.O. Box 10, Reno, Nevada, USA.

Glenn Leasher's 1962 *Infinity:* following the fatal accident on 10 September 1962, the wreckage was removed from Bonneville and taken to the Utah Highway Maintenance Yard in Wendover, where it still stands today as a sobering reminder of a project that became a tragic statistic.

Art Arfon's 1964-66 *Green Monster:* rebuilt by Arfons in 1968, it was subsequently purchased by Slick Gardner of Santa Ines Valley, California USA and renamed *Andersen's Pea Soup Monster.*

Craig Breedlove's 1964 *Spirit of America:* Museum of Science and Industry, Jackson Park, Chicago, USA.

Craig Breedlove's 1965 *Spirit of America – Sonic 1:* Indianapolis Motor Speedway – Hall of Fame, Indianapolis, Indiana, USA.

Bob Summers' 1965 *Goldenrod:* owned by Utah businessman Richard Dixon and on permanent display at his famed Bonneville Speedway Museum, PO Box 39, Wendover, Utah, USA.

Mickey Thompson's 1968 *Autolite Special:* recently repurchased by Thompson for an assault on the Summers Brothers' wheel-driven record in 1987, and renamed *Conquest I.*

Gary Gabelich's 1970 *The Blue Flame:* now on permanent display at the Auto & Technic Museum e.V D-6920 Sinsheim, Kraichgau, West Germany.

Bill Fredrick's 1971 *'Courage of Australia':* owned by the Wynn's Oil Company, now on permanent display in the Birdwood Mill Museum, Shannon Street, Birdwood, Adelaide, South Australia 5234.

Kitty Hambleton's (née O'Neil) 1976 *SMI Motivator:* original vehicle dismantled and utilized in the construction of the *Budweiser Rocket.* A full scale engineering mock-up of the vehicle can be seen on permanent display at Paul J. Meyer's, Success Motivation Institute, PO Box 7411, Waco, Texas, USA.

The late Gary Gabelich's 1970 The Blue Flame *now on permanent display at the Auto + Technik Museum e.V, Sinsheim, Kraichgau, West Germany.*

Stan Barrett's 1979 *Budweiser Rocket:* donated to the American people by owner Hal Needham, and is now on permanent display at the National Museum of American History, Smithsonian Institution, Washington DC, USA.

Richard Noble's 1981-83 *Thrust 2:* currently at the Project Thrust workshop in Fishbourne on the Isle of Wight being prepared for her final resting place at the National Motor Museum, Beaulieu, Hampshire, England.

Appendix 3

LSR Vehicle Categories and Groups

Categories and Vehicle Groups	Classes

CATEGORY A
Special Automobiles:

Group I: Engine with reciprocating Otto cycle, with or without supercharger

Group II: Engine with reciprocating Otto cycle, without supercharger

Group III: Engine with Diesel cycle with or without supercharger

Group IV: Engine with Diesel cycle without supercharger
Group V: Engine with rotative Otto cycle with or without supercharger
Group VI: Engine with rotative Otto cycle without supercharger

Group VII: Rotary piston-engined with single or multiple rotors

1. Up to 250 cc
2. From 250 cc to 350 cc
3. From 350 cc to 500 cc
4. From 500 cc to 750 cc
5. From 750 cc to 1,100 cc
6. From 1,100 cc to 1,500 cc
7. From 1,500 cc to 2,000 cc
8. From 2,000 cc to 3,000 cc
9. From 3,000 cc to 5,000 cc
10. From 5,000 cc to 8,000 cc
11. Over 8,000

Group VIII: Electrical engine

Group IX: Turbine engine

Group X: Steam engine

Unloaded weight:

1. Up to 500 kg
2. 500 kg to 1,000 kg
3. Over 1,000 kg

CATEGORY B

Automobiles:
Recognised series produced
    Touring cars (5,000 units)

1. Up to 1,000 cc
2. From 1,000 cc to 2,000 cc
3. From 2,000 cc to 3,000 cc
4. From 3,000 cc to 5,000 cc
5. From 5,000 cc to 7,000 cc
6. Over 7,000 cc

CATEGORY C

Special Vehicles or Projectiles
These records may be subdivided, if necessary, according
to the type of engine propulsion used (jet, rocket, etc)

Unlimited

CATEGORY D

Ground Effect Vehicles subdivided, if necessary, according to
any criterion the CSI would judge or evaluate appropriate

Unlimited

LSR Attempts ~ FIA
Operating Procedures

**LAND
SPEED
RACERS**

1.1.   Safety Inspection

Safety inspection must be completely and satisfactorily passed by each participating vehicle (regardless of class) before any qualifying runs will be allowed. Vehicles competing in classes in which the existing record exceeds 200 mph shall be inspected by at least two Safety Inspectors; vehicles competing in classes in which the record exceeds 250 mph shall be inspected by at least three Inspectors. Where applicable, vehicles should be inspected with body panels off and to verify the driver can reach all levers, switches, etc., when the body is seated. Limb restraint systems must be demonstrated to be effective.

Any body or engine class change will necessitate re-inspection. Failure to obtain such re-inspection will result in the loss of all times recorded in the new class. Vehicles exhibiting ill-handling (such as spins, fires, etc.,) on the course must be re-inspected and may be barred from further competition at the discretion of the Contest Board. Decisions by the Contest Board are final.

1.2.   Classification

It is assumed that the owner and/or driver has entered a vehicle in its proper class. However, a vehicle is subject to class verification by the Contest Board at any time and first place vehicles must be verified. All vehicles will run only in the lowest primary class for which they are legal. Any vehicle which is not legal for any class, but meets all safety regulations, may run for time only. No trophies will be awarded.

1.3.   Starter

An Official Starter and Assistant Starter shall be appointed by the Contest Board and shall have the authority to bar a vehicle from the course even though it has passed inspection. Such action may be appealed to the Contest Board, which shall have the power to overrule the appointed Starters.

1.4.   Weather

The Contest Board assumes no responsibility whatsover for delays, postponements, and cancellation of all or parts of an event because of inclement weather, unsafe course conditions, and/or any other reason. The Starter shall close the race course in whole or in part when the wind velocity at any point exceeds 15 mph or any other unsafe condition arises.

1.5.   Course

The straightaway speed course, conditions permitting, will be an overall distance of seven miles. There will be an approach of two miles from the starting line to the four timing traps placed as follows: One trap timing the first quarter mile of the third mile, one trap timing the full third mile, one trap timing the full fourth mile, and one trap timing the full fifth mile. There will be a warm up area available.

1.6. Qualifying

To qualify for a record attempt, a vehicle must exceed the existing record by at least .001 mph. Only one person will be allowed in a vehicle during competition, except for motorcycles with sidecars. The number of qualifying runs allowed to each vehicle is unlimited; however, any vehicle or driver considered by the Contest Board to be detrimental to the safety of the event may be barred from the course at any time. All qualifying runs will be timed through the first quarter of the third measured mile and, at the drivers' option, the full third mile. Vehicles which have exceeded 175 mph in the quarter, at the CURRENT Nationals, will be timed through at the full five miles. Class change will not necessitate requalification for the long course for attempts at records in excess of 200 mph.

1.7. Record Runs

Records are established by a two way average over the same relative mile depending on the course length. Qualifiers over 175 mph and Streamliners may be timed through three miles and may choose over which of the three available relative miles his/her average speed will be calculated.

All vehicles that have qualified for record runs must be at the starting line and ready to run at 8:00 a.m. of the following day (local time). The starting line access road will be closed at 8:00 a.m. Any vehicle unable to run by that time will be disqualified for record runs and will have to requalify. In the event that record runs are cancelled for that day, eligible vehicles need not requalify. After a vehicle leaves the starting line on a record run, any interruptions, such as spins, loss of engine power, premature deployment of braking parachutes, etc., will terminate the record attempt. Official (sanctioned) fuel shall be used on record runs and tanks/chambers sealed under scrutiny of the appointed official. Petroleum vehicles must report to the fueling area with empty fuel tanks.

1.8. Record Body and Class Inspection

All record breaking vehicles must report immediately after their return record run to the designated area to be inspected by an appointed official for compliance with body class, engine displacement, and safety requirements. Record breaking engines may not be removed from the chassis prior to displacement inspection, which shall be made by direct measurement of bore and stroke or swept volume in one revolution. All components shall be available for inspection upon request.

Any infraction of the above may result in disqualification.

1.9. Protests

All protests must be made in writing to the Contest Board before the end of qualifying runs for the meet. Any protest which shall require the disassembly of an assembled engine must be accompanied by an appropriate fee determined by the Contest Board, which shall be awarded to the owner and/or driver of the protested engine in the event the protest is not upheld.

1.10. Trophies

Class and record trophies will be sent to the winners by mail after the conclusion of a meet. Class trophies will be awarded only to those entries who run within 5% of the record or record minimum. When a record setter is also first in class, only a record trophy will be awarded. Additional trophies may be obtained through the Contest Board office only.

1.11. Timing Plaque

A timing plaque showing the fastest qualifying speed and a result sheet will be sent to all entries upon request to the Contest Board. Record setting entries will receive a timing plaque showing the record speed.

1.12. Temperance

Any participant who shows any signs of intoxication will be barred immediately from an event and the matter will be referred to the Contest Board for such action as it deems necessary. This rule will be strictly enforced.

1.13. Driver Licensing

All drivers/riders must have a current competition license, issued by the Contest Board or sanctioning authority. These may be obtained by application to the Contest Board office after meeting requirements listed below.

Experienced drivers/riders holding licenses in a slower category may qualify for the next faster category by satisfactorily completing one or more runs at a speed within the minimum and maximum for the next faster category and having a timing slip verified by a Contest Board official. The categories are as follows:-

Category A   200 mph and faster
Category B   175 to 199 mph
Category C   150 to 174 mph
Category D   125 to 149 mph
Category E   124 mph and slower

Drivers/riders may not advance more than one category per qualification attempt. Any driver/rider operating a competition vehicle faster than his/her category license (except while attempting to qualify for the next faster category) shall be barred from further competition until the circumstances are reviewed by the Contest Board.

Licensing requirements are:-
Category E   Full Drivers' License
Category D   E License and certified timing slip between 125 and 149 mph
Category C   D License and certified timing slip between 150 and 174 mph
Category B   C License and certified timing slip between 175 and 199 mph
Category A   B License and certified timing slip over 200 mph

Licenses will be periodically reviewed and reduced one license category for each two years of inactive competition.

Bibliography

Villa, Leo *The Record Breakers, Sir Malcolm & Donald Campbell, Land and Water-speed Kings of the 20th Century.* Paul Hamlyn, London, New York, Sydney, Toronto, 1969.

Goddard, Robert *Rocket Development.* Prentice-Hall, New York, 1948.

Posthumus, Cyril *Land Speed Record.* Osprey Publishing Ltd, London, 1971.

Baker, David *The Rocket – The History and Development of Rocket & Missile Technology.* New Cavendish Books, London, 1978.

Clifton, Paul *The Fastest Men on Earth.* Herbert Jenkins Ltd, London, 1964.

Zarem, Lewis *New Dimensions of Flight.* E.P. Dutton & Co, New York, 1959.

Wolfe, Tom *The Right Stuff.* Jonathan Cape, New York, 1979.

Katz, Frederic *Art Arfons: Fastest Man on Wheels.* Rutledge, London, New York, Toronto, 1965.

Pearson, John *Bluebird and the Dead Lake.* Collins Publishers, London, 1965.

Houlgate, Deke *The Fastest Men in the World-on Wheels.* The World Publishing Co, New York, 1971.

Wentworth Day, J. *Speed. The Authentic Life of Malcolm Campbell.* Hutchinson, London, 1931.

Sutton, George P. *Rocket Propulsion Elements,* John Wiley & Sons, New York, 1963.

Jenkins, Ab and Ashton, Wendell, J. *The Salt of the Earth.* Clymer Motors, Los Angeles, 1945.

Pearson, John *The Last Hero. The Gallant Story of Donald Campbell and the Land-Speed Record.* Davis McKay Company, New York, 1966.

Clark, John D. *Ignition.* Rutgers University Press, New Brunswick, 1972.

Campbell, Sir Malcolm *Speed on Wheels.* Sampson Low, Marston & Co. Ltd, London, 1949.

Sox, Ronnie and Martin, Buddy *The Sox & Martin Book of Drag Racing.* Henry Regnery Company, Chicago, 1974.

Hardcastle, David and Jones, Peter *Drive it! The Complete Book of British Drag Racing,* Haynes Publishing Group, Sparkford, Nr. Yeovil, 1981.

Isenberg, Hans G. *Rakcten auf Rädern* (Rockets on Wheels). Falken-Verlag GmbH, Niedernhausen/Ts, 1981.

Breedlove, Craig. *Spirit of America.* Henry Regnery Company, Chicago, 1971.

Davis, S.H.C. *The John Cobb Story.* G.T. Foulis & Co. Limited, London, 1953.

Eyston, George E.T. *Speed on Salt.* Floyd Clymer, Los Angeles, 1939.

Campbell, Sir Malcolm *My Thirty Years of Speed.* Hutchinson, London, 1935.

Käsmann, Ferdinand C.W. *Weltrekord-fahrzeuge 1898 bis heute.* Verlag W. Kohlhammer GmbH, Stuttgart, 1984.

Montagu, Lord E.J. *The Gordon Bennett Races.* Cassell, London, 1963.

Pershing, Bernard *Aerodynamics and Racing Cars.* AIAA, Los Angeles, 1974.

Tours, Hugh *Parry Thomas – Designer – Driver.* Batsford, London, 1959.

Boddy, William *The Story of Brooklands.* Grenville, London, 1948.

Thompson, Mickey *Challenger.* Prentice-Hall, New Jersey, NY, 1964.

Knudson, Richard L. *Land Speed Record Breakers.* Lerner, Minneapolis, 1981.

Horsley, Fred *The World's Fastest Cars.* Trend Books, Los Angeles, 1955.

Day, J. Wentworth *The Life of Sir Henry Segrave.* Hutchinson, London, 1931.

Stambler, Irwin *The Supercars and the Men Who Race Them.* Putnam's & Sons, New York, 1975.

Bochroch, Albert R. *American Automobile Racing.* Patrick Stephens Ltd, Cambridge, 1974

Beckh, H.J. von *Technical Note AFMDC 58-11.* U.S. Air Force Missile Development Center, Holloman, New Mexico, 1958.

Acknowledgements

Books aren't written overnight. This one was the product of four years of research. My humble thanks go to the many people who have helped along the way and without whose help and valued assistance this book would not have been possible.

H.R.H. Prince Majid bin Abdul Aziz
former Minister for Municipal and Rural Affairs
The Kingdom of Saudi Arabia

August A. Busch III
Chairman of the Board and President
Anheuser-Busch Companies Inc

Jack MacDonough
Vice President
Brand Management
Anheuser-Busch Companies Inc

Art Arfons
Art Arfons Associates

Craig Arfons
G.M. Enterprises of Manatee County Inc

Walt Arfons

Susan Arnold
Bob Thomas & Associates Inc

Gary Baim
World Speed Record Association

Stan Barrett
Penny Barrett
David Barrett
Stanton Barrett
Melissa Barrett

Ferdinand Beickler
Adam Opel AG

Dan Bisher
Vice President
Rocketman Productions Inc

Chris Bladon
Bladon Bros

Craig Breedlove
Spirit of America Enterprises

Norm C. Breedlove

Derek C. Guy
Public Relations Manager
Burmah-Castrol (UK) Limited

Pearl M. Bloomfield
Public Relations Assistant
Burmah-Castrol (UK) Limited

Gary A. Cagle
President
Southern California Timing Association Inc

Miriam Carroll
Vauxhall Motors Limited

Robert A. Stranahan, JR
President and Chairman of the Board
Champion Spark Plug Company

Martyn F.T. Brownhill
Director – International Advertising
Champion Spark Plug Company

Günther Claassen
Direktor
MESSE ESSEN GmbH

Mike Collins

Ron Crawley
Managing Director
Valvoline Oil Company Limited

Victor J. Danilov
President and Director
Museum of Science and Industry
Chicago, USA

Baron Guy de Caters

Jim Deist
President
Deist Safety

Richard Dixon
Bonneville Speedway Museum

Timothy J. Donnay
Lesotho National Parks

Professor E.R. Ellis
Automotive Studies Group
Cranfield Institute of Technology

Carl Ericson
American Gas Association

Brig. General Hratch Etyemezian
Royal Automobile Club of Jordan

The late Earl 'Pappy' Evans

Gene Evans
Consultant – Marketing and Promotions
William F. Harrah Automobile Museum

Mike Flack
Civil Aviation Authority

Jim Foster
Daytona International Speedway

Bill Fredrick
Fredrick's Inc

Tony Fox
President
Foxjet International Inc

The late Gary Gabelich

Rae Gabelich

R.A. Galuzevski
Aerojet Tactical Systems

Robert W. Galvin
Chairman of the Board
Motorola Inc

Slick Gardner

Bill Gaynor
Project 1000 Inc

Henri Girod-Eymery
Président de la Commission Historique
Automobile Club de France

G. Brian Sisak
Goodyear International Corporation

Christopher J. Aked
The Goodyear Tyre & Rubber Co. (GB)
Limited

Zeldine Graham

Edward Z. Gray
NASA

Frank & Beattie Heath

John A. Holloway
Director Press & PR Services
Smiths Industries PLC

George Hurst
Hurst Performance, Inc

Ron Hussey

Ermie & Marvin Immerso
Ermie Immerso Enterprises Inc

Ed & Ron Iskenderian
Ed Iskenderian Racing Cams

Donald Fleming
Director
Institute of Gas Technology
Chicago

Robert L. Mount
Senior Advisor
Institute of Gas Technology
Chicago

Forrest W. Anderson
Coordinator, Communications
Institute of Gas Technology
Chicago

Mark Jones
Novosti Press Agency

Bob Kachler

Bruce N. Kaliser
Utah Geological Survey

Ferdinand C.W. Käsmann

J. Phillip Keene III
Director
Utah Travel Council

Lee Kelly
Hot Rod Magazine

Col. Joe Kittinger
High Velocity Inc

Col. William J. Knight – Vice Commander
USAF Flight Test Center
Edwards Air Force Base

James Knowles
Mobil Oil Company Limited

Charles F. Kreiner
Director – Public Relations
Bell Aerospace Textron, Inc

Dr S.S. Kumar

Rick Lawrance
State of California
Department of Economic and Business
Development

Hermann Layher
Auto + Technik Museum e.V.

Joyce Lee
IPC Video Limited

Dr Bron Lipkin

Françoise MAISON
Conservateur
Musée National du Château de Compiègne

Jack L. Martin
Director
Indianapolis Motor Speedway Corporation

Randy Mason
Curator
The Edison Institute
Henry Ford Museum

W.R. McCrary
The Firestone Tire & Rubber Company

Rosco McGlashan
Australian Land Speed Challenge

Billy Meyer

Paul Meyer
Success Motivation Institute

Ky Michaelson
Space Age Racing, Inc

Ak Miller

Brian A. Miller
Head of Marketing
Martin-Baker Aircraft Co. Limited

Sammy Miller
Wayne, New Jersey

The Lord Montagu of Beaulieu
The National Motor Museum

Dean Moon
Moon Equipment Company

Mel Moore
Public Relations Manager
Kawasaki Motors Corporation., USA

Gregg B. Morgan
Outdoor Recreation Planner
Salt Lake District Officer
Bureau of Land Management

Hal Needham

Vladimir K. Nikitin
Soviet Institute for Automobiles and Roads
Kharkov, USSR

Richard Noble
Thrust Cars Limited

Jay Ohrberg

Kitty Hambleton (née O'Neil)

The late Dr Nathan Ostich

Romeo Palamides

Wally Parks
President
National Hot Rod Association

John Paxson

Air Vice-Marshal Peter Howard OBE, QHP,
MB, BS, PhD, FRCP, FFOM, FRAeS, RAF
Commandant
RAF Institute of Aviation Medicine

Group Captain D.H. Glaister
Head, Biodynamics Division
Consultant in Aviation Medicine
RAF Institute of Aviation Medicine

Squadron Leader A.R.J. Prior
RAF Institute of Aviation Medicine

Nina Rindt

J. Sarrut
Assistant Secretary General
Fédération Internationale de l'Automobile

Hans – Joachim Schilder
Hobby Magazin der technik
Ehapa Verlag GmbH

Bruno Selmi
Bruno's Country Club
Gerlach, Nevada

Mike Spitzer
President
Mike Spitzer Race Cars

Garth Stewart
Western Cafe
Wendover, Utah

Bill and Bob Summers
Summers Brothers Inc

Mickey & Danny Thompson
Mickey Thompson Entertainment Group, Inc

Alex Tremulis

Mr. A. Trewenneck
Editor
Westmorland Gazette

Robert C. Truax
Truax Engineering, Inc

Stuart Turner
Ford Motor Company Limited

General Sir Harry Tuzo
Chairman
Marconi Space & Defence Systems Limited

The late Jo Petrali
United States Automobile Club

Dave Petrali
United States Automobile Club

Don & Marcia Vesco

Peter J. Viererbl
Daimler-Benz AG

The late Leo Villa

Tom Palm
V.P. Research, Inc

Paul Vickroy
V.P. Research, Inc

James V. White
Chrysler Corporation

Roger White
Curatorial Assistant
Smithsonian Institution
Washington, DC

Gordon Williams
Boeing Commercial Airplane Co

Vic Wilson

William L. Withuhn
Curator of Transportation
Smithsonian Institution
Washington, DC

Monte Wolfe
Chairman of the Board
Bonneville Nationals, Inc

Chuck Yeager
USAF Brigadier General (retired)

Dr Abbas Hassan Yehir
Tsuring et Automobile Club d'Iran

With special thanks to Geoffrey Corbett and
his staff at Rank Video Services Limited for
their generous and professional assistance
in converting my American NTSC tapes to
PAL.

LSR

Index

Y

Yeager, Captain Charles E. 'Chuck' 88, 96,
   147, 149, 150

Z

Zboröwsky, Count Louis 25

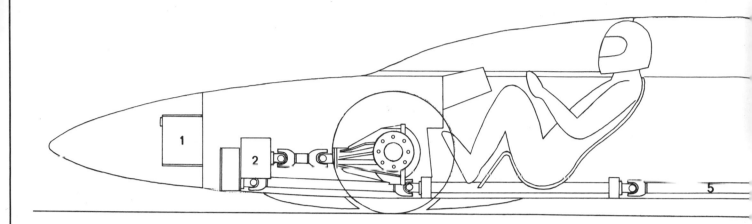

*A line drawing showing the
configuration of the
Minnesota Land Speed
Record Project vehicle.*

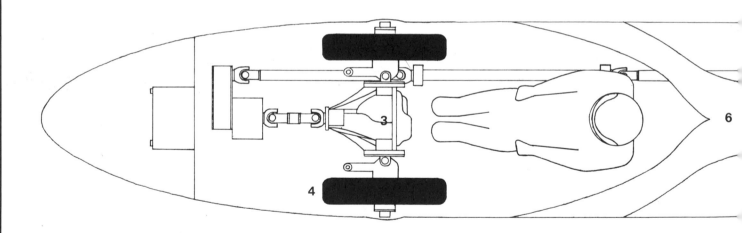

1. Battery

2. Front Transfer Case Assembly

3. Front Dana-60 Differential

4. High Speed Tyres

5. Main Driveshafts

6. Engine Air Intake

7. Water Injection Tank

8. Fuel Cell

9. G.E. T-58 Turbine Engine

10. Rear Transfer Case Assembly

11. Rear Dana-60 Differential

12. Braking Parachutes

13. Dual Tail Fins

14. Engine Exhaust Duct